1968

The Fate of Innocence

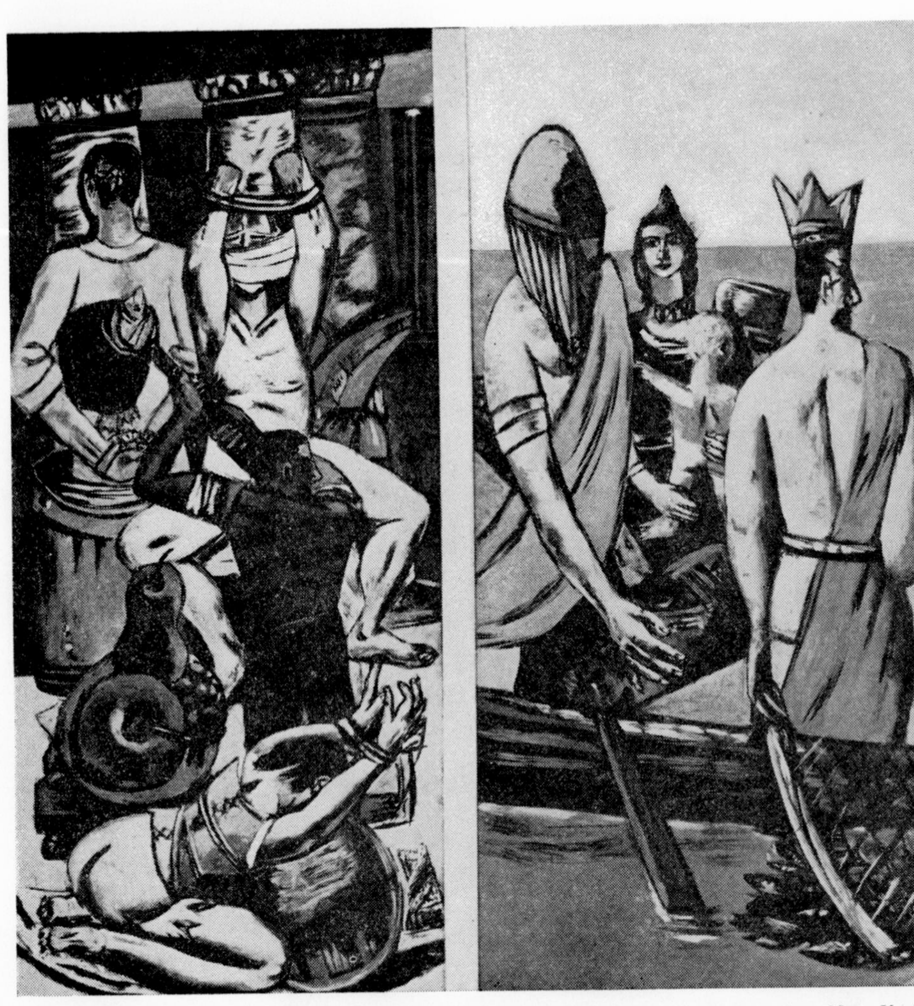

Max Beckmann, *Departure* (1932-35). Collection, The Museum of Modern Art, New York.

The Fate of Innocence

edited by
GERALD JAY GOLDBERG
University of California, Los Angeles

Prentice-Hall, Inc.
Englewood Cliffs, N.J.

PRENTICE-HALL INTERNATIONAL, INC., *London*
PRENTICE-HALL OF AUSTRALIA, PTY., LTD., *Sydney*
PRENTICE-HALL OF CANADA, LTD., *Toronto*
PRENTICE-HALL OF INDIA (PRIVATE), LTD., *New Delhi*
PRENTICE-HALL OF JAPAN, INC., *Tokyo*

Library of Congress Catalog Card Number: 65-17808

Printed in the United States of America [30818-C]

Preface

This "seminar book" is designed to provide capable college students with the materials for a challenging course of study during their initial instruction in English. Although usually associated with advanced work, the seminar system has in recent years been used with notable success in introductory courses, and it allows for independence in learning, variety in departmental offerings, and flexibility of scope not ordinarily found in English courses at the lower division level. The seminar method aids learning in depth; the student, and not the nature of the course, is the limiting factor.

The text contains significant English and American primary works drawn from different historical periods and selected in accordance with a shared literary theme. The chronological arrangement of the material places the theme in the perspective of literary history. By comparing and contrasting the philosophic assumptions of the different works, the teacher may comment on the beliefs of an author, and to some extent an age, as well as reveal the continuity of a literary theme. The Introduction is intended to function as a general discussion of the theme and to provide a context, rather than a prescriptive explication of the specific works included.

Poetry, drama, and prose fiction are represented in this collection, and it should be possible, following the suggested seminar paper topics, to use this text for basic instruction in the characteristics of the principal literary genres. The diverse nature of the works lends itself to considerations of prosody, dramatic convention, point of view, symbolism, imagery, diction, irony, and discussions of problems in formal analysis. Thus, through the use of such material as that gathered together in this "seminar book," the teacher will find it possible, in the course of directing an intensive study of the varied but thematically linked individual works, to instruct his class in literary types, the principal theme in relation to the history of ideas, and of course, relevant literary criticism. In investigating the last, the student will familiarize himself with the techniques of independent research and the facilities of his school's library.

Since this book is planned to function centrifugally—directing the student beyond the confines of the works included to related materials and areas of concentration—two important features which it contains are the suggested research topics for both seminar and term papers and a bibliographical check list. Regarding the former, the seminar paper assignments are intended to explore the principal texts of the course and to acquaint the researcher with the available criticism that has already been done on his topic. These papers might well be presented as in-class reports for discussion. The broader term paper assignments, for the most part, require reading in other, related works of literature. A supplementary list of primary materials is included for this purpose and to provide amplification and flexibility for the teacher who wishes either to vary the works or to increase their number. The bibliographical checklist is a suggestive aid to the student beginning research in English and American literature. Since independent library research should be an important objective of those using this text, the bibliography is in no sense complete but merely a starting point.

Many of my former colleagues at Dartmouth College have made useful suggestions in the course of my work on this book, and their help was greatly appreciated. But the most continuous, provocative, and influential assistance that I have received has come from my seminar students themselves, and I wish to acknowledge my debt to them.

G.J.G.

Contents

The Fate of Innocence

Introduction

For all of its brutality, sadism, and incisory anger, Max Beckmann's triptych "Departure" is finally an idyl of innocence, replete with the prophetic dream of some better life—perfect in calm and order—just beyond the horizon. The two side panels, their crowded interior scenes agitated with mutilated and bound figures enveloped in a cacophony of bass drum and muffled cry, open onto a center panel of daylight, boundless silent space, and a classically composed royal entourage, epic in their verticality, serene in their skins. If man can be vicious in "Departure," nature is seen to be benevolent. And so under clear skies and the benediction of the monarch's upraised fingers, innocence, embodied handsomely in the royal mother and child grouping, rejects the surrounding world of evil and sails off to some remote earthly paradise of the human spirit, but not before it has italicized its plight in a postlapsarian universe.

Although it is possible to argue, citing Milton's Satan as a case in point, that evil must be at least externally attractive if it is to function seductively, one notes that traditionally and overwhelmingly the iconography of evil has been composed of repellent images, from the demons of Hieronymous Bosch to the grotesques of Goya. Conversely, physical beauty, such as that found in the central panel of the Beckmann triptych, is the typical visual manifestation of innocence and represents an established association that finds its counterpart in literature.[1] In spite of the relatively

[1] Oscar Wilde cleverly exploits this association in his famous study of decadence, *The Picture of Dorian Gray*. Dorian, Wilde's depraved hero, possesses a diabolical lure in his unblemished physical beauty, for his corruption is mirrored not in the man but, miraculously, in his portrait.

unimportant role that Plato himself ascribed to bodies in his doctrines (their purpose being merely to house and transport souls), Plotinus and the seventeenth-century Neoplatonists conceived of the body in much more exalted terms. The Renaissance statesman and writer, Castiglione, in fact goes so far as to posit a causal relationship between the unblemished soul and its fleshly shape when, in *The Courtier,* he writes, ". . . and we may say that the good and the beautiful are in a way one and the same thing, and especially in the human body; of whose beauty I think the most immediate cause is beauty of the soul. . . ." [2] Similarly, Edmund Spenser in "An Hymne in Honour of Beautie" expresses the informing aspect of the soul:

> For of the soule the bodie forme doth take:
> For soule is forme, and doth the bodie make.[3]

That physical perfection should come to stand for moral perfection—a sort of homiletic shorthand—seems to be, ironically because of a limitation of the medium, a development of the visual arts.

The correlation between body and soul is a literary commonplace when innocence is conceived of as moral purity. Spenser's Britomart, Shakespeare's Miranda, Milton's Adam and Eve, Fielding's Fanny Andrews and Sophia Western, and Melville's Billy Budd all share an external perfection. But clarification is needed when innocence comes in such varied guises as those of Fielding's paragon, Joseph Andrews, and his inimitable clown, Parson Adams. The essential distinction is that though Adams like Andrews is morally untainted and represents a standard by which his society is to be judged, Fielding, in treating the former, also emphasizes the cleric's lack of self-knowledge and social ignorance, for as he says of him, "simplicity was his characteristic." It is this emphasis on an aspect of innocence other than moral purity that may help to explain the odd figure and idiosyncratic style of the good Parson. Analogously, Joe Gargery in Dickens' *Great Expectations* and Benjy Compson in Faulkner's *The Sound and the Fury* are hardly apollonian conceptions. Benjy is a hulking, slobbering mental de-

[2] Count Baldesar Castiglione, *The Book of the Courtier,* trans. Leonard Eckstein Opdycke (New York, 1929), p. 292.

[3] *The Works of Edmund Spenser,* eds. Edwin Greenlaw, Charles G. Osgood, Frederick M. Padelford, Ray Heffner, I (Baltimore, Md., 1943), 207.

fective; Joe, though physically powerful, is uxorious, his weakness reflected in the pale blue of his eye and the pale yellow of his hair. In both instances the reader is presented with simple humanity. Yet their simplicity—the innocence they share—takes different forms; for example, the ignorantly artless Joe (although admirable in his fidelity) is wanting in manners, whereas Benjy is deficient in intelligence.

The saintly fool, a divine outsider ridiculed by a fallen and uncomprehending world, represents another manifestation of simplicity. Like Jesus mocked for his unworldliness, the holy innocent is a figure whose stature is defined in these words of Saint Paul:

> If any man among you seemeth to be wise in this world, let him become a fool, that he may be wise.
> For the wisdom of this world is foolishness with God.[4]

Surely Billy Budd is Christlike in his death, but in his life he is the Handsome Sailor, a cynosure admired by his fellows for his strength as well as his beauty and vain enough to believe that he is being summoned by Captain Vere to be rewarded for his prowess. Not vanity but humility best characterizes the saintly fool who is derided and held apart by society as somehow unfit. Dostoevsky's stated desire in creating the protagonist of his novel, *The Idiot,* was "to portray a truly beautiful soul," and though Myshkin's language seems gibberish and his ideas nonsensical (or worse) to those around him, he so far transcends them in wisdom and understanding that there is a sublimity in his alienation. Myshkin's innocence is, of course, not stupidity but an affirmation of unfashionable truths, and if he chooses a life of suffering, it is out of his deep love of humanity and his willingness (one might, in keeping with the singular obsession of the saint, almost say need) to sacrifice himself to realize that love. No matter how the saintly fool is abused by society, his life nevertheless represents the triumph of innocence after the Fall. "It is written, better to be a fool all your days than for one hour to be evil," says the rabbi to Isaac Singer's Gimpel, whose tenacious faith, compassionate nature, and freedom from self-pity identify him ironically as a fool in a world of wise guys.

Obviously, innocence may be interpreted and presented in literature in a variety of ways depending upon the author's particular

[4] 1 Corinthians 3:18-19.

predilection. Moral purity, simplicity, these represent two significant areas of stress in treating the concept of innocence, but they are not the only ones. Leslie Fiedler's statement:

> In an age which no longer believes in sin, crime becomes the capital concern of the moral imagination. Questions of innocence and guilt are thought of as being resolved in the public arena of the courtroom rather than in the privacy of the confessional or the heart,[5]

is suggestive of another likely point of emphasis—legal innocence. Although freedom from specific guilt will inevitably suggest detective fiction, it might equally well direct one to a consideration of works of greater pretension, such as Albert Camus' *The Stranger,* Arthur Miller's *The Crucible,* or Theodore Dreiser's *An American Tragedy* in which the fate of Clyde Griffiths is, in effect, an elaborate study in degrees of culpability.

Not guilt but evil is the subject of William Golding's *Lord of the Flies,* indicating that even the young are not untainted in these post-Freudian days. But it was not always so. There have been times formerly in literature when the period most closely associated with innocence was childhood. "Heaven lies about us in our infancy!" says Wordsworth in his "Ode: Intimations of Immortality," believing as does his contemporary Blake that "Shades of the prison-house begin to close / Upon the growing Boy. . . ." And still today, in spite of the fact that we have been somewhat disillusioned by modern psychology and are reluctant to equate grace with childhood as does Wordsworth, the association of innocence and youth is found in our literature. But it is essentially the innocence of the immature, the inexperienced, the unworldly, and characteristic of that genre that has as its protagonist the young man who is apprentice to life, the *Bildungsroman.*

It would seem that the dependent state of childhood is at least partially responsible for the attribution of helplessness to innocence. Further strengthening the connection between the two is that tradition of Judaic-Christian thought which has its origin in the fatal exposure of Adam and Eve to the blandishments of Satan. A visual manifestation of this relationship may be found in the work of the Renaissance painter, Angelo Bronzino, whose allegorical composi-

---

[5] "Leopold and Loeb: A Perspective in Time," *No! in Thunder: Essays on Myth and Literature* (Boston, 1960), p. 209.

tion, "L'Innocentia," depicts a female figure symbolic of innocence cowering—typically defenseless—as she is beset by four wild animals, perhaps as Erwin Panofsky contends, representing the worldly evils of Envy, Fury, Greed, and Perfidy.[6] Hard pressed, the helpless lady lifts her eyes in supplication and discovers her rescuer in the armor-clad figure of Justice. It would be unwise, however, to conclude that innocence and weakness are one, for not infrequently the innocent is presented as potent in his own right or, as in the Bronzino composition, capable of eliciting strong (in some instances magical) protection from others.[7] To illustrate, the idealized world of the fairy tale reveals that the young heroine of "East of the Sun and West of the Moon" has her support in the three miraculous hags, Cinderella her wonder-working godmother, and Little Briar-Rose the good wish of the twelfth Wise Woman. Outside the realm of fairy tale and total dependence are such formidable figures as Gawain (*Gawain and the Green Knight*) and the Lady (*Comus*) whose innocence—chastity—imbues them with personal strength in addition to the protection of magic.

If the classic age of innocence is youth, its traditional setting may be said to be the country. As civilization has its roots in the city, the landscape of innocence represents a longing for and idealization of the past and finds its best expression in pastoral poetry with its implied contrast between the rural and the urban. Alluding to Theocritus, the first great poet in this genre, W. W. Greg holds it to be significant that his work was "directly born of the contrast between the recollections of a childhood spent among the Sicilian uplands and the crowded social and intellectual city-life of Alexandria." [8] The shepherds who populate the pastoral milieu are primarily singers and not farmers; they are a dream of simplicity, a vision of innocence created by a complex mind acutely aware of the shortcomings of its urban environment. It is specifically in the Virgilian pastoral that we discover the magnitude of civilized man's degeneration in the pathetic disparity between then and now, between a spring garden of delight in which the conditions of life are

---

[6] *Studies in Iconology* (New York, 1962), p. 84.

[7] See Northrop Frye's discussion of the "analogy of innocence" in his *Anatomy of Criticism* (Princeton, N.J., 1957), pp. 151ff.

[8] *Pastoral Poetry and Pastoral Drama* (London, 1906), p. 5.

dominated by the harmony of man with nature and a winter world traumatized by the struggle for survival.[9] The Golden Age which Virgil's *Eclogues* re-create is a pagan Eden, a reflection of that myth, common to most cultures, of perfection in the past.[10] The remoteness and timelessness characteristic of both the pastoral and the Golden Age enhance not only the appeal but the credibility of ideal simplicity for the complicated individual long accustomed to evil. Even in our own century the concept of the Earthly Paradise still maintains its hold on man's imagination. Pastoral poetry, however, is clearly no longer a viable form in an era when the city has evolved into megalopolis, and now, for the most part, romantic fiction, utopian fantasies, and the comic are the realms of the ideal. Thus, for example, in Mary Chase's contemporary comedy, *Harvey,* the world-weary psychiatrist, Dr. Chumley, longs to exploit the invisible pooka's amazing ability to overcome time so that he may free himself from his responsibilities and escape to a suburban grove of maple trees outside Pittsburgh in order to sip beer and have some beautiful young woman stroke his head and say, "Poor thing! Oh, you poor, poor thing!" The impetus for this idyl is as old as man, but when compared with earlier notions of the splendor of the Golden Age, Dr. Chumley's modern vision of innocent bliss is comically pathetic.

In his study of the theme of the Earthly Paradise in nineteenth-century art, Werner Hofmann cites two distinct conceptions of the Golden Age, one conservative and the other revolutionary:

> . . . in the latter man actively takes possession of the world, in the former he is given over to idleness and pleasure. There are memories of a peaceful state of nature and visions of a communal spirit leading man on to ever higher stages of civilization. The socialist utopias exalted the active planning of human happiness, but the dreams of

---

[9] According to Hallett Smith, *Elizabethan Poetry* (Cambridge, Mass., 1952), p. 14, "The identification of the pastoral life with the conditions of the Golden Age was natural enough. One was a criticism of life by means of adopting the point of view of its simplest and purest elements; the other was a criticism of the present way of life by describing an ideal past."

[10] The pastoral setting of the Golden Age, a period in which innocence was the condition of man, is to be seen in such paintings as Hans von Marées' "The Golden Age I," Ingres' "The Golden Age," and Gauguin's *"D'où venons-nous? Que sommes-nous? Où allons-nous?"* An interesting account of the Golden Age is François Hemsterhuis' *Alexis or The Golden Age* (1782). Among later literary works linking this ideal world and the pastoral are Tasso's *Aminta,* Browne's *Britannia's Pastoral,* and Sidney's *Arcadia.*

> purely subjective bliss were satisfied with the voluntary choice of a rich life lived to the full, and their escapist worlds were modelled on the legendary extravagances of antiquity.[11]

Hofmann's dichotomy of active and passive states of perfection is suggestive of two possible spheres of innocence—time-bound and timeless. Apropos of the latter is the Christian Golden Age, Paradise, which has occurred in pre-history (Eden) and will occur again in eternity (Heaven), but not in time's covenant. This Paradise, as described by Milton, is a harmonious garden of plenty whose inhabitants, if not completely idle, yet have no need to labor for survival. The lushness of the setting precludes strenuous work, and Adam and Eve experience their surroundings as a manifestation of God's grace, very much like the sailors in Andrew Marvell's "Bermudas":

> He lands us on a grassy Stage;
> Safe from the Storms, and Prelat's rage.
> He gave us this eternal Spring,
> Which here enamells every thing;
> And sends the Fowl's to us in care,
> On daily Visits through the Air.
> He hangs in shades the Orange bright,
> Like golden Lamps in a green Night.
> And does in the Pomgranates close,
> Jewels more rich than *Ormus* shows.
> He makes the Figs our mouths to meet;
> And throws the Melons at our feet.[12]

Whether Paradise, the Golden Age, Arcadia, or the Islands of the Blessed, the idyllic environment is conducive to leisure and is free of both time and corruption.

Originating no doubt as myths, archetypal conceptions of environmental excellence are omnipresent in human thought and, perhaps in an attempt to make such perfect worlds less remote, they have been translated into elaborate fictional societies that might possibly function in time.[13] Utopias, then, endeavor to establish the

---

[11] *The Earthly Paradise: Art in the Nineteenth Century* (New York, 1961), p. 364.

[12] *The Poems of Andrew Marvell,* ed. Hugh Macdonald (Cambridge, Mass., 1952), p. 13.

[13] Glenn Negley and J. Max Patrick, *The Quest for Utopia* (New York, 1952), p. 251.

New Jerusalem on earth and within the province of history, despite self-interest, war, religious skepticism, and corruption. By and large, however, the utopist demands an active contribution from the members of his society as do Plato, More, Bacon, and Morris; and even Wells, in his *Modern Utopia* with all its emphasis on science and technology, has not completely eliminated labor. In this context, the extremity of Gonzalo's famous utopian plan in *The Tempest* is clear:

> I' th' commonwealth I would by contraries
> Execute all things; for no kind of traffic
> Would I admit; no name of magistrate;
> Letters should not be known; riches, poverty,
> And use of service, none; contract, succession,
> Bourn, bound of land, tilth, vineyard, none;
> No use of metal, corn, or wine, or oil;
> No occupation; all men idle, all;
> And women too, but innocent and pure. . . .

That his naïve dream of idleness is mocked by Antonio and Sebastian is understandable, for they are ambitious men, practical opportunists who recognize the importance of power in government and covet it. Moreover, the ironic literal meaning of Utopia, that is, "not a place," would seem to be tacit in their cynicism.[14] Gonzalo's impetuosity is a further irony, for although Utopias exist in time, they are never of the present moment but rather set backward or forward chronologically, providing their creators with the possibility of exercising their imaginations. In the Postscript to his well-known work, *Looking Backward* (1888), Edward Bellamy wrote:

> All thoughtful men agree that the present aspect of society is portentous of great changes. The only question is, whether they will be for the better or the worse. Those who believe in man's essential nobleness lean to the former view, those who believe in his essential baseness to the latter. For my part, I hold to the former opinion. *Looking Backward* was written in the belief that the Golden Age lies before us and not behind us, and is not far away.

Although perhaps historically close, as Bellamy hopefully believes, the ideal setting for innocence always appears to be beyond man's

---

[14] William Morris' fictional Utopia is significantly called *News from Nowhere;* and Samuel Butler's *Erewhon* depicts a land where not only values are inverted but names as well, and hence, in this instance too, the title itself conveys the essential truth that Erewhon is nowhere.

grasp (whether in time or otherwise), an unfulfilled wish, a romantic yearning for something different and better, and this may well be its significance.

Scholars have determined that Shakespeare in creating Gonzalo's ideal commonwealth no doubt had recourse to John Florio's 1603 translation of Montaigne's *Essays*, for there are striking similarities between ideas expressed in the thirty-first essay, "Of Cannibals," and the aged courtier's Utopia. It was Montaigne who, fascinated by the discoveries of new worlds during his lifetime and by way of making a critical judgment on his own society, reinforced the association of exotic lands with innocence. "I am sorry that Lycurgus and Plato did not have this knowledge," he writes in the above essay, commenting on the revelation of communities of natives in Brazil,

> for it seems to me that what we actually see in these nations surpasses not only all the pictures in which poets have embellished the golden age, and all their ingenuity in imagining a happy state of man, but also the conceptions and the very desire of philosophy. They could not imagine a naturalness so pure and simple as that which we see by experience. . . .[15]

During the Renaissance, the Americas were typically envisaged as a fertile garden whose inhabitants were likened to Adam before the Fall. Arthur Barlow, dispatched by Sir Walter Raleigh to determine the suitability of Virginia for colonization, recorded that he found "the people most gentle, loving, and faithful, void of all guile and treason, and such as live after the manner of the golden age. . . ."[16]

But just as the unknown can elicit thoughts of perfection, it can also fill the hearts of men with dread, and so we see during the Renaissance another attitude toward strange lands. In Howes'

[15] Michel de Montaigne, *Selected Essays*, trans. Donald M. Frame (New York, 1943), p. 78.

[16] E. J. Payne, *Voyages of Elizabethan Seamen* (London, 1900, second series), pp. 62-63. Discussing the image of America as a garden, Leo Marx in his essay, "Shakespeare's American Fable," *The Massachusetts Review* (Autumn 1960), p. 45, notes that "When Elizabethan voyagers described Virginia in this image they were drawing upon utopian aspirations that Europeans always had cherished, and that had given rise, long before the discovery of America, to a whole series of idealized, imaginary worlds. Besides the Golden Age and Arcadia, we are reminded of Elysium, Atlantis, the enchanted gardens, Eden and Tirnanoque, and the fragrant bower where the Hesperides stood watch over the golden apples."

Annals[17] there is an account of an expedition of eight vessels to Virginia in 1609 during which, as a consequence of a sudden, violent storm, the flagship is damaged severely and separated from its companions:

> Sir George Somers, sitting at the stern, seeing the ship desperate of relief, looking every minute when the ship would sink, he espied land, which according to his and Captain Newport's opinion they judged it should be that dreadful coast of the Bermodes, which islands were of all nations said and supposed to be enchanted and inhabited with witches and devils, which grew by reason of accustomed monstrous thunder, storm, and tempest, near unto those islands.

This quotation would seem to lend support to the thesis that "On the spectrum of Elizabethan ideas of America the hideous wilderness appears at one end and the garden at the other." [18]

These poles—nature as abundant storehouse or inhospitable wasteland—constitute an interesting dichotomous interpretation of strange lands that finds its counterpart in the attitudes toward those creatures who inhabit them. It became commonplace during the sixteenth and seventeenth centuries to regard the natives who lived far beyond the shores of Europe essentially in one of two ways, either pagan savages out of God's grace or admirable innocents at one with nature. And even in the eighteenth century, while Rousseau was expounding his belief in the noble savage (the peacefulness of his character! his freedom from vice!), others held the view that those "who had not received the light of the Christian revelation were all in much the same sort of idolatrous ignorance. . . ." [19]

Against a conceptual background of alternatives such as I have been describing, *The Tempest* assumes new meaning. Not only does Shakespeare find fault with Montaigne's notion of the socio-political perfection of uncultivated societies in this play, but he also seems to take exception to the French essayist's characterization of the innocent savage as well as the idyllic landscape in which he plays out his days. There is, after all, little of nobility in the misshapen and savage Caliban who schemes with Stephano to have a nail driven into his sleeping master's head. Rather he is, as Prospero

[17] See John Stow, *The Annales, or Generall Chronicle of England,* continued and augmented by Edmund Howes (London, 1615).

[18] Marx, *op. cit.,* p. 47.

[19] See Benjamin Bissell, *The American Indian in English Literature of the Eighteenth Century* (New Haven, Conn., 1925), p. 31.

informs us, a cunning coward, a thing of darkness upon whom nurture fails totally. Although in his final speech Caliban may say, "I'll be wise hereafter, / And seek for grace," this statement in the context of his obvious fear of punishment must be read as an expedient gesture rather than a true enlightenment.

In literature the isolated setting may have a therapeutic function, either as a garden of delight (a *"locus amoenus"*) or, as in *The Tempest,* a retreat for purgation.[20] It is following the period of his enforced island exile that Prospero succeeds in mastering himself and rising above petty vindictiveness. The speaker in Marvell's "The Garden," however, has voluntarily sought out his place of seclusion in order to come in contact with the restorative powers of primeval truths, and so his tone is one of wonder as he observes,

> Fair quiet, have I found thee here
> And Innocence thy Sister dear! [21]

Although conceived of in vastly different ways in these two instances, nature, directly or indirectly, is seen to have a regenerative influence in both. The quest for innocence through a redemptive journey into uncharted regions, so characteristic of American literature from Cooper and Thoreau to Faulkner and Bellow, is related to this phenomenon of the virtue of physical isolation.

Among the structural devices used in the literature of innocence is the encounter. In the pastoral, the relationship between the simple country and the cultivated town is often dramatized through a confrontation of rustic and courtier, a rivalry in which innocence, in the person of the former, customarily triumphs. Horace, emphasizing the potency of innocence, writes:

> He who is innocent and pure
> Needs not to go equipped
> With spear or quiver of the Moor
> And arrows poison-tipped.[22]

---

[20] Describing the revolutionary change in garden theory (i.e., the movement from the formal to the picturesque) that occurred during the eighteenth century and the influence of Milton's Eden, Martin Price (*To the Palace of Wisdom* [New York, 1964], p. 376) portrays the function of the garden as "an occasion of an aesthetic awareness and a theater of thought; it suggests meanings as much as it starts trains of sensation or sentiment."

[21] *Op. cit.,* p. 51.

[22] *Latin Poetry in Verse Translation,* ed. L. R. Lind (Boston, 1957), p. 105.

As implied previously, however, innocence has not always had things its own way. A variation on the Aesopian description of life among the Greek rodents is the Romanian fable of the town-mouse who visits the field-mouse and, beneath a cool exterior, warmly regards his country cousin's wealth of grains and nuts. Urbanely, he proffers a reciprocal invitation with the alleged intention of showing off the luxury of town living, the ease of life in a grocery store. When he returns the visit, the simple field-mouse is much impressed; enjoying himself thoroughly sampling the wares of the city, he is more curious than frightened when the grocer's huge cat walks in menacingly. Between nibbles, the field-mouse casually inquires of his cousin who the gentleman is. "That," says the town-mouse, slipping gingerly into his hole, "is our priest. Go and kiss his hand." Thus, the shrewd town-mouse achieves his end of eliminating his innocent cousin and thereby becomes the owner of a peaceful rural estate. Whether essentially comic or tragic, the fate of innocence is commonly revealed by the encounter.

For Milton, who could not praise a "fugitive and cloistered virtue," it is crucial that the innocence of the heroine in *Comus* be tried, as it is by the son of Bacchus and Circe. However, despite Comus' ingenuity in assuming the disguise of a simple shepherd, the Lady succeeds in championing her cause vis-à-vis the seductive arguments of her adversary. Melville's *Billy Budd* is another work in which an encounter constitutes the dramatic climax of the action. The confrontation of the two forces representing natural depravity and Adamic innocence in the presence of the helpless Captain Vere may be said to be the obligatory scene in the *novella*. As in such other American fiction as Faulkner's *A Fable* and Nathanael West's *Miss Lonelyhearts* in which innocence is destroyed, here, too, the innocent man meets an inexplicable and irredeemable adversary "in the very condition of life—an evil exceeding any social ill and something for which nothing in the man's view of life has prepared him. In that sense Billy Budd is really the prototype of the Puritan tragic hero: the innocent man encountering evil 'for which the creator alone is responsible'. . . ." [23] Of Henry James's novels, *Roderick Hudson, The American, The Portrait of a Lady* and, his last three, *The Wings of the Dove, The Ambassadors,* and *The Golden Bowl*

---

[23] Ursula Brumm, "The Figure of Christ in American Literature," *Partisan Review,* XXIV (Summer 1957), 411-12.

deal with the impact of the older, more corrupt civilization of Europe upon the ingenuous American. James develops his international theme by utilizing the encounter of the socially innocent American with the sophisticated European or Europeanized American, as in *Daisy Miller*. Daisy and Frederick Winterbourne, the character who functions as the central intelligence in the story, are thrown together repeatedly subsequent to their chance meeting in the garden of the "Trois Couronnes" in Vevey. Significantly, in this garden milieu it is the charm of Daisy's freshness that is uppermost in Winterbourne's mind. But when they meet in Rome, he becomes increasingly more dubious of her innocence. That the irrepressible Daisy's end should be tragic is in part a consequence of Winterbourne's understandable difficulty in distinguishing manners from morality after his long residence abroad.

Daisy Miller and the other works included in this volume have been selected in an attempt to reveal collectively the nature and fate of innocence. If the presence of innocence is problematical for Winterbourne, it is ironically no less difficult to experience in our own lives. For it is the innocents—the Gimpels of the literary universe—who, having somehow wandered out of their natural habitat in the Golden Age, simultaneously confront us with the knowledge of our tainted humanity and the reality of the idyllic dream.

Adam and Eve in the Garden of Eden: The Fall

Although Adam and Eve's fall from innocence may be regarded as an actual event that occurred some time in the past, it is also possible to interpret their disobedience as an act that is continually being repeated, a mythic explanation of the presence of evil in the world. So, too, their garden home of Eden when viewed as myth is revealed as an archetypical setting for innocence. "If we believe the Scripture," writes Sir William Temple in the eighteenth century, "we must allow that God Almighty esteemed the life of a man in a garden the happiest he could give him, or else he would not have placed Adam in that of Eden; that it was the state of innocence and pleasure; and that the life of husbandry and cities came after the fall, with guilt and with labor." * We know that early gardens were conceived of as imitations of paradise, and in literature they also represent a typical ambience for innocence, from the vale of Enna in which Persephone gathered flowers to T. S. Eliot's Rose Garden.

The excerpt from the Book of Genesis reprinted here is based upon the King James Bible.

And the Lord God planted a garden eastward in Eden; and there he put the man whom he had formed. And out of the ground made the Lord God to grow every tree that is pleasant to the sight, and good for food; the tree of life also in the midst of the garden, and the tree of knowledge of good and evil.

And a river went out of Eden to water the garden; and from thence it was parted, and became into four heads. The name of the first is Pison: that is it which compasseth the whole land of Havilah, where there is gold. And the gold of that land is good: there is bdellium and the onyx stone. And the name of the second river is

* "Upon the Gardens of Epicurus," *The Garden as Considered in Literature,* ed. Walter Howe (New York, 1890), p. 89.

Gihon: the same is it that compasseth the whole land of Ethiopia. And the name of the third river is Hiddekel: that is it which goeth toward the east of Assyria. And the fourth river is Euphrates.

And the Lord God took the man, and put him into the garden of Eden to dress it and keep it. And the Lord God commanded the man, saying, Of every tree of the garden thou mayest freely eat: But of the tree of the knowledge of good and evil, thou shalt not eat of it: for in the day that thou eatest thereof thou shalt surely die.

And the Lord God said, It is not good that the man should be alone; I will make him a help meet for him. And out of the ground the Lord God formed every beast of the field, and every fowl of the air; and brought them unto Adam to see what he would call them: and whatsoever Adam called every living creature, that was the name thereof. And Adam gave names to all cattle, and to the fowl of the air, and to every beast of the field; but for Adam there was not found a help meet for him.

And the Lord God caused a deep sleep to fall upon Adam, and he slept; and he took one of his ribs, and closed up the flesh instead thereof. And the rib, which the Lord God had taken from man, made he a woman, and brought her unto the man.

And Adam said, This is now bone of my bones, and flesh of my flesh: she shall be called Woman, because she was taken out of man. Therefore shall a man leave his father and his mother, and shall cleave unto his wife: and they shall be one flesh. And they were both naked, the man and his wife, and were not ashamed.

Now the serpent was more subtile than any beast of the field which the Lord God had made. And he said unto the woman, Yea, hath God said, Ye shall not eat of every tree of the garden? And the woman said unto the serpent, We may eat of the fruit of the trees of the garden: But of the fruit of the tree which is in the midst of the garden, God hath said, Ye shall not eat of it, neither shall ye touch it, lest ye die. And the serpent said unto the woman, Ye shall not surely die: For God doth know that in the day ye eat thereof, then your eyes shall be opened, and ye shall be as gods, knowing good and evil.

And when the woman saw that the tree was good for food, and that it was pleasant to the eyes, and a tree to be desired to make one wise, she took of the fruit thereof, and did eat, and gave also unto her husband with her; and he did eat. And the eyes of them both were opened, and they knew that they were naked; and they sewed fig leaves together, and made themselves aprons.

And they heard the voice of the Lord God walking in the garden in the cool of the day: and Adam and his wife hid themselves from the presence of the Lord God amongst the trees of the garden. And the Lord God called unto Adam, and said unto him, Where art thou?

And he said, I heard thy voice in the garden, and I was afraid, because I was naked; and I hid myself.

And he said, Who told thee that thou wast naked? Hast thou eaten of the tree, whereof I commanded thee that thou shouldest not eat?

And the man said, The woman whom thou gavest to be with me, she gave me of the tree, and I did eat.

And the Lord God said unto the woman, What is this that thou hast done? And the woman said, The serpent beguiled me, and I did eat.

And the Lord God said unto the serpent, Because thou hast done this, thou art cursed above all cattle, and above every beast of the field; upon thy belly shalt thou go, and dust shalt thou eat all the days of thy life: And I will put enmity between thee and the woman, and between thy seed and her seed; it shall bruise thy head, and thou shalt bruise his heel.

Unto the woman he said, I will greatly multiply thy sorrow and thy conception; in sorrow thou shalt bring forth children; and thy desire shall be to thy husband, and he shall rule over thee.

And unto Adam he said, Because thou hast hearkened unto the voice of thy wife, and hast eaten of the tree, of which I commanded thee, saying, Thou shalt not eat of it: cursed is the ground for thy sake; in sorrow shalt thou eat of it all the days of thy life; Thorns also and thistles shall it bring forth to thee; and thou shalt eat the herb of the field; In the sweat of thy face shalt thou eat bread, till thou return unto the ground; for out of it wast thou taken: for dust thou art, and unto dust shalt thou return.

And Adam called his wife's name Eve; because she was the mother of all living. Unto Adam also and to his wife did the Lord God make coats of skins, and clothed them.

And the Lord God said, Behold, the man is become as one of us, to know good and evil: and now, lest he put forth his hand, and take also of the tree of life, and eat, and live for ever: Therefore the Lord God sent him forth from the garden of Eden, to till the ground from whence he was taken. So he drove out the man: and he placed at the east of the garden of Eden cherubim, and a flaming sword which turned every way, to keep the way of the tree of life.

The Tempest

WILLIAM SHAKESPEARE

In Shakespeare's *Tempest* the rebirth motif against a background of nature and the extensive use of music and dance suggest the influence of both the pastoral and the court masque.* Milton's masque, *Comus,* also contains features drawn from the pastoral tradition, and the heroines of both works share in common their chastity, even though Miranda's virtue appears somewhat less militant than that of the Lady. But it is the early ignorance of Prospero in giving away his ducal powers and the subsequent wisdom he achieves that is the area of innocence most significant for full insight into the meaning of Shakespeare's play.

The Tempest is the last of the plays wholly written by Shakespeare, and the date of composition—based upon internal and external evidence—is generally assumed to be 1611. Because this work seems to represent the end of the creative career of the most prodigious talent the stage has ever known, there is little wonder that critics have long been tempted to read *The Tempest* as an autobiographical statement by the author, so that for them Prospero's final renunciation of his magic becomes Shakespeare's parting farewell to the theater. Although this interpretation is appealing in its tidiness, modern critics have tended to emphasize aspects of the play other than the biographical, with current discussion given over to such subjects as the operation of forgiveness, reconciliation, and the purgative function of the isolated setting.

This edition, with certain minor exceptions, follows the text of Shakespeare's First Folio of 1623, but the spelling and punctuation have been modernized.

* These influences are discussed by Frank Kermode in his Introduction to the Arden edition of the play, pp. lix-lxxvi.

Names of the Actors

ALONSO, *King of Naples*
SEBASTIAN, *his brother*
PROSPERO, *the right Duke of Milan*
ANTONIO, *his brother, the usurping Duke of Milan*
FERDINAND, *son to the King of Naples*
GONZALO, *an honest old councillor*
ADRIAN *and* FRANCISCO, *lords*
CALIBAN, *a savage and deformed slave*
TRINCULO, *a jester*
STEPHANO, *a drunken butler*
MASTER OF A SHIP
BOATSWAIN
MARINERS
MIRANDA, *daughter to* PROSPERO
ARIEL, *an airy spirit*
IRIS, CERES, JUNO, NYMPHS, REAPERS } [*presented by*] SPIRITS
[*Other* SPIRITS *attending on* PROSPERO]

The Scene

[*A ship at sea*] *an uninhabited island*

Act I

SCENE I [*A ship at sea*]

A tempestuous noise of thunder and lightning heard. Enter a SHIPMASTER *and a* BOATSWAIN.

MASTER. Boatswain!

BOATSWAIN. Here, master. What cheer?

MASTER. Good, speak to th' mariners; fall to't yarely, or we run ourselves aground. Bestir, bestir! *Exit.*

Enter MARINERS.

BOATSWAIN. Heigh, my hearts! Cheerly, cheerly, my hearts! 5
Yare, yare! Take in the topsail! Tend to th' master's whistle! Blow till thou burst thy wind, if room enough!

Enter ALONSO, SEBASTIAN, ANTONIO, FERDINAND, GONZALO, *and others.*

ALONSO. Good boatswain, have care. Where's the master? Play the men.

BOATSWAIN. I pray now, keep below. 10

ANTONIO. Where is the master, boatswain?

BOATSWAIN. Do you not hear him? You mar our labor. Keep your cabins: you do assist the storm.

GONZALO. Nay, good, be patient.

BOATSWAIN. When the sea is. Hence! What cares these roar- 15

I,i,3 *yarely:* briskly. 6 *Tend:* attend. 7 *if room enough:* i.e., so long as we have sea-room. 9 *Play the men:* act like men. 15 *roarers:* waves.

ers for the name of king? To cabin! Silence! Trouble us not.

GONZALO. Good, yet remember whom thou hast aboard.

BOATSWAIN. None that I more love than myself. You are a councillor: if you can command these elements to silence, and work the peace of the present, we will not hand a rope more; 20 use your authority. If you cannot, give thanks you have lived so long, and make yourself ready in your cabin for the mischance of the hour, if it so hap. Cheerly, good hearts! Out of our way, I say. *Exit.*

GONZALO. I have great comfort from this fellow: methinks 25 he hath no drowning mark upon him; his complexion is perfect gallows. Stand fast, good Fate, to his hanging! Make the rope of his destiny our cable, for our own doth little advantage. If he be not born to be hanged, our case is miserable.

Exeunt.

[*Re-*]*enter* BOATSWAIN.

BOATSWAIN. Down with the topmast! Yare! Lower, lower! 30 Bring her to try with main-course. *A cry within.* A plague upon this howling! They are louder than the weather or our office.

[*Re-*]*enter* SEBASTIAN, ANTONIO, *and* GONZALO.

Yet again? What do you here? Shall we give o'er and drown? Have you a mind to sink? 35

SEBASTIAN. A pox o' your throat, you bawling, blasphemous, incharitable dog!

BOATSWAIN. Work you, then.

ANTONIO. Hang, cur! hang, you whoreson, insolent noisemaker. We are less afraid to be drowned than thou art. 40

GONZALO. I'll warrant him for drowning, though the ship were no stronger than a nutshell and as leaky as an unstanched wench.

BOATSWAIN. Lay her ahold, ahold! Set her two courses! Off to sea again! Lay her off! 45

Enter MARINERS *wet.*

MARINERS. All lost! To prayers, to prayers! All lost!

BOATSWAIN. What, must our mouths be cold?

---

20 *work . . . present:* end this storm at once. 29 Gonzalo alludes to the proverb "He that is born to be hanged will never be drowned." 31 *try with main-course:* to lie almost stationary by using only the mainsail. 33 *our office:* (the noise that we make in accomplishing) our work. 41 *warrant . . . drowning:* guarantee him against drowning. 44 *Lay her ahold:* i.e., the boaswain, seeing the ship drift toward the rocks, changes this order to heave-to and commands that more sail be put on in a desperate attempt to clear the shore; *two courses:* the foresail and the mainsail.

GONZALO. The King and Prince at prayers! Let's assist them,
For our case is as theirs.
SEBASTIAN. I am out of patience.
ANTONIO. We are merely cheated of our lives by drunkards. 50
This wide-chopped rascal—would thou mightst lie drowning
The washing of ten tides!
GONZALO. He'll be hanged yet,
Though every drop of water swear against it
And gape at wid'st to glut him.
A confused noise within: "Mercy on us!"— 55
"We split, we split!"—"Farewell, my wife and children!"
—"Farewell, brother!"—"We split, we split, we split!"
ANTONIO. Let's all sink wi' th' King.
SEBASTIAN. Let's take leave of him.
Exeunt [ANTONIO *and* SEBASTIAN].
GONZALO. Now would I give a thousand furlongs of sea for
an acre of barren ground—long heath, brown furze, anything. 60
The wills above be done, but I would fain die a dry death.
Exeunt.

SCENE II [*The island. Before Prospero's cell*]

Enter PROSPERO *and* MIRANDA.

MIRANDA. If by your art, my dearest father, you have
Put the wild waters in this roar, allay them.
The sky, it seems, would pour down stinking pitch
But that the sea, mounting to th' welkin's cheek,
Dashes the fire out. O, I have suffered 5
With those that I saw suffer! a brave vessel
(Who had no doubt some noble creature in her)
Dashed all to pieces! O, the cry did knock
Against my very heart! Poor souls, they perished!
Had I been any god of power, I would 10
Have sunk the sea within the earth or ere
It should the good ship so have swallowed and
The fraughting souls within her.
PROSPERO. Be collected.
No more amazement. Tell your piteous heart
There's no harm done.

---

50 *merely:* completely. 51 *wide-chopped:* wide-jawed. 52 *washing . . . tides:* an exaggeration of the English practice of leaving the hanging bodies of pirates on the shore until three high tides had passed. 54 *glut:* swallow. I,ii,4 *welkin:* sky. 11 *or ere:* before. 13 *fraughting:* cargo of; *collected:* calm.

MIRANDA. O, woe the day!

PROSPERO. No harm. 15

I have done nothing but in care of thee,
Of thee my dear one, thee my daughter, who
Art ignorant of what thou art, naught knowing
Of whence I am; nor that I am more better
Than Prospero, master of a full poor cell, 20
And thy no greater father.

MIRANDA. More to know
Did never meddle with my thoughts.

PROSPERO. 'Tis time
I should inform thee farther. Lend thy hand
And pluck my magic garment from me. So:

[*Lays down his robe.*]

Lie there, my art. Wipe thou thine eyes; have comfort. 25
The direful spectacle of the wreck, which touched
The very virtue of compassion in thee,
I have with such provision in mine art
So safely ordered that there is no soul—
No, not so much perdition as an hair 30
Betid to any creature in the vessel
Which thou heard'st cry, which thou saw'st sink. Sit down;
For thou must now know farther.

MIRANDA. You have often
Begun to tell me what I am; but stopped
And left me to a bootless inquisition, 35
Concluding, "Stay: not yet."

PROSPERO. The hour's now come;
The very minute bids thee ope thine ear.
Obey, and be attentive. Canst thou remember
A time before we came unto this cell?
I do not think thou canst, for then thou wast not 40
Out three years old.

MIRANDA. Certainly, sir, I can.

PROSPERO. By what? By any other house or person?
Of any thing the image tell me that
Hath kept with thy remembrance.

MIRANDA. 'Tis far off,
And rather like a dream than an assurance 45

---

19 *more better:* the double comparative, usually employed for emphasis, was common in Early Modern English. 22 *meddle:* mingle. 28 *provision:* foresight. 30 *perdition:* loss. 35 *bootless inquisition:* vain inquiry. 41 *out:* fully.

That my remembrance warrants. Had I not
Four or five women once that tended me?
PROSPERO. Thou hadst, and more, Miranda. But how is it
That this lives in thy mind? What seest thou else
In the dark backward and abysm of time? 50
If thou remembrest aught ere thou cam'st here,
How thou cam'st here thou mayst.
MIRANDA. But that I do not.
PROSPERO. Twelve year since, Miranda, twelve year since,
Thy father was the Duke of Milan, and
A prince of power.
MIRANDA. Sir, are not you my father? 55
PROSPERO. Thy mother was a piece of virtue, and
She said thou wast my daughter; and thy father
Was Duke of Milan; and his only heir
A princess—no worse issued.
MIRANDA. O the heavens!
What foul play had we that we came from thence? 60
Or blessed was't we did?
PROSPERO. Both, both, my girl!
By foul play, as thou say'st, were we heaved thence,
But blessedly holp hither.
MIRANDA. O, my heart bleeds
To think o' th' teen that I have turned you to,
Which is from my remembrance! Please you, farther. 65
PROSPERO. My brother, and thy uncle, called Antonio—
I pray thee mark me—that a brother should
Be so perfidious!—he whom next thyself
Of all the world I loved, and to him put
The manage of my state, as at that time 70
Through all the signories it was the first,
And Prospero the prime duke, being so reputed
In dignity, and for the liberal arts
Without a parallel; those being all my study,
The government I cast upon my brother 75
And to my state grew stranger, being transported
And rapt in secret studies. Thy false uncle—
Dost thou attend me?
MIRANDA. Sir, most heedfully.

---

50 *backward:* past. 56 *piece:* masterpiece. 63 *holp:* helped. 64 *teen:* pain. 65 *from:* out of. 69-70 *put the manage:* entrusted the management. 71 *signories:* states of northern Italy governed by a signior, or lord.

PROSPERO. Being once perfected how to grant suits,
How to deny them, who t' advance, and who 80
To trash for over-topping, new-created
The creatures that were mine, I say, or changed 'em,
Or else new-formed 'em; having both the key
Of officer and office, set all hearts i' th' state
To what tune pleased his ear, that now he was 85
The ivy which had hid my princely trunk
And sucked my verdure out on't. Thou attend'st not!
MIRANDA. O, good sir, I do.
PROSPERO. I pray thee, mark me.
I thus neglecting worldly ends, all dedicated
To closeness, and the bettering of my mind 90
With that which, but by being so retired,
O'er-prized all popular rate, in my false brother
Awaked an evil nature, and my trust,
Like a good parent, did beget of him
A falsehood in its contrary, as great 95
As my trust was, which had indeed no limit,
A confidence sans bound. He being thus lorded
Not only with what my revenue yielded
But what my power might else exact, like one
Who having unto truth, by telling of it, 100
Made such a sinner of his memory
To credit his own lie, he did believe
He was indeed the Duke, out o' th' substitution
And executing th' outward face of royalty
With all prerogative. Hence his ambition growing— 105
Dost thou hear?
MIRANDA. Your tale, sir, would cure deafness.
PROSPERO. To have no screen between this part he played
And him he played it for, he needs will be
Absolute Milan. Me (poor man) my library
Was dukedom large enough. Of temporal royalties 110
He thinks me now incapable; confederates
(So dry he was for sway) wi' th' King of Naples
To give him annual tribute, do him homage,

---

79 *perfected:* practiced in. 81 *trash for over-topping:* check for exceeding authority. 82-83 *or . . . Or:* either . . . or. 90 *closeness:* seclusion. 92 *O'er-prized . . . rate:* was worth more than is thought or understood by the commonality. 97 *sans bound:* limitless. 102 *To:* as to. 103 *out:* as a result. 109 *Absolute Milan:* Duke of Milan in fact. 111 *confederates:* conspires. 112 *dry:* (thirsty), eager.

Subject his coronet to his crown, and bend
The dukedom yet unbowed (alas, poor Milan!) 115
To most ignoble stooping.

MIRANDA. O the heavens!

PROSPERO. Mark his condition, and th' event; then tell me
If this might be a brother.

MIRANDA. I should sin
To think but nobly of my grandmother.
Good wombs have borne bad sons.

PROSPERO. Now the condition. 120
This King of Naples, being an enemy
To me inveterate, hearkens my brother's suit;
Which was, that he, in lieu o' th' premises
Of homage and I know not how much tribute,
Should presently extirpate me and mine 125
Out of the dukedom, and confer fair Milan,
With all the honors, on my brother. Whereon,
A treacherous army levied, one midnight
Fated to th' purpose, did Antonio open
The gates of Milan; and, i' th' dead of darkness, 130
The ministers for th' purpose hurried thence
Me and thy crying self.

MIRANDA. Alack, for pity!
I, not rememb'ring how I cried out then,
Will cry it o'er again; it is a hint
That wrings mine eyes to't.

PROSPERO. Hear a little further, 135
And then I'll bring thee to the present business
Which now's upon's; without the which, this story
Were most impertinent.

MIRANDA. Wherefore did they not
That hour destroy us?

PROSPERO. Well demanded, wench.
My tale provokes that question. Dear, they durst not, 140
So dear the love my people bore me; nor set
A mark so bloody on the business; but
With colors fairer painted their foul ends.
In few, they hurried us aboard a bark,

---

114 *his crown:* the authority of the King of Naples. 117 *condition:* i.e., the pact made with Naples; *event:* outcome. 123 *in . . . premises:* in return for these conditions. 125 *presently:* immediately; *extirpate:* remove. 131 *ministers:* i.e., those employed. 134 *hint:* occasion. 138 *impertinent:* irrelevant. 144 *In few:* in short.

Bore us some leagues to sea; where they prepared 145
A rotten carcass of a butt, not rigged,
Nor tackle, sail, nor mast; the very rats
Instinctively have quit it. There they hoist us,
To cry to th' sea that roared to us; to sigh
To th' winds, whose pity, sighing back again, 150
Did us but loving wrong.

MIRANDA. Alack, what trouble
Was I then to you!

PROSPERO. O, a cherubin
Thou wast that did preserve me! Thou didst smile,
Infused with a fortitude from heaven,
When I have decked the sea with drops full salt, 155
Under my burden groaned; which raised in me
An undergoing stomach, to bear up
Against what should ensue.

MIRANDA. How came we ashore?

PROSPERO. By providence divine.
Some food we had, and some fresh water, that 160
A noble Neapolitan, Gonzalo,
Out of his charity, who being then appointed
Master of this design, did give us, with
Rich garments, linens, stuffs, and necessaries
Which since have steaded much. So, of his gentleness, 165
Knowing I loved my books, he furnished me
From mine own library with volumes that
I prize above my dukedom.

MIRANDA. Would I might
But ever see that man!

PROSPERO. Now I arise.
[*Dons his robe once more.*]
Sit still, and hear the last of our sea-sorrow. 170
Here in this island we arrived; and here
Have I, thy schoolmaster, made thee more profit
Than other princess can, that have more time
For vainer hours, and tutors not so careful.

MIRANDA. Heavens thank you for't! And now I pray you, sir, 175
For still 'tis beating in my mind, your reason
For raising this sea-storm?

PROSPERO. Know thus far forth.

---

146 *butt:* tub. 157 *undergoing stomach:* courage to endure. 165 *steaded:* benefited. 172 *more profit:* profit more. 173 *princess:* princesses.

By accident most strange, bountiful Fortune
(Now my dear lady) hath mine enemies
Brought to this shore; and by my prescience 180
I find my zenith doth depend upon
A most auspicious star, whose influence
If now I court not, but omit, my fortunes
Will ever after droop. Here cease more questions.
Thou art inclined to sleep. 'Tis a good dulness, 185
And give it way. I know thou canst not choose.

[MIRANDA *sleeps.*]

Come away, servant, come! I am ready now.
Approach, my Ariel: come!

Enter ARIEL.

ARIEL. All hail, great master! Grave sir, hail! I come
To answer thy best pleasure; be't to fly, 190
To swim, to dive into the fire, to ride
On the curled clouds. To thy strong bidding task
Ariel and all his quality.

PROSPERO. Hast thou, spirit,
Performed to point the tempest that I bade thee?

ARIEL. To every article. 195
I boarded the King's ship: now on the beak,
Now in the waist, the deck, in every cabin,
I flamed amazement: sometime I'ld divide
And burn in many places; on the topmast,
The yards, and bowsprit would I flame distinctly, 200
Then meet and join. Jove's lightnings, the precursors
O' th' dreadful thunder-claps, more momentary
And sight-outrunning were not. The fire and cracks
Of sulphurous roaring the most mighty Neptune
Seem to besiege, and make his bold waves tremble; 205
Yea, his dread trident shake.

PROSPERO. My brave spirit!
Who was so firm, so constant, that this coil
Would not infect his reason?

ARIEL. Not a soul
But felt a fever of the mad and played
Some tricks of desperation. All but mariners 210
Plunged in the foaming brine and quit the vessel,

---

181 *zenith:* i.e., the height of my fortune. 183 *omit:* ignore. 193 *quality:* lesser spirits led by Ariel. 194 *to point:* exactly. 196 *beak:* prow. 197 *waist*: midship; *deck:* poop. 198 *flamed amazement:* struck fear by appearing as flames. 207 *coil:* turmoil.

Then all afire with me: the King's son Ferdinand,
With hair up-staring (then like reeds, not hair),
Was the first man that leapt; cried "Hell is empty,
And all the devils are here!"

PROSPERO. Why, that's my spirit! 215
But was not this nigh shore?

ARIEL. Close by, my master.

PROSPERO. But are they, Ariel, safe?

ARIEL. Not a hair perished.
On their sustaining garments not a blemish,
But fresher than before; and as thou bad'st me,
In troops I have dispersed them 'bout the isle. 220
The King's son have I landed by himself,
Whom I left cooling of the air with sighs
In an odd angle of the isle, and sitting,
His arms in this sad knot.

PROSPERO. Of the King's ship,
The mariners, say how thou hast disposed, 225
And all the rest o' th' fleet.

ARIEL. Safely in harbor
Is the King's ship; in the deep nook where once
Thou call'dst me up at midnight to fetch dew
From the still-vexed Bermoothes, there she's hid;
The mariners all under hatches stowed, 230
Who, with a charm joined to their suffered labor,
I have left asleep; and for the rest o' th' fleet,
Which I dispersed, they all have met again,
And are upon the Mediterranean flote
Bound sadly home for Naples, 235
Supposing that they saw the King's ship wrecked,
And his great person perish.

PROSPERO. Ariel, thy charge
Exactly is performed; but there's more work.
What is the time o' th' day?

ARIEL. Past the mid season.

PROSPERO. At least two glasses. The time 'twixt six and now 240
Must by us both be spent most preciously.

ARIEL. Is there more toil? Since thou dost give me pains,
Let me remember thee what thou hast promised,

---

213 *up-staring:* standing on end. 218 *sustaining:* which bore them up in the water. 224 *in . . . knot:* thus (with a gesture by Ariel) sadly folded. 229 *still-vexed Bermoothes:* tempestuous Bermudas. 234 *flote:* sea. 239 *mid season:* noon. 240 *glasses:* hours. 243 *remember:* remind.

Which is not yet performed me.
PROSPERO. How now? moody?
What is't thou canst demand?
ARIEL. My liberty. 245
PROSPERO. Before the time be out? No more!
ARIEL. I prithee,
Remember I have done thee worthy service,
Told thee no lies, made no mistakings, served
Without or grudge or grumblings. Thou did promise
To bate me a full year.
PROSPERO. Dost thou forget 250
From what a torment I did free thee?
ARIEL. No.
PROSPERO. Thou dost; and think'st it much to tread the ooze
Of the salt deep,
To run upon the sharp wind of the North,
To do me business in the veins o' th' earth 255
When it is baked with frost.
ARIEL. I do not, sir.
PROSPERO. Thou liest, malignant thing! Hast thou forgot
The foul witch Sycorax, who with age and envy
Was grown into a hoop? Hast thou forgot her?
ARIEL. No, sir.
PROSPERO. Thou hast. Where was she born? Speak! Tell me! 260
ARIEL. Sir, in Argier.
PROSPERO. O, was she so? I must
Once in a month recount what thou hast been,
Which thou forget'st. This damned witch Sycorax,
For mischiefs manifold, and sorceries terrible
To enter human hearing, from Argier, 265
Thou know'st, was banished. For one thing she did
They would not take her life. Is not this true?
ARIEL. Ay, sir.
PROSPERO. This blue-eyed hag was hither brought with child
And here was left by th' sailors. Thou, my slave, 270
As thou report'st thyself, was then her servant;
And, for thou wast a spirit too delicate
To act her earthy and abhorred commands,
Refusing her grand hests, she did confine thee,
By help of her more potent ministers, 275

---

250 *bate me:* lessen my period of service. 261 *Argier:* Algiers. 274 *hests:* commands.

And in her most unmitigable rage,
Into a cloven pine; within which rift
Imprisoned thou didst painfully remain
A dozen years; within which space she died
And left thee there, where thou didst vent thy groans 280
As fast as mill-wheels strike. Then was this island
(Save for the son that she did litter here,
A freckled whelp, hag-born) not honored with
A human shape.

ARIEL. Yes, Caliban her son.

PROSPERO. Dull thing, I say so; he, that Caliban, 285
Whom now I keep in service. Thou best know'st
What torment I did find thee in: thy groans
Did make wolves howl and penetrate the breasts
Of ever-angry bears. It was a torment
To lay upon the damned, which Sycorax 290
Could not again undo. It was mine art,
When I arrived and heard thee, that made gape
The pine, and let thee out.

ARIEL. I thank thee, master.

PROSPERO. If thou more murmur'st, I will rend an oak
And peg thee in his knotty entrails till 295
Thou hast howled away twelve winters.

ARIEL. Pardon, master.
I will be correspondent to command,
And do my spriting gently.

PROSPERO. Do so; and after two days
I will discharge thee.

ARIEL. That's my noble master!
What shall I do? Say what? What shall I do? 300

PROSPERO. Go make thyself like a nymph o' th' sea. Be subject
To no sight but thine and mine; invisible
To every eyeball else. Go take this shape
And hither come in't. Go! Hence with diligence!

Exit [ARIEL].

Awake, dear heart, awake! Thou hast slept well. 305
Awake!

MIRANDA. The strangeness of your story put
Heaviness in me.

PROSPERO. Shake it off. Come on.

---

281 *mill-wheels:* i.e., the buckets on turning water wheels. 295 *his:* its. 297 *correspondent:* obedient. 298 *spriting gently:* my work as a spirit graciously.

We'll visit Caliban, my slave, who never
Yields us kind answer.
MIRANDA. 'Tis a villain, sir,
I do not love to look on.
PROSPERO. But, as 'tis, 310
We cannot miss him: he does make our fire,
Fetch in our wood, and serves in offices
That profit us. What, ho! slave! Caliban!
Thou earth, thou! Speak!
CALIBAN. *within.* There's wood enough within.
PROSPERO. Come forth, I say! There's other business for thee. 315
Come, thou tortoise! When?
[*Re-*]*enter* ARIEL *like a water nymph.*
Fine apparition! My quaint Ariel,
Hark in thine ear.
ARIEL. My lord, it shall be done. *Exit.*
PROSPERO. Thou poisonous slave, got by the devil himself
Upon thy wicked dam, come forth! 320
Enter CALIBAN.
CALIBAN. As wicked dew as e'er my mother brushed
With raven's feather from unwholesome fen
Drop on you both! A south-west blow on ye
And blister you all o'er!
PROSPERO. For this, be sure, to-night thou shalt have cramps, 325
Side-stitches that shall pen thy breath up; urchins
Shall, for that vast of night that they may work,
All exercise on thee; thou shalt be pinched
As thick as honeycomb, each pinch more stinging
Than bees that made 'em.
CALIBAN. I must eat my dinner. 330
This island's mine by Sycorax my mother,
Which thou tak'st from me. When thou cam'st first,
Thou strok'st me and made much of me; wouldst give me
Water with berries in't; and teach me how
To name the bigger light, and how the less, 335
That burn by day and night; and then I loved thee
And showed thee all the qualities o' th' isle,
The fresh springs, brine-pits, barren place and fertile.
Cursed be I that did so! All the charms
Of Sycorax—toads, beetles, bats, light on you! 340
For I am all the subjects that you have,

---

311 *miss:* do without. 317 *quaint:* remarkable. 319 *got:* begotten. 326 *urchins:* goblins in the shape of hedgehogs. 327 *vast:* desolate period.

Which first was mine own king; and here you sty me
In this hard rock, whiles you do keep from me
The rest o' th' island.

PROSPERO. Thou most lying slave,
Whom stripes may move, not kindness! I have used thee 345
(Filth as thou art) with humane care, and lodged thee
In mine own cell, till thou didst seek to violate
The honor of my child.

CALIBAN. O ho, O ho! Would't had been done!
Thou didst prevent me; I had peopled else 350
This isle with Calibans.

MIRANDA. Abhorred slave,
Which any print of goodness wilt not take,
Being capable of all ill! I pitied thee,
Took pains to make thee speak, taught thee each hour
One thing or other: when thou didst not, savage, 355
Know thine own meaning, but wouldst gabble like
A thing most brutish, I endowed thy purposes
With words that made them known. But thy vile race,
Though thou didst learn, had that in't which good natures
Could not abide to be with; therefore wast thou 360
Deservedly confined into this rock,
Who hadst deserved more than a prison.

CALIBAN. You taught me language, and my profit on't
Is, I know how to curse. The red plague rid you
For learning me your language!

PROSPERO. Hag-seed, hence! 365
Fetch us in fuel; and be quick, thou'rt best,
To answer other business. Shrug'st thou, malice?
If thou neglect'st or dost unwillingly
What I command, I'll rack thee with old cramps,
Fill all thy bones with aches, make thee roar 370
That beasts shall tremble at thy din.

CALIBAN. No, pray thee.
[*Aside.*] I must obey. His art is of such pow'r,
It would control my dam's god, Setebos,
And make a vassal of him.

PROSPERO. So, slave; hence! *Exit* CALIBAN.

Enter FERDINAND; *and* ARIEL (*invisible*), *playing and singing.*

---

342 *sty:* imprison. 345 *stripes:* lashes. 352 *print:* imprint. 364 *red plague:* bubonic plague; *rid:* destroy. 369 *old cramps:* i.e., the cramps typical of the old.

Ariel's Song

Come unto these yellow sands, 375
And then take hands.
Curtsied when you have and kissed,
The wild waves whist,
Foot it featly here and there;
And, sweet sprites, the burden bear. 380
Hark, hark!
Burden, dispersedly. Bow-wow.
The watchdogs bark.
Burden, dispersedly. Bow-wow.
Hark, hark! I hear 385
The strain of strutting chanticleer
Cry cock-a-diddle-dow.

FERDINAND. Where should this music be? I' th' air or th' earth?
It sounds no more; and sure it waits upon
Some god o' th' island. Sitting on a bank, 390
Weeping again the King my father's wreck.
This music crept by me upon the waters,
Allaying both their fury and my passion
With its sweet air. Thence I have followed it,
Or it hath drawn me rather; but 'tis gone. 395
No, it begins again.

Ariel's Song

Full fathom five thy father lies;
Of his bones are coral made;
Those are pearls that were his eyes;
Nothing of him that doth fade 400
But doth suffer a sea-change
Into something rich and strange.
Sea-nymphs hourly ring his knell:
Burden. Ding-dong.
Hark! now I hear them—Ding-dong bell. 405

FERDINAND. The ditty does remember my drowned father.
This is no mortal business, nor no sound
That the earth owes. I hear it now above me.
PROSPERO. The fringed curtains of thine eye advance

---

378 *whist:* silent. 379 *featly:* nimbly. 380 *burden:* refrain. 406 *remember:* allude to. 408 *owes:* owns. 409 *advance:* raise.

And say what thou seest yond. 410
MIRANDA. What is't? a spirit?
Lord, how it looks about! Believe me, sir,
It carries a brave form. But 'tis a spirit.
PROSPERO. No, wench: it eats, and sleeps, and hath such senses
As we have, such. This gallant which thou seest
Was in the wreck; and, but he's something stained 415
With grief (that's beauty's canker), thou mightst call him
A goodly person. He hath lost his fellows,
And strays about to find 'em.
MIRANDA. I might call him
A thing divine; for nothing natural
I ever saw so noble.
PROSPERO. [*Aside.*] It goes on, I see, 420
As my soul prompts it. Spirit, fine spirit, I'll free thee
Within two days for this.
FERDINAND. Most sure, the goddess
On whom these airs attend! Vouchsafe my prayer
May know if you remain upon this island,
And that you will some good instruction give 425
How I may bear me here. My prime request,
Which I do last pronounce, is (O you wonder!)
If you be maid or no?
MIRANDA. No wonder, sir,
But certainly a maid.
FERDINAND. My language? Heavens!
I am the best of them that speak this speech, 430
Were I but where 'tis spoken.
PROSPERO. How? the best?
What wert thou if the King of Naples heard thee?
FERDINAND. A single thing, as I am now, that wonders
To hear thee speak of Naples. He does hear me;
And that he does I weep. Myself am Naples, 435
Who with mine eyes, never since at ebb, beheld
The King my father wrecked.
MIRANDA. Alack, for mercy!
FERDINAND. Yes, faith, and all his lords, the Duke of Milan
And his brave son being twain.

---

420 *It:* i.e., Prospero's plan. 423 *Vouchsafe:* grant. 424 *remain:* dwell. 426 *bear me:* conduct myself. 428 *maid or no:* Ferdinand is uncertain whether Miranda is a mortal woman or a goddess. 439 *brave . . . twain:* refers to alleged drowning of Antonio and his son; no further mention is made of the latter in the play.

PROSPERO. [*Aside.*] The Duke of Milan
And his more braver daughter could control thee, 440
If now 'twere fit to do't. At the first sight
They have changed eyes. Delicate Ariel,
I'll set thee free for this. [*To* FERDINAND.] A word, good sir.
I fear you have done yourself some wrong: a word.
MIRANDA. Why speaks my father so ungently? This 445
Is the third man that e'er I saw; the first
That e'er I sighed for. Pity move my father
To be inclined my way!
FERDINAND. O, if a virgin,
And your affection not gone forth, I'll make you
The Queen of Naples.
PROSPERO. Soft, sir! one word more. 450
[*Aside.*] They are both in either's pow'rs. But this swift business
I must uneasy make, lest too light winning
Make the prize light. [*To* FERDINAND.] One word more! I charge thee
That thou attend me. Thou dost here usurp
The name thou ow'st not, and hast put thyself 455
Upon this island as a spy, to win it
From me, the lord on't.
FERDINAND. No, as I am a man!
MIRANDA. There's nothing ill can dwell in such a temple.
If the ill spirit have so fair a house,
Good things will strive to dwell with't.
PROSPERO. Follow me.— 460
Speak not you for him; he's a traitor.—Come!
I'll manacle thy neck and feet together;
Sea water shalt thou drink; thy food shall be
The fresh-brook mussels, withered roots, and husks
Wherein the acorn cradled. Follow!
FERDINAND. No. 465
I will resist such entertainment till
Mine enemy has more power.
He draws, and is charmed from moving.
MIRANDA. O dear father,
Make not too rash a trial of him, for
He's gentle, and not fearful.
PROSPERO. What! I say,

---

442 *changed eyes:* fallen in love. 458 *temple:* i.e., handsome body. 466 *entertainment:* treatment. 469 *gentle:* of noble birth; *fearful:* cowardly.

My foot my tutor?—Put thy sword up, traitor! 470
Who mak'st a show, but dar'st not strike, thy conscience
Is so possessed with guilt. Come from thy ward!
For I can here disarm thee with this stick
And make thy weapon drop.

MIRANDA. Beseech you, father!

PROSPERO. Hence! Hang not on my garments.

MIRANDA. Sir, have pity. 475
I'll be his surety.

PROSPERO. Silence! One word more
Shall make me chide thee, if not hate thee. What!
An advocate for an impostor? Hush!
Thou think'st there is no more such shapes as he,
Having seen but him and Caliban. Foolish wench! 480
To th' most of men this is a Caliban,
And they to him are angels.

MIRANDA. My affections
Are then most humble. I have no ambition
To see a goodlier man.

PROSPERO. Come on, obey!
Thy nerves are in their infancy again 485
And have no vigor in them.

FERDINAND. So they are,
My spirits, as in a dream, are all bound up.
My father's loss, the weakness which I feel,
The wreck of all my friends, nor this man's threats
To whom I am subdued, are but light to me, 490
Might I but through my prison once a day
Behold this maid. All corners else o' th' earth
Let liberty make use of. Space enough
Have I in such a prison.

PROSPERO. [*Aside.*] It works. [*To* FERDINAND.]
Come on.—
Thou hast done well, fine Ariel! [*To* FERDINAND.] Follow me. 495
[*To* ARIEL.] Hark what thou else shalt do me.

MIRANDA. Be of comfort.
My father's of a better nature, sir,
Than he appears by speech. This is unwonted
Which now came from him.

PROSPERO. Thou shalt be as free
As mountain winds; but then exactly do 500

---

470 *My . . . tutor:* i.e., Shall an inferior instruct me? 472 *ward:* stance of guard in fighting. 485 *nerves:* sinews.

All points of my command.

ARIEL. To th' syllable.

PROSPERO. Come, follow.—Speak not for him. *Exeunt.*

Act II

SCENE I [*Another part of the island*]

Enter ALONSO, SEBASTIAN, ANTONIO, GONZALO, ADRIAN, FRANCISCO, *and others.*

GONZALO. Beseech you, sir, be merry. You have cause
(So have we all) of joy; for our escape
Is much beyond our loss. Our hint of woe
Is common: every day some sailor's wife,
The masters of some merchant, and the merchant, 5
Have just our theme of woe; but for the miracle,
I mean our preservation, few in millions
Can speak like us. Then wisely, good sir, weigh
Our sorrow with our comfort.

ALONSO. Prithee, peace.

SEBASTIAN. [*Aside to* ANTONIO.] He receives comfort like cold 10
porridge.

ANTONIO. [*Aside to* SEBASTIAN.] The visitor will not give him
o'er so.

SEBASTIAN. [*Aside to* ANTONIO.] Look, he's winding up the
watch of his wit; by and by it will strike. 15

GONZALO. Sir—

SEBASTIAN. [*Aside to* ANTONIO.] One. Tell.

GONZALO. When every grief is entertained that's offered,
Comes to th' entertainer—

SEBASTIAN. A dollar. 20

GONZALO. Dolor comes to him, indeed. You have spoken
truer than you purposed.

SEBASTIAN. You have taken it wiselier than I meant you
should.

GONZALO. Therefore, my lord— 25

ANTONIO. Fie, what a spendthrift is he of his tongue!

ALONSO. I prithee, spare.

GONZALO. Well, I have done. But yet—

SEBASTIAN. He will be talking.

ANTONIO. Which, of he or Adrian, for a good wager, first 30
begins to crow?

II,i,5 *masters . . . merchant:* masters of a merchant ship; *the merchant:* the owner. 17 *Tell:* count.

SEBASTIAN. The old cock.
ANTONIO. The cockerel.
SEBASTIAN. Done! The wager?
ANTONIO. A laughter. 35
SEBASTIAN. A match!
ADRIAN. Though this island seem to be desert—
ANTONIO. Ha, ha, ha!
SEBASTIAN. So, you're paid.
ADRIAN. Uninhabitable and almost inaccessible— 40
SEBASTIAN. Yet—
ADRIAN. Yet—
ANTONIO. He could not miss't.
ADRIAN. It must needs be of subtle, tender, and delicate temperance. 45
ANTONIO. Temperance was a delicate wench.
SEBASTIAN. Ay, and a subtle, as he most learnedly delivered.
ADRIAN. The air breathes upon us here most sweetly.
SEBASTIAN. As if it had lungs, and rotten ones.
ANTONIO. Or as 'twere perfumed by a fen. 50
GONZALO. Here is everything advantageous to life.
ANTONIO. True; save means to live.
SEBASTIAN. Of that there's none, or little.
GONZALO. How lush and lusty the grass looks! how green!
ANTONIO. The ground, indeed, is tawny. 55
SEBASTIAN. With an eye of green in't.
ANTONIO. He misses not much.
SEBASTIAN. No; he doth but mistake the truth totally.
GONZALO. But the rarity of it is—which is indeed almost beyond credit— 60
SEBASTIAN. As many vouched rarities are.
GONZALO. That our garments, being, as they were, drenched in the sea, hold, notwithstanding, their freshness and gloss, being rather new-dyed than stained with salt water.
ANTONIO. If but one of his pockets could speak, would it not say he lies? 65
SEBASTIAN. Ay, or very falsely pocket up his report.
GONZALO. Methinks our garments are now as fresh as when we put them on first in Afric, at the marriage of the King's fair daughter Claribel to the King of Tunis. 70

---

35 *A laughter:* the winner laughs at the loser. 39 *you're paid:* i.e., you've had your laugh as winner. 45 *temperance:* climate. 46 *Temperance:* here used as proper noun (a girl's name). 56 *eye:* touch. 61 *vouched:* affirmed.

SEBASTIAN. 'Twas a sweet marriage, and we prosper well in our return.

ADRIAN. Tunis was never graced before with such a paragon to their queen.

GONZALO. Not since widow Dido's time. 75

ANTONIO. Widow? A pox o' that! How came that "widow" in? Widow Dido!

SEBASTIAN. What if he had said "widower Aeneas" too? Good Lord, how you take it!

ADRIAN. "Widow Dido," said you? You make me study of 80 that. She was of Carthage, not of Tunis.

GONZALO. This Tunis, sir, was Carthage.

ADRIAN. Carthage?

GONZALO. I assure you, Carthage.

ANTONIO. His word is more than the miraculous harp. 85

SEBASTIAN. He hath raised the wall and houses too.

ANTONIO. What impossible matter will he make easy next?

SEBASTIAN. I think he will carry this island home in his pocket and give it his son for an apple.

ANTONIO. And, sowing the kernels of it in the sea, bring 90 forth more islands.

GONZALO. Ay!

ANTONIO. Why, in good time.

GONZALO. Sir, we were talking that our garments seem now as fresh as when we were at Tunis at the marriage of your 95 daughter, who is now Queen.

ANTONIO. And the rarest that e'er came there.

SEBASTIAN. Bate, I beseech you, widow Dido.

ANTONIO. O, widow Dido? Ay, widow Dido!

GONZALO. Is not, sir, my doublet as fresh as the first day I 100 wore it? I mean, in a sort.

ANTONIO. That "sort" was well fished for.

GONZALO. When I wore it at your daughter's marriage.

ALONSO. You cram these words into mine ears against
The stomach of my sense. Would I had never 105
Married my daughter there! for, coming thence,

---

74 *to:* for. 75 *widow Dido:* Dido, Queen of Carthage, was the widow of Sychaeus. The story of her love for Aeneas and subsequent suicide at his departure is told by Virgil. 85 *His . . . harp:* Amphion's harp "miraculously" raised the walls of Thebes; but even more wonderful, according to Antonio, is Gonzalo who can make two cities one. 98 *Bate:* except. 101 *in a sort:* comparatively.

My son is lost; and, in my rate, she too,
Who is so far from Italy removed
I ne'er again shall see her. O thou mine heir
Of Naples and of Milan, what strange fish 110
Hath made his meal on thee?

FRANCISCO. Sir, he may live.
I saw him beat the surges under him
And ride upon their backs. He trod the water,
Whose enmity he flung aside, and breasted
The surge most swol'n that met him. His bold head 115
'Bove the contentious waves he kept, and oared
Himself with his good arms in lusty stroke
To th' shore, that o'er his wave-worn basis bowed,
As stooping to relieve him. I not doubt
He came alive to land.

ALONSO. No, no, he's gone. 120

SEBASTIAN. Sir, you may thank yourself for this great loss,
That would not bless our Europe with your daughter,
But rather lose her to an African,
Where she, at least, is banished from your eye,
Who hath cause to wet the grief on't.

ALONSO. Prithee, peace. 125

SEBASTIAN. You were kneeled to and importuned otherwise
By all of us; and the fair soul herself
Weighed, between loathness and obedience, at
Which end o' th' beam should bow. We have lost your son,
I fear, for ever. Milan and Naples have 130
Mo widows in them of this business' making
Than we bring men to comfort them:
The fault's your own.

ALONZO. So is the dear'st o' th' loss.

GONZALO. My Lord Sebastian,
The truth you speak doth lack some gentleness, 135
And time to speak it in. You rub the sore
When you should bring the plaster.

SEBASTIAN. Very well.

ANTONIO. And most chirurgeonly.

GONZALO. It is foul weather in us all, good sir,
When you are cloudy.

SEBASTIAN. Foul weather?

---

107 *rate:* opinion. 128 *Weighed:* balanced. 131 *Mo:* more. 133 *dear'st . . . loss:* i.e., most grief. 138 *chirurgeonly:* like a surgeon.

ANTONIO. Very foul. 140
GONZALO. Had I plantation of this isle, my lord—
ANTONIO. He'd sow't with nettle-seed.
SEBASTIAN. Or docks, or mallows.
GONZALO. And were the king on't, what would I do?
SEBASTIAN. Scape being drunk for want of wine.
GONZALO. I' th' commonwealth I would by contraries 145
Execute all things; for no kind of traffic
Would I admit; no name of magistrate;
Letters should not be known; riches, poverty,
And use of service, none; contract, succession,
Bourn, bound of land, tilth, vineyard, none; 150
No use of metal, corn, or wine, or oil;
No occupation; all men idle, all;
And women too, but innocent and pure;
No sovereignty.
SEBASTIAN. Yet he would be king on't.
ANTONIO. The latter end of his commonwealth forgets the 155
beginning.
GONZALO. All things in common nature should produce
Without sweat or endeavor. Treason, felony,
Sword, pike, knife, gun, or need of any engine
Would I not have; but nature should bring forth, 160
Of it own kind, all foison, all abundance,
To feed my innocent people.
SEBASTIAN. No marrying 'mong his subjects?
ANTONIO. None, man, all idle—whores and knaves.
GONZALO. I would with such perfection govern, sir, 165
T' excel the golden age.
SEBASTIAN. 'Save his Majesty!
ANTONIO. Long live Gonzalo!
GONZALO. And—do you mark me, sir?
ALONSO. Prithee, no more. Thou dost talk nothing to me.
GONZALO. I do well believe your Highness; and did it to
minister occasion to these gentlemen, who are of such sensible 170
and nimble lungs that they always use to laugh at nothing.
ANTONIO. 'Twas you we laughed at.
GONZALO. Who in this kind of merry fooling am nothing

---

141 *plantation:* colonization (but used by Antonio to mean "planting"). 145 *by contraries:* in contrast to customary practices. 146 *traffic:* trade. 149 *use of service:* servant class; *succession:* inheritance of property. 150 *bound of land:* i.e., private ownership; *tilth:* tillage. 159 *engine:* instrument of war. 160 *it:* its; *foison:* plenty. 170 *minister occasion:* afford opportunity; *sensible:* sensitive.

to you: so you may continue, and laugh at nothing still.
ANTONIO. What a blow was there given! 175
SEBASTIAN. An it had not fallen flatlong.
GONZALO. You are gentlemen of brave mettle: you would lift the moon out of her sphere if she would continue in it five weeks without changing.

Enter ARIEL [*invisible*] *playing solemn music.*

SEBASTIAN. We would so, and then go a-batfowling. 180
ANTONIO. Nay, good my lord, be not angry.
GONZALO. No, I warrant you: I will not adventure my discretion so weakly. Will you laugh me asleep, for I am very heavy?
ANTONIO. Go sleep, and hear us.

[*All sleep except* ALONSO, SEBASTIAN, *and* ANTONIO.]

ALONSO. What, all so soon asleep? I wish mine eyes 185
Would, with themselves, shut up my thoughts. I find
They are inclined to do so.
SEBASTIAN. Please you, sir,
Do not omit the heavy offer of it.
It seldom visits sorrow; when it doth,
It is a comforter.
ANTONIO. We two, my lord, 190
Will guard your person while you take your rest,
And watch your safety.
ALONSO. Thank you. Wondrous heavy.

[ALONSO *sleeps. Exit* ARIEL.]

SEBASTIAN. What a strange drowsiness possesses them!
ANTONIO. It is the quality o' th' climate.
SEBASTIAN. Why
Doth it not then our eyelids sink? I find not 195
Myself disposed to sleep.
ANTONIO. Nor I: my spirits are nimble.
They fell together all, as by consent.
They dropped, as by a thunder-stroke. What might,
Worthy Sebastian—O, what might?—No more!
And yet methinks I see it in thy face, 200
What thou shouldst be. Th' occasion speaks thee, and
My strong imagination sees a crown
Dropping upon thy head.

---

176 *An:* if; *flatlong:* a sword's flat side. 178 *sphere:* orbit. 180 *a-batfowling:* bird hunting at night with a lantern (here, the moon); the clubs used were called "bats." 182-83 *adventure . . . weakly:* risk my reputation for good sense by taking offense at such feeble jibes. 188 *omit:* neglect; *heavy offer:* i.e., the oblivion of sleep. 201 *speaks:* summons.

SEBASTIAN. What? Art thou waking?
ANTONIO. Do you not hear me speak?
SEBASTIAN. I do; and surely
It is a sleepy language, and thou speak'st 205
Out of thy sleep. What is it thou didst say?
This is a strange repose, to be asleep
With eyes wide open; standing, speaking, moving,
And yet so fast asleep.
ANTONIO. Noble Sebastian,
Thou let'st thy fortune sleep—die, rather; wink'st 210
Whiles thou art waking.
SEBASTIAN. Thou dost snore distinctly;
There's meaning in thy snores.
ANTONIO. I am more serious than my custom. You
Must be so too, if heed me; which to do
Trebles thee o'er.
SEBASTIAN. Well, I am standing water. 215
ANTONIO. I'll teach you how to flow.
SEBASTIAN. Do so. To ebb
Hereditary sloth instructs me.
ANTONIO. O,
If you but knew how you the purpose cherish
Whiles thus you mock it! how, in stripping it,
You more invest it! Ebbing men indeed 220
(Most often) do so near the bottom run
By their own fear or sloth.
SEBASTIAN. Prithee, say on.
The setting of thine eye and cheek proclaim
A matter from thee; and a birth, indeed,
Which throes thee much to yield.
ANTONIO. Thus, sir: 225
Although this lord of weak remembrance, this,
Who shall be of as little memory
When he is earthed, hath here almost persuaded
(For he's a spirit of persuasion, only
Professes to persuade) the King his son's alive, 230
'Tis as impossible that he's undrowned
As he that sleeps here swims.
SEBASTIAN. I have no hope

---

215 *Trebles thee o'er:* improves your status threefold; *standing water:* i.e., between tides (undecided). 217 *Hereditary sloth:* natural laziness. 224 *matter:* something of importance. 225 *throes . . . yield:* is brought forth with pain. 227-28 *as . . . earthed:* as little remembered when he is buried.

That he's undrowned.
ANTONIO. O, out of that "no hope"
What great hope have you! No hope that way is
Another way so high a hope that even 235
Ambition cannot pierce a wink beyond,
But doubt discovery there. Will you grant with me
That Ferdinand is drowned?
SEBASTIAN. He's gone.
ANTONIO. Then tell me,
Who's the next heir of Naples?
SEBASTIAN. Claribel.
ANTONIO. She that is Queen of Tunis; she that dwells 240
Ten leagues beyond man's life; she that from Naples
Can have no note, unless the sun were post—
The man i' th' moon's too slow—till new-born chins
Be rough and razorable; she that from whom
We all were sea-swallowed, though some cast again, 245
And by that destiny, to perform an act
Whereof what's past is prologue; what to come,
In yours and my discharge.
SEBASTIAN. What stuff is this? How say you?
'Tis true my brother's daughter's Queen of Tunis;
So is she heir of Naples; 'twixt which regions 250
There is some space.
ANTONIO. A space whose ev'ry cubit
Seems to cry out "How shall that Claribel
Measure us back to Naples? Keep in Tunis,
And let Sebastian wake!" Say this were death
That now hath seized them; why, they were no worse 255
Than now they are. There be that can rule Naples
As well as he that sleeps; lords that can prate
As amply and unnecessarily
As this Gonzalo; I myself could make
A chough of as deep chat. O, that you bore 260
The mind that I do! What a sleep were this
For your advancement! Do you understand me?
SEBASTIAN. Methinks I do.
ANTONIO. And how does your content

235-38 *even . . . there:* even your ambition cannot look beyond your great prospects of being King. 241 *Ten . . . life:* i.e., "at the end of the earth." 242 *post:* messenger. 245 *cast:* thrown up. 248 *discharge:* business. 253 *us:* i.e., the cubits; *Keep:* let her remain. 259-60 *make . . . chat:* teach a jackdaw to talk as he does.

Tender your own good fortune?
SEBASTIAN. I remember
You did supplant your brother Prospero.
ANTONIO. True. 265
And look how well my garments sit upon me,
Much feater than before. My brother's servants
Were then my fellows; now they are my men.
SEBASTIAN. But, for your conscience—
ANTONIO. Ay, sir, where lies that? If 'twere a kibe, 270
'Twould put me to my slipper; but I feel not
This deity in my bosom. Twenty consciences
That stand 'twixt me and Milan, candied be they
And melt, ere they molest! Here lies your brother,
No better than the earth he lies upon 275
If he were that which now he's like—that's dead;
Whom I with this obedient steel (three inches of it)
Can lay to bed for ever; whiles you, doing thus,
To the perpetual wink for aye might put
This ancient morsel, this Sir Prudence, who 280
Should not upbraid our course. For all the rest,
They'll take suggestion as a cat laps milk;
They'll tell the clock to any business that
We say befits the hour.
SEBASTIAN. Thy case, dear friend,
Shall be my precedent. As thou got'st Milan, 285
I'll come by Naples. Draw thy sword. One stroke
Shall free thee from the tribute which thou payest,
And I the King shall love thee.
ANTONIO. Draw together;
And when I rear my hand, do you the like,
To fall it on Gonzalo. *[They draw.]*
SEBASTIAN. O, but one word! *[They talk apart.]* 290

[Re-]enter ARIEL *[invisible] with music and song.*

ARIEL. My master through his art foresees the danger
That you, his friend, are in, and sends me forth
(For else his project dies) to keep them living.
Sings in GONZALO'*s ear.*

While you here do snoring lie,
Open-eyed conspiracy 295

267 *feater:* more appropriately. 268 *fellows:* equals; *men:* servants. 270 *kibe:* chilblain. 273 *candied:* frozen. 279 *wink:* sleep. 283-84 *tell . . . hour:* do as they are told. 290 *fall it:* let it fall.

His time doth take.
If of life you keep a care,
Shake off slumber and beware.
Awake, awake!

ANTONIO. Then let us both be sudden.
GONZALO. [*Wakes.*] Now good angels 300
Preserve the King! [*The others wake.*]
ALONSO. Why, how now?—Ho, awake?—Why are you drawn?
Wherefore this ghastly looking?
GONZALO. What's the matter?
SEBASTIAN. Whiles we stood here securing your repose,
Even now, we heard a hollow burst of bellowing 305
Like bulls, or rather lions. Did't not wake you?
It struck mine ear most terribly.
ALONSO. I heard nothing.
ANTONIO. O, 'twas a din to fright a monster's ear,
To make an earthquake! Sure it was the roar
Of a whole herd of lions.
ALONSO. Heard you this, Gonzalo? 310
GONZALO. Upon mine honor, sir, I heard a humming,
And that a strange one too, which did awake me.
I shaked you, sir, and cried. As mine eyes opened,
I saw their weapons drawn. There was a noise,
That's verily. 'Tis best we stand upon our guard, 315
Or that we quit this place. Let's draw our weapons.
ALONSO. Lead off this ground, and let's make further search
For my poor son.
GONZALO. Heavens keep him from these beasts!
For he is, sure, i' th' island.
ALONSO. Lead away.
ARIEL. Prospero my lord shall know what I have done. 320
So, King, go safely on to seek thy son. *Exeunt.*

SCENE II [*Another part of the island*]

Enter CALIBAN *with a burden of wood. A noise of thunder heard.*

CALIBAN. All the infections that the sun sucks up
From bogs, fens, flats, on Prosper fall, and make him
By inch-meal a disease! His spirits hear me,
And yet I needs must curse. But they'll nor pinch,

304 *securing:* protecting. 315 *verily:* in truth. II,ii,3 *By inch-meal:* inch by inch.

Fright me with urchin-shows, pitch me i' th' mire, 5
Nor lead me, like a firebrand, in the dark
Out of my way, unless he bid 'em; but
For every trifle are they set upon me;
Sometime like apes that mow and chatter at me,
And after bite me; then like hedgehogs which 10
Lie tumbling in my barefoot way and mount
Their pricks at my footfall; sometime am I
All wound with adders, who with cloven tongues
Do hiss me into madness.

Enter TRINCULO.

Lo, now, lo!
Here comes a spirit of his, and to torment me 15
For bringing wood in slowly. I'll fall flat.
Perchance he will not mind me. [*Lies down.*]

TRINCULO. Here's neither bush nor shrub to bear off any weather at all, and another storm brewing: I hear it sing i' th' wind. Yond same black cloud, yond huge one, looks like a foul 20 bombard that would shed his liquor. If it should thunder as it did before, I know not where to hide my head. Yond same cloud cannot choose but fall by pailfuls. What have we here? a man or a fish? dead or alive? A fish: he smells like a fish; a very ancient and fishlike smell; a kind of, not of the newest 25 poor-John. A strange fish! Were I in England now, as once I was, and had but this fish painted, not a holiday fool there but would give a piece of silver. There would this monster make a man: any strange beast there makes a man. When they will not give a doit to relieve a lame beggar, they will lay out ten 30 to see a dead Indian. Legged like a man! and his fins like arms! Warm, o' my troth! I do now let loose my opinion, hold it no longer: this is no fish, but an islander, that hath lately suffered by a thunderbolt. [*Thunder.*] Alas, the storm is come again! My best way is to creep under his gaberdine: there is no other 35 shelter hereabout. Misery acquaints a man with strange bedfellows. I will here shroud till the dregs of the storm be past.

Enter STEPHANO, *singing;* [*a bottle in his hand*].

STEPHANO. I shall no more to sea, to sea;
Here shall I die ashore.

---

5 *urchin-shows:* supernatural apparitions. 6 *firebrand:* will-o'-the-wisp. 9 *mow:* make faces. 21 *bombard:* large leather jug. 26 *poor-John:* dried hake. 27 *painted:* i.e., pictured on a signboard. 28-29 *make a man:* i.e., make a man's fortune. 30 *doit:* Dutch coin of small value. 35 *gaberdine:* cloak. 37 *shroud:* cover myself.

This is a very scurvy tune to sing at a man's funeral. Well, here's my comfort. *Drinks.* 40

The master, the swabber, the boatswain, and I,
The gunner, and his mate,
Loved Mall, Meg, and Marian, and Margery,
But none of us cared for Kate. 45
For she had a tongue with a tang,
Would cry to a sailor "Go hang!"
She loved not the savor of tar nor of pitch;
Yet a tailor might scratch her where'er she did itch.
Then to sea, boys, and let her go hang! 50

This is a scurvy tune too; but here's my comfort. *Drinks.*

CALIBAN. Do not torment me! O!

STEPHANO. What's the matter? Have we devils here? Do you put tricks upon 's with savages and men of Inde, ha? I have not scaped drowning to be afeard now of your four legs; for it 55 hath been said, "As proper a man as ever went on four legs cannot make him give ground"; and it shall be said so again, while Stephano breathes at nostrils.

CALIBAN. The spirit torments me. O!

STEPHANO. This is some monster of the isle, with four legs, 60 who hath got, as I take it, an ague. Where the devil should he learn our language? I will give him some relief, if it be but for that. If I can recover him, and keep him tame, and get to Naples with him, he's a present for any emperor that ever trod on neat's-leather. 65

CALIBAN. Do not torment me, prithee; I'll bring my wood home faster.

STEPHANO. He's in his fit now, and does not talk after the wisest. He shall taste of my bottle: if he have never drunk wine afore, it will go near to remove his fit. If I can recover 70 him and keep him tame, I will not take too much for him; he shall pay for him that hath him, and that soundly.

CALIBAN. Thou dost me yet but little hurt. Thou wilt anon; I know it by thy trembling. Now Prosper works upon thee.

STEPHANO. Come on your ways: open your mouth: here is 75 that which will give language to you, cat. Open your mouth. This will shake your shaking, I can tell you, and that soundly.

---

56 *proper:* able. 63 *recover:* cure. 65 *neat's-leather:* i.e., shoes. 71 *I . . . him:* no price will be high enough for him. 73 *anon:* soon. 76 *cat:* the proverbial expression is "Liquor will make a cat speak."

[*Gives* CALIBAN *drink.*] You cannot tell who's your friend. Open your chaps again.

TRINCULO. I should know that voice. It should be—but he is drowned; and these are devils. O, defend me! 80

STEFANO. Four legs and two voices—a most delicate monster! His forward voice now is to speak well of his friend; his backward voice is to utter foul speeches and to detract. If all the wine in my bottle will recover him, I will help his ague. Come! 85 [*Gives drink.*] Amen! I will pour some in thy other mouth.

TRINCULO. Stephano!

STEPHANO. Doth thy other mouth call me? Mercy, mercy! This is a devil, and no monster. I will leave him; I have no long spoon. 90

TRINCULO. Stephano! If thou beest Stephano, touch me and speak to me; for I am Trinculo—be not afeard—thy good friend Trinculo.

STEPHANO. If thou beest Trinculo, come forth. I'll pull thee by the lesser legs. If any be Trinculo's legs, these are they. 95 [*Draws him out from under* CALIBAN'S *garment.*] Thou art very Trinculo indeed: how cam'st thou to be the siege of this moon-calf? Can he vent Trinculos?

TRINCULO. I took him to be killed with a thunder-stroke. But art thou not drowned, Stephano? I hope now thou art not 100 drowned. Is the storm over-blown? I hid me under the dead moon-calf's gaberdine for fear of the storm. And art thou living, Stephano? O Stephano, two Neapolitans scaped!

STEPHANO. Prithee, do not turn me about: my stomach is not constant. 105

CALIBAN. [*Aside.*] These be fine things, an if they be not sprites.
That's a brave god and bears celestial liquor.
I will kneel to him.

STEPHANO. How didst thou scape? How cam'st thou hither? Swear, by this bottle, how thou cam'st hither. I escaped upon 110 a butt of sack, which the sailors heaved o'erboard, by this bottle, which I made of the bark of a tree with mine own hands since I was cast ashore.

CALIBAN. I'll swear upon that bottle to be thy true subject, for the liquor is not earthly. 115

---

79 *chaps:* jaws. 89-90 *I . . . spoon:* the proverbial expression is "He who sups with the devil must have a long spoon." 97 *siege:* excrement. 98 *moon-calf:* monster. 111 *butt of sack:* barrel of Spanish wine.

STEPHANO. Here! Swear then how thou escapedst.

TRINCULO. Swum ashore, man, like a duck. I can swim like a duck, I'll be sworn.

STEPHANO. Here, kiss the book. [*Gives him drink.*] Though thou canst swim like a duck, thou art made like a goose. 120

TRINCULO. O Stephano, hast any more of this?

STEPHANO. The whole butt, man: my cellar is in a rock by th' seaside, where my wine is hid. How now, moon-calf! How does thine ague?

CALIBAN. Hast thou not dropped from heaven? 125

STEPHANO. Out o' th' moon, I do assure thee. I was the Man i' th' Moon when time was.

CALIBAN. I have seen thee in her, and I do adore thee.
My mistress showed me thee, and thy dog, and thy bush.

STEPHANO. Come, swear to that; kiss the book. I will furnish 130 it anon with new contents. Swear. [CALIBAN *drinks.*]

TRINCULO. By this good light, this is a very shallow monster! I afeard of him? A very weak monster! The Man i' th' Moon? A most poor credulous monster!—Well drawn, monster, in good sooth! 135

CALIBAN. I'll show thee every fertile inch o' th' island;
And I will kiss thy foot. I prithee, be my god.

TRINCULO. By this light, a most perfidious and drunken monster! When's god's asleep, he'll rob his bottle.

CALIBAN. I'll kiss thy foot. I'll swear myself thy subject. 140

STEPHANO. Come on, then. Down, and swear!

TRINCULO. I shall laugh myself to death at this puppy-headed monster. A most scurvy monster! I could find in my heart to beat him—

STEPHANO. Come, kiss. 145

TRINCULO. But that the poor monster's in drink. An abominable monster!

CALIBAN. I'll show thee the best springs; I'll pluck thee berries.
I'll fish for thee, and get thee wood enough.
A plague upon the tyrant that I serve! 150
I'll bear him no more sticks, but follow thee,
Thou wondrous man.

TRINCULO. A most ridiculous monster, to make a wonder of a poor drunkard!

CALIBAN. I prithee, let me bring thee where crabs grow; 155

---

119 *book:* i.e., bottle. 127 *when time was:* once upon a time. 134 *drawn:* drunk. 155 *crabs:* crab apples.

And I with my long nails will dig thee pignuts,
Show thee a jay's nest, and instruct thee how
To snare the nimble marmoset; I'll bring thee
To clustering filberts, and sometimes I'll get thee
Young scamels from the rock. Wilt thou go with me? 160

STEPHANO. I prithee now, lead the way without any more talking. Trinculo, the King and all our company else being drowned, we will inherit here. Here, bear my bottle. Fellow Trinculo, we'll fill him by and by again.

CALIBAN *sings drunkenly.*

CALIBAN. Farewell, master; farewell, farewell! 165

TRINCULO. A howling monster! a drunken monster!

CALIBAN. No more dams I'll make for fish,
Nor fetch in firing
At requiring,
Nor scrape trenchering, nor wash dish. 170
'Ban, 'Ban, Cacaliban
Has a new master:—get a new man.
Freedom, high-day! high-day, freedom! freedom, high-day, freedom!

STEPHANO. O brave monster! lead the way. *Exeunt.* 175

Act III

SCENE I [*Before* PROSPERO'*s cell*]

Enter FERDINAND, *bearing a log.*

FERDINAND. There be some sports are painful, and their labor
Delight in them sets off; some kinds of baseness
Are nobly undergone, and most poor matters
Point to rich ends. This my mean task
Would be as heavy to me as odious, but 5
The mistress which I serve quickens what's dead
And makes my labors pleasures. O, she is
Ten times more gentle than her father's crabbed;
And he's composed of harshness! I must remove
Some thousands of these logs and pile them up, 10
Upon a sore injunction. My sweet mistress
Weeps when she sees me work, and says such baseness

---

160 *scamels:* of uncertain meaning, but most probably sea gulls. 170 *trenchering:* trenchers, wooden plates. III,i,1-2 *There . . . off:* i.e., there are difficult tasks in which the pleasure derived is heightened by the arduousness. 6 *quickens:* brings to life. 11 *Upon . . . injunction:* i.e., under pain of harsh punishment.

Had never like executor. I forget;
But these sweet thoughts do even refresh my labors
Most busy least, when I do it.

Enter MIRANDA; *and* PROSPERO [*at a distance, unseen*].

MIRANDA. Alas, now pray you 15
Work not so hard! I would the lightning had
Burnt up those logs that you are enjoined to pile!
Pray set it down and rest you. When this burns,
'Twill weep for having wearied you. My father
Is hard at study: pray now rest yourself. 20
He's safe for these three hours.

FERDINAND. O most dear mistress,
The sun will set before I shall discharge
What I must strive to do.

MIRANDA. If you'll sit down,
I'll bear your logs the while. Pray give me that:
I'll carry it to the pile.

FERDINAND. No, precious creature: 25
I had rather crack my sinews, break my back,
Than you should such dishonor undergo
While I sit lazy by.

MIRANDA. It would become me
As well as it does you; and I should do it
With much more ease; for my good will is to it, 30
And yours it is against.

PROSPERO. [*Aside.*] Poor worm, thou art infected!
This visitation shows it.

MIRANDA. You look wearily.

FERDINAND. No, noble mistress: 'tis fresh morning with me
When you are by at night. I do beseech you,
Chiefly that I might set it in my prayers, 35
What is your name?

MIRANDA. Miranda. O my father,
I have broke your hest to say so!

FERDINAND. Admired Miranda!
Indeed the top of admiration, worth
What's dearest to the world! Full many a lady
I have eyed with best regard, and many a time 40
Th' harmony of their tongues hath into bondage
Brought my too diligent ear; for several virtues
Have I liked several women; never any

---

15 *least:* i.e., least engaged by my work. 19 *weep:* i.e., drip resin. 32 *visitation:* visit. 37 *hest:* command. 42 *several:* different.

With so full soul, but some defect in her
Did quarrel with the noblest grace she owed, 45
And put it to the foil. But you, O you,
So perfect and so peerless, are created
Of every creature's best.

MIRANDA. I do not know
One of my sex; no woman's face remember,
Save, from my glass, mine own; nor have I seen 50
More that I may call men than you, good friend,
And my dear father. How features are abroad
I am skilless of; but, by my modesty
(The jewel in my dower), I would not wish
Any companion in the world but you; 55
Nor can imagination form a shape,
Besides yourself, to like of. But I prattle
Something too wildly, and my father's precepts
I therein do forget.

FERDINAND. I am, in my condition,
A prince, Miranda; I do think, a king 60
(I would not so), and would no more endure
This wooden slavery than to suffer
The flesh-fly blow my mouth. Hear my soul speak!
The very instant that I saw you, did
My heart fly to your service; there resides, 65
To make me slave to it; and for your sake
Am I this patient log-man.

MIRANDA. Do you love me?

FERDINAND. O heaven, O earth, bear witness to this sound,
And crown what I profess with kind event
If I speak true! if hollowly, invert 70
What best is boded me to mischief! I,
Beyond all limit of what else i' th' world,
Do love, prize, honor you.

MIRANDA. I am a fool
To weep at what I am glad of.

PROSPERO. [*Aside.*] Fair encounter
Of two most rare affections! Heavens rain grace 75
On that which breeds between 'em!

FERDINAND. Wherefore weep you?

MIRANDA. At mine unworthiness, that dare not offer

---

46 *put . . . foil:* bring it to nothing. 52 *abroad:* elsewhere. 53 *skilless:* uninformed. 62 *wooden slavery:* i.e., imposed task of carrying wood. 63 *blow:* sully. 69 *kind event:* happy outcome.

What I desire to give, and much less take
What I shall die to want. But this is trifling;
And all the more it seeks to hide itself, 80
The bigger bulk it shows. Hence, bashful cunning,
And prompt me, plain and holy innocence!
I am your wife, if you will marry me;
If not, I'll die your maid. To be your fellow
You may deny me; but I'll be your servant, 85
Whether you will or no.

FERDINAND. My mistress, dearest,
And I thus humble ever.

MIRANDA. My husband then?

FERDINAND. Ay, with a heart as willing
As bondage e'er of freedom. Here's my hand.

MIRANDA. And mine, with my heart in't; and now farewell 90
Till half an hour hence.

FERDINAND. A thousand thousand!

Exeunt [FERDINAND *and* MIRANDA *severally*].

PROSPERO. So glad of this as they I cannot be,
Who are surprised withal; but my rejoicing
At nothing can be more. I'll to my book;
For yet, ere supper time, must I perform 95
Much business appertaining. *Exit.*

SCENE II [*Another part of the island*]

Enter CALIBAN, STEPHANO, *and* TRINCULO.

STEPHANO. Tell not me! When the butt is out, we will drink water; not a drop before. Therefore bear up and board 'em! Servant-monster, drink to me.

TRINCULO. Servant-monster? The folly of this island! They say there's but five upon this isle: we are three of them. If th' 5 other two be brained like us, the state totters.

STEPHANO. Drink, servant-monster, when I bid thee: thy eyes are almost set in thy head.

TRINCULO. Where should they be set else? He were a brave monster indeed if they were set in his tail. 10

STEPHANO. My man-monster hath drowned his tongue in sack. For my part, the sea cannot drown me. I swam, ere I could recover the shore, five-and-thirty leagues off and on. By this

---

79 *want:* lack. 84 *fellow:* equal. 89 *of freedom:* i.e., to obtain freedom. 91 *thousand thousand:* i.e., farewells. 93 *Who . . . withal:* they who are taken unaware by love. III,ii,2 *bear . . . 'em:* drink up. 8 *set:* i.e., closed from drink. 13 *recover:* reach.

light, thou shalt be my lieutenant, monster, or my standard.

TRINCULO. Your lieutenant, if you list; he's no standard. 15

STEPHANO. We'll not run, Monsieur Monster.

TRINCULO. Nor go neither; but you'll lie like dogs, and yet say nothing neither.

STEPHANO. Moon-calf, speak once in thy life, if thou beest a good moon-calf. 20

CALIBAN. How does thy honor? Let me lick thy shoe.
I'll not serve him; he is not valiant.

TRINCULO. Thou liest, most ignorant monster: I am in case to justle a constable. Why, thou deboshed fish thou, was there ever man a coward that hath drunk so much sack as I to-day? 25 Wilt thou tell a monstrous lie, being but half a fish and half a monster?

CALIBAN. Lo, how he mocks me! Wilt thou let him, my lord?

TRINCULO. "Lord" quoth he? That a monster should be such a natural! 30

CALIBAN. Lo, lo, again! Bite him to death, I prithee.

STEPHANO. Trinculo, keep a good tongue in your head. If you prove a mutineer—the next tree! The poor monster's my subject, and he shall not suffer indignity.

CALIBAN. I thank my noble lord. Wilt thou be pleased 35
To hearken once again to the suit I made to thee?

STEPHANO. Marry, will I. Kneel and repeat it; I will stand, and so shall Trinculo.

Enter ARIEL, *invisible.*

CALIBAN. As I told thee before, I am subject to a tyrant, a sorcerer, that by his cunning hath cheated me of the island. 40

ARIEL. Thou liest.

CALIBAN. "Thou liest," thou jesting monkey thou!
I would my valiant master would destroy thee.
I do not lie.

STEPHANO. Trinculo, if you trouble him any more in's tale, by this hand, I will supplant some of your teeth. 45

TRINCULO. Why, I said nothing.

STEPHANO. Mum then, and no more.—Proceed.

CALIBAN. I say by sorcery he got this isle;
From me he got it. If thy greatness will
Revenge it on him—for I know thou dar'st, 50
But this thing dare not—

---

14 *standard:* standard-bearer. 23 *in case:* in a condition. 24 *deboshed:* debauched. 30 *natural:* an idiot. 45 *supplant:* knock out. 51 *this thing:* either himself or Trinculo.

STEPHANO. That's most certain.
CALIBAN. Thou shalt be lord of it, and I'll serve thee.
STEPHANO. How now shall this be compassed?
Canst thou bring me to the party? 55
CALIBAN. Yea, yea, my lord! I'll yield him thee asleep,
Where thou mayst knock a nail into his head.
ARIEL. Thou liest; thou canst not.
CALIBAN. What a pied ninny's this! Thou scurvy patch!
I do beseech thy greatness give him blows 60
And take his bottle from him. When that's gone,
He shall drink nought but brine, for I'll not show him
Where the quick freshes are.
STEPHANO. Trinculo, run into no further danger: interrupt the monster one word further and, by this hand, I'll turn my 65 mercy out o' doors and make a stockfish of thee.
TRINCULO. Why, what did I? I did nothing. I'll go farther off.
STEPHANO. Didst thou not say he lied?
ARIEL. Thou liest.
STEPHANO. Do I so? Take thou that! [*Strikes* TRINCULO.] As 70 you like this, give me the lie another time.
TRINCULO. I did not give the lie. Out o' your wits, and hearing too? A pox o' your bottle! This can sack and drinking do. A murrain on your monster, and the devil take your fingers!
CALIBAN. Ha, ha, ha! 75
STEPHANO. Now, forward with your tale.—Prithee, stand further off.
CALIBAN. Beat him enough. After a little time
I'll beat him too.
STEPHANO. Stand farther.—Come, proceed.
CALIBAN. Why, as I told thee, 'tis a custom with him 80
I' th' afternoon to sleep: there thou mayst brain him,
Having first seized his books, or with a log
Batter his skull, or paunch him with a stake,
Or cut his wezand with thy knife. Remember
First to possess his books; for without them 85
He's but a sot, as I am, nor hath not
One spirit to command. They all do hate him
As rootedly as I. Burn but his books.
He has brave utensils (for so he calls them)

---

54 *compassed:* achieved. 59 *pied ninny:* as jester, Trinculo wears motley; *patch:* fool. 63 *quick freshes:* springs of fresh water. 66 *stockfish:* dried cod, requiring beating in preparation. 74 *murrain:* plague. 83 *paunch:* stab in the belly. 84 *wezand:* windpipe. 86 *sot:* fool. 89 *brave utensils:* handsome furnishings.

Which, when he has a house, he'll deck withal. 90
And that most deeply to consider is
The beauty of his daughter. He himself
Calls her a nonpareil. I never saw a woman
But only Sycorax my dam and she;
But she as far surpasseth Sycorax 95
As great'st does least.

STEPHANO. Is it so brave a lass?

CALIBAN. Ay, lord. She will become thy bed, I warrant,
And bring thee forth brave brood.

STEPHANO. Monster, I will kill this man: his daughter and I will be king and queen, save our Graces! and Trinculo and 100 thyself shall be viceroys. Dost thou like the plot, Trinculo?

TRINCULO. Excellent.

STEPHANO. Give me thy hand. I am sorry I beat thee; but while thou liv'st, keep a good tongue in thy head.

CALIBAN. Within this half hour will he be asleep. 105
Wilt thou destroy him then?

STEPHANO. Ay, on mine honor.

ARIEL. This will I tell my master.

CALIBAN. Thou mak'st me merry; I am full of pleasure.
Let us be jocund. Will you troll the catch
You taught me but while-ere? 110

STEPHANO. At thy request, monster, I will do reason, any reason. Come on, Trinculo, let us sing. *Sings.*

Flout 'em and scout 'em
And scout 'em and flout 'em;
Thought is free. 115

CALIBAN. That's not the tune.

ARIEL *plays the tune on a tabor and pipe.*

STEPHANO. What is this same?

TRINCULO. This is the tune of our catch, played by the picture of Nobody.

STEPHANO. If thou beest a man, show thyself in thy likeness. 120
If thou beest a devil, take't as thou list.

TRINCULO. O, forgive me my sins!

STEPHANO. He that dies pays all debts. I defy thee.
Mercy upon us!

---

109 *troll the catch:* sing the round. 110 *while-ere:* just now. 113 *flout:* mock; *scout:* deceive. 118-19 *picture of Nobody:* i.e., an invisible musician (allusion to contemporary pictures of figures with no bodies).

CALIBAN. Art thou afeard? 125
STEPHANO. No, monster, not I.
CALIBAN. Be not afeard: the isle is full of noises,
Sounds and sweet airs that give delight and hurt not.
Sometimes a thousand twangling instruments
Will hum about mine ears; and sometime voices 130
That, if I then had waked after long sleep,
Will make me sleep again; and then, in dreaming,
The clouds methought would open and show riches
Ready to drop upon me, that, when I waked,
I cried to dream again. 135
STEPHANO. This will prove a brave kingdom to me, where
I shall have my music for nothing.
CALIBAN. When Prospero is destroyed.
STEPHANO. That shall be by and by: I remember the story.
TRINCULO. The sound is going away: let's follow it, and 140
after do our work.
STEPHANO. Lead, monster; we'll follow. I would I could see
this taborer: he lays it on.
TRINCULO. Wilt come? I'll follow, Stephano. *Exeunt.*

SCENE III [*Another part of the island*]

Enter ALONSO, SEBASTIAN, ANTONIO, GONZALO, ADRIAN, FRANCISCO, *&c.*

GONZALO. By'r Lakin, I can go no further, sir:
My old bones ache: here's a maze trod indeed
Through forthrights and meanders. By your patience,
I needs must rest me.
ALONSO. Old lord, I cannot blame thee,
Who am myself attached with weariness 5
To th' dulling of my spirits. Sit down and rest.
Even here I will put off my hope, and keep it
No longer for my flatterer: he is drowned
Whom thus we stray to find; and the sea mocks
Our frustrate search on land. Well, let him go. 10
ANTONIO. [*Aside to* SEBASTIAN.] I am right glad that he's so out of hope
Do not for one repulse forgo the purpose
That you resolved t' effect.
SEBASTIAN. [*Aside to* ANTONIO.] The next advantage

---

139 *by and by:* soon. 143 *taborer:* drummer. III,iii,1 *By're Lakin:* by Our Lady. 3 *forthrights:* straight paths; *meanders:* winding paths. 5 *attached:* seized. 10 *frustrate:* vain.

Will we take throughly.

ANTONIO. [*Aside to* SEBASTIAN.] Let it be to-night;
For, now they are oppressed with travel, they 15
Will not nor cannot use such vigilance
As when they are fresh.

SEBASTIAN. [*Aside to* ANTONIO.] I say to-night. No more.

Solemn and strange music; and PROSPERO *on the top (invisible). Enter several strange Shapes, bringing in a banquet; and dance about it with gentle actions of salutations; and, inviting the King &c. to eat, they depart.*

ALONSO. What harmony is this? My good friends, hark!

GONZALO. Marvellous sweet music!

ALONSO. Give us kind keepers, heavens! What were these? 20

SEBASTIAN. A living drollery. Now I will believe
That there are unicorns; that in Arabia
There is one tree, the phoenix' throne; one phoenix
At this hour reigning there.

ANTONIO. I'll believe both;
And what does else want credit, come to me, 25
And I'll be sworn 'tis true. Travellers ne'er did lie,
Though fools at home condemn 'em.

GONZALO. If in Naples
I should report this now, would they believe me
If I should say I saw such islanders?
(For certes these are people of the island) 30
Who, though they are of monstrous shape, yet note,
Their manners are more gentle, kind, than of
Our human generation you shall find
Many—nay, almost any.

PROSPERO. [*Aside.*] Honest lord,
Thou has said well; for some of you there present 35
Are worse than devils.

ALONSO. I cannot too much muse
Such shapes, such gesture, and such sound, expressing
(Although they want the use of tongue) a kind
Of excellent dumb discourse.

PROSPERO. [*Aside.*] Praise in departing.

---

14 *throughly:* thoroughly. 17 S.D. *on the top:* perhaps a reference to an upper level of the theater's tiring-house. 20 *keepers:* guardian angels. 21 *living drollery:* puppet show with live figures. 23 *phoenix:* a mythical bird born every five hundred years from the ashes of its own pyre. 25 *want credit:* lack credibility. 36 *muse:* wonder at. 39 *Praise in departing:* a proverbial expression meaning "Save your praise until you see how all will end."

FRANCISCO. They vanished strangely.
SEBASTIAN. No matter, since 40
They have left their viands behind; for we have stomachs.
Will't please you taste of what is here?
ALONSO. Not I.
GONZALO. Faith, sir, you need not fear. When we were boys,
Who would believe that there were mountaineers
Dew-lapped like bulls, whose throats had hanging at 'em 45
Wallets of flesh? or that there were such men
Whose heads stood in their breasts? which now we find
Each putter-out of five for one will bring us
Good warrant of.
ALONSO. I will stand to, and feed;
Although my last, no matter, since I feel 50
The best is past. Brother, my lord the Duke,
Stand to, and do as we.

Thunder and lightning. Enter ARIEL, *like a harpy; claps his wings upon the table; and with a quaint device the banquet vanishes.*

ARIEL. You are three men of sin, whom destiny—
That hath to instrument this lower world
And what is in't—the never-surfeited sea 55
Hath caused to belch up you, and on this island,
Where man doth not inhabit, you 'mongst men
Being most unfit to live, I have made you mad;
And even with such-like valor men hang and drown
Their proper selves.
[ALONSO, SEBASTIAN, *&c. draw their swords.*]
You fools: I and my fellows 60
Are ministers of Fate. The elements,
Of whom your swords are tempered, may as well
Wound the loud winds, or with bemocked-at stabs
Kill the still-closing waters, as diminish
One dowle that's in my plume. My fellow ministers 65
Are like invulnerable. If you could hurt,
Your swords are now too massy for your strengths
And will not be uplifted. But remember
(For that's my business to you) that you three

---

48 *putter-out . . . one:* a common practice in Shakespeare's England was for a prospective traveler to deposit a sum with an underwriter, and upon his safe return, the traveler would receive five times the original amount. 52 S.D. *quaint device:* ingenious stage machine. 54 *to:* i.e., as its. 60 *proper:* own. 64 *still:* always. 65 *dowle:* small feather. 66 *like:* likewise. 67 *massy:* weighty.

From Milan did supplant good Prospero; 70
Exposed unto the sea, which hath requit it,
Him and his innocent child; for which foul deed
The powers, delaying, not forgetting, have
Incensed the seas and shores, yea, all the creatures,
Against your peace. Thee of thy son, Alonso, 75
They have bereft; and do pronounce by me
Ling'ring perdition (worse than any death
Can be at once) shall step by step attend
You and your ways; whose wraths to guard you from,
Which here, in this most desolate isle, else falls 80
Upon your heads, is nothing but heart's sorrow
And a clear life ensuing.

He vanishes in thunder; then, to soft music, enter the Shapes again, and dance with mocks and mows, and carrying out the table.

PROSPERO. Bravely the figure of this harpy hast thou
Performed, my Ariel; a grace it had, devouring.
Of my instruction hast thou nothing bated 85
In what thou hadst to say. So, with good life
And observation strange, my meaner ministers
Their several kinds have done. My high charms work,
And these, mine enemies, are all knit up
In their distractions: they now are in my power; 90
And in these fits I leave them, while I visit
Young Ferdinand, whom they suppose is drowned,
And his and mine loved darling. [*Exit above.*]

GONZALO. I' th' name of something holy, sir, why stand you
In this strange stare?

ALONSO. O, it is monstrous, monstrous! 95
Methought the billows spoke and told me of it;
The winds did sing it to me; and the thunder,
That deep and dreadful organ pipe, pronounced
The name of Prosper; it did bass my trespass.
Therefore my son i' th' ooze is bedded; and 100
I'll seek him deeper than e'er plummet sounded
And with him there lie mudded. *Exit.*

---

71 *requit it:* i.e., avenged the deed. 77 *perdition:* destruction. 82 *clear:* innocent. S.D. *mocks and mows:* mocking gestures and grimaces. 84 *devouring:* i.e., devouring the banquet (making it disappear). 85 *bated:* omitted. 86 *good life:* realistic acting. 87 *observation strange:* unusual fidelity. 88 *several kinds:* particular tasks. 89 *knit:* bound. 96 *it:* i.e., my sin. 99 *bass my trespass:* proclaim my sin in deep tones.

SEBASTIAN. But one fiend at a time,
I'll fight their legions o'er!
ANTONIO. I'll be thy second.
Exeunt [SEBASTIAN *and* ANTONIO].

GONZALO. All three of them are desperate: their great guilt, 105
Like poison given to work a great time after,
Now 'gins to bite the spirits. I do beseech you,
That are of suppler joints, follow them swiftly
And hinder them from what this ecstasy
May now provoke them to.
ADRIAN. Follow, I pray you.
Exeunt omnes.

Act IV

SCENE I [*Before* PROSPERO'*s cell*]

Enter PROSPERO, FERDINAND, *and* MIRANDA.

PROSPERO. If I have too austerely punished you,
Your compensation makes amends; for I
Have given you here a third of mine own life,
Or that for which I live; who once again
I tender to thy hand. All thy vexations 5
Were but my trials of thy love, and thou
Hast strangely stood the test. Here, afore heaven,
I ratify this my rich gift. O Ferdinand,
Do not smile at me that I boast her off,
For thou shalt find she will outstrip all praise 10
And make it halt behind her.
FERDINAND. I do believe it
Against an oracle.
PROSPERO. Then, as my gift, and thine own acquisition
Worthily purchased, take my daughter. But
If thou dost break her virgin-knot before 15
All sanctimonious ceremonies may
With full and holy rite be ministered,
No sweet aspersion shall the heavens let fall
To make this contract grow; but barren hate,
Sour-eyed disdain, and discord shall bestrew 20

---

108 *ecstasy:* madness. IV,i,7 *strangely:* exceptionally well. 9 *boast her off:* i.e., boast of her. 11 *halt:* limp. 12 *Against an oracle:* though an oracle should deny it. 16 *sanctimonious:* holy. 18 *aspersion:* blessing. 19 *grow:* prosper.

The union of your bed with weeds so loathly
That you shall hate it both. Therefore take heed,
As Hymen's lamp shall light you.

FERDINAND. As I hope
For quiet days, fair issue, and long life,
With such love as 'tis now, the murkiest den, 25
The most opportune place, the strong'st suggestion
Our worser genius can, shall never melt
Mine honor into lust, to take away
The edge of that day's celebration
When I shall think or Phoebus' steeds are foundered 30
Or Night kept chained below.

PROSPERO. Fairly spoke.
Sit then and talk with her; she is thine own.
What, Ariel! my industrious servant, Ariel!

Enter ARIEL.

ARIEL. What would my potent master? Here I am.

PROSPERO. Thou and thy meaner fellows your last service 35
Did worthily perform; and I must use you
In such another trick. Go bring the rabble,
O'er whom I give thee pow'r, here to this place.
Incite them to quick motion; for I must
Bestow upon the eyes of this young couple 40
Some vanity of mine art: it is my promise,
And they expect it from me.

ARIEL. Presently?

PROSPERO. Ay, with a twink.

ARIEL. Before you can say "Come" and "Go,"
And breathe twice and cry, "So, so," 45
Each one, tripping on his toe,
Will be here with mop and mow.
Do you love me, master? No?

PROSPERO. Dearly, my delicate Ariel. Do not approach
Till thou dost hear me call.

ARIEL. Well: I conceive. *Exit.* 50

PROSPERO. Look thou be true: do not give dalliance
Too much the rein: the strongest oaths are straw
To th' fire i' th' blood. Be more abstemious,
Or else good night your vow!

---

23 *Hymen:* the god of marriage who carried a bridal torch. 24 *issue:* children. 27 *worser genius can:* bad angel can make. 31 *or . . . below:* i.e., that night will never come. 41 *vanity:* show. 42 *presently:* immediately. 50 *conceive:* understand.

FERDINAND. I warrant you, sir.
The white cold virgin snow upon my heart 55
Abates the ardor of my liver.

PROSPERO. Well.
Now come, my Ariel: bring a corollary
Rather than want a spirit. Appear, and pertly!
No tongue! All eyes! Be silent. *Soft music.*

Enter IRIS.

IRIS. Ceres, most bounteous lady, thy rich leas 60
Of wheat, rye, barley, vetches, oats, and pease;
Thy turfy mountains, where live nibbling sheep,
And flat meads thatched with stover, them to keep;
Thy banks with pioned and twilled brims,
Which spongy April at thy hest betrims 65
To make cold nymphs chaste crowns; and thy broom groves,
Whose shadow the dismissed bachelor loves,
Being lass-lorn; thy pole-clipt vineyard;
And thy sea-marge, sterile and rocky-hard,
Where thou thyself dost air—the queen o' th' sky, 70
Whose wat'ry arch and messenger am I,
Bids thee leave these, and with her sovereign grace,

JUNO *descends.*

Here on this grass-plot, in this very place,
To come and sport: her peacocks fly amain.
Approach, rich Ceres, her to entertain. 75

Enter CERES.

CERES. Hail, many-colored messenger, that ne'er
Dost disobey the wife of Jupiter,
Who, with thy saffron wings, upon my flowers
Diffusest honey drops, refreshing showers,
And with each end of thy blue bow dost crown 80
My bosky acres and my unshrubbed down,
Rich scarf to my proud earth—why hath thy queen
Summoned me hither to this short-grassed green?

IRIS. A contract of true love to celebrate
And some donation freely to estate 85
On the blessed lovers.

---

56 *liver:* passion. 57 *corollary:* surplus. 58 *want:* lack; *pertly:* quickly. 60 *Iris:* goddess of the rainbow as well as female messenger of the gods; *Ceres:* goddess of plenty; *leas:* fields. 63 *stover:* grass used for fodder. 65 *betrims:* i.e., with flowers. 66 *broom:* gorse. 67 *dismissed:* rejected. 68 *pole-clipt:* pruned. 69 *sea-marge:* shore. 70 *queen:* Jupiter's wife, the goddess Juno. 74 *peacocks:* birds sacred to Juno. 81 *bosky:* wooded. 82 *scarf:* i.e., adornment. 85 *estate:* bestow.

CERES. Tell me, heavenly bow,
If Venus or her son, as thou dost know,
Do now attend the queen? Since they did plot
The means that dusky Dis my daughter got,
Her and her blind boy's scandalled company 90
I have forsworn.

IRIS. Of her society
Be not afraid: I met her Deity
Cutting the clouds towards Paphos, and her son
Dove-drawn with her. Here thought they to have done
Some wanton charm upon this man and maid, 95
Whose vows are, that no bed-right shall be paid
Till Hymen's torch be lighted; but in vain.
Mars's hot minion is returned again;
Her waspish-headed son has broke his arrows,
Swears he will shoot no more, but play with sparrows 100
And be a boy right out.

CERES. Highest queen of state,
Great Juno comes; I know her by her gait.

JUNO. How does my bounteous sister? Go with me
To bless this twain, that they may prosperous be
And honored in their issue. 105

They sing.

JUNO. Honor, riches, marriage blessing,
Long continuance, and increasing,
Hourly joys be still upon you!
Juno sings her blessings on you.

CERES. Earth's increase, foison plenty, 110
Barns and garners never empty,
Vines with clust'ring bunches growing,
Plants with goodly burden bowing;
Spring come to you at the farthest
In the very end of harvest. 115
Scarcity and want shall shun you,
Ceres' blessing so is on you.

FERDINAND. This is a most majestic vision, and
Harmonious charmingly. May I be bold
To think these spirits?

---

87 *her son:* the blind Cupid. 89 *dusky Dis:* the god of the underworld, Pluto, who abducted Persephone, Ceres' daughter. 90 *scandalled:* scandalous. 93 *Paphos:* the center of Venus's cult in Cyprus. 98 *Mars's . . . minion:* the lustful mistress of Mars, i.e., Venus. 99 *waspish-headed:* spiteful.

PROSPERO. Spirits, which by mine art 120
I have from their confines called to enact
My present fancies.

FERDINAND. Let me live here ever!
So rare a wondered father and a wise
Makes this place Paradise.

JUNO and CERES whisper, and send IRIS on employment.

PROSPERO. Sweet now, silence!
Juno and Ceres whisper seriously. 125
There's something else to do. Hush and be mute,
Or else our spell is marred.

IRIS. You nymphs, called Naiades, of the windring brooks,
With your sedged crowns and ever-harmless looks,
Leave your crisp channels, and on this green land 130
Answer your summons; Juno does command.
Come, temperate nymphs, and help to celebrate
A contract of true love: be not too late.

Enter certain NYMPHS.

You sunburned sicklemen, of August weary,
Come hither from the furrow and be merry. 135
Make holiday: your rye-straw hats put on,
And these fresh nymphs encounter every one
In country footing.

Enter certain REAPERS, properly habited. They join with the NYMPHS in a graceful dance; towards the end whereof PROSPERO starts suddenly and speaks; after which, to a strange, hollow, and confused noise, they heavily vanish.

PROSPERO. [*Aside.*] I had forgot that foul conspiracy
Of the beast Caliban and his confederates 140
Against my life: the minute of their plot
Is almost come. [*To the* SPIRITS.] Well done! Avoid! No more!

FERDINAND. This is strange. Your father's in some passion
That works him strongly.

MIRANDA. Never till this day
Saw I him touched with anger so distempered. 145

PROSPERO. You do look, my son, in a moved sort,
As if you were dismayed: be cheerful, sir.
Our revels now are ended. These our actors,
As I foretold you, were all spirits and
Are melted into air, into thin air; 150

---

123 *wondered:* wonderful. 128 *windring:* winding and wandering. 130 *crisp:* rippling. 132 *temperate:* chaste. 138 *footing:* dancing. S.D. *heavily:* dejectedly. 142 *Avoid:* be gone. 146 *moved sort:* troubled state.

And, like the baseless fabric of this vision,
The cloud-capped towers, the gorgeous palaces,
The solemn temples, the great globe itself,
Yea, all which it inherit, shall dissolve,
And, like this insubstantial pageant faded, 155
Leave not a rack behind. We are such stuff
As dreams are made on, and our little life
Is rounded with a sleep. Sir, I am vexed.
Bear with my weakness: my old brain is troubled.
Be not disturbed with my infirmity. 160
If you be pleased, retire into my cell
And there repose. A turn or two I'll walk
To still my beating mind.

FERDINAND, MIRANDA. We wish your peace. *Exeunt.*

PROSPERO. Come with a thought. I thank thee, Ariel. Come.

Enter ARIEL.

ARIEL. Thy thoughts I cleave to. What's thy pleasure?

PROSPERO. Spirit,
We must prepare to meet with Caliban. 165

ARIEL. Ay, my commander: when I presented Ceres,
I thought to have told thee of it, but I feared
Lest I might anger thee.

PROSPERO. Say again, where didst thou leave these varlets?

ARIEL. I told you, sir, they were red-hot with drinking; 170
So full of valor that they smote the air
For breathing in their faces, beat the ground
For kissing of their feet; yet always bending
Towards their project. Then I beat my tabor;
At which, like unbacked colts, they pricked their ears, 175
Advanced their eyelids, lifted up their noses
As they smelt music. So I charmed their ears
That calf-like they my lowing followed through
Toothed briers, sharp furzes, pricking goss, and thorns,
Which entered their frail shins. At last I left them 180
I' th' filthy mantled pool beyond your cell,
There dancing up to th' chins, that the foul lake
O'erstunk their feet.

PROSPERO. This was well done, my bird.

---

151 *baseless:* unreal. 156 *rack:* wisp of cloud. 157 *on:* of. 158 *rounded:* crowned. 167 *presented:* either acted the part of or introduced. 170 *varlets:* knaves. 176 *unbacked:* unbroken. 177 *Advanced:* lifted up. 178 *As:* as if. 180 *goss:* gorse. 182 *filthy mantled:* covered with scum.

Thy shape invisible retain thou still. 185
The trumpery in my house, go bring it hither
For stale to catch these thieves.

ARIEL. I go, I go. *Exit.*

PROSPERO. A devil, a born devil, on whose nature
Nurture can never stick: on whom my pains,
Humanely taken, all, all lost, quite lost! 190
And as with age his body uglier grows,
So his mind cankers. I will plague them all,
Even to roaring.

[*Re-*]*enter* ARIEL, *loaden with glistering apparel, &c.*

Come, hang them on this line.

[PROSPERO *and* ARIEL *remain, invisible.*] *Enter* CALIBAN, STEPHANO, *and* TRINCULO, *all wet.*

CALIBAN. Pray you, tread softly, that the blind mole may not
Hear a foot fall. We now are near his cell. 195

STEPHANO. Monster, your fairy, which you say is a harmless fairy, has done little better than played the Jack with us.

TRINCULO. Monster, I do smell all horse-piss, at which my nose is in great indignation.

STEPHANO. So is mine. Do you hear, monster? If I should 200 take a displeasure against you, look you—

TRINCULO. Thou wert but a lost monster.

CALIBAN. Good my lord, give me thy favor still.
Be patient, for the prize I'll bring thee to
Shall hoodwink this mischance. Therefore speak softly. 205
All's hushed as midnight yet.

TRINCULO. Ay, but to lose our bottles in the pool—

STEPHANO. There is not only disgrace and dishonor in that, monster, but an infinite loss.

TRINCULO. That's more to me than my wetting. Yet this is 210 your harmless fairy, monster.

STEPHANO. I will fetch off my bottle, though I be o'er ears for my labor.

CALIBAN. Prithee, my king, be quiet. Seest thou here?
This is the mouth o' th' cell. No noise, and enter. 215
Do that good mischief which may make this island
Thine own for ever, and I, thy Caliban,
For aye thy foot-licker.

---

187 *stale:* decoy. 189 *Nurture:* education. 192 *cankers:* decays. 193 *line:* lime tree. 197 *Jack:* knave, will-o'-the-wisp. 205 *hoodwink:* i.e., make us forget. 212 *o'er ears:* i.e., soaked.

STEPHANO. Give me thy hand. I do begin to have bloody thoughts.

TRINCULO. O King Stephano! O peer! O worthy Stephano, look what a wardrobe here is for thee! 220

CALIBAN. Let it alone, thou fool! It is but trash.

TRINCULO. O, ho, monster! we know what belongs to a frippery. O King Stephano!

STEPHANO. Put off that gown, Trinculo: by this hand, I'll have that gown! 225

TRINCULO. Thy Grace shall have it.

CALIBAN. The dropsy drown this fool! What do you mean
To dote thus on such luggage? Let't alone,
And do the murder first. If he awake, 230
From toe to crown he'll fill our skins with pinches,
Make us strange stuff.

STEPHANO. Be you quiet, monster. Mistress line, is not this my jerkin? Now is the jerkin under the line. Now, jerkin, you are like to lose your hair and prove a bald jerkin. 235

TRINCULO. Do, do! We steal by line and level, an't like your Grace.

STEPHANO. I thank thee for that jest. Here's a garment for't. Wit shall not go unrewarded while I am king of this country. "Steal by line and level" is an excellent pass of pate. There's another garment for't. 240

TRINCULO. Monster, come put some lime upon your fingers, and away with the rest.

CALIBAN. I will have none on't. We shall lose our time
And all be turned to barnacles, or to apes 245
With foreheads villainous low.

STEPHANO. Monster, lay-to your fingers: help to bear this away where my hogshead of wine is, or I'll turn you out of my kingdom. Go to, carry this.

TRINCULO. And this. 250

STEPHANO. Ay, and this.

A noise of hunters heard. Enter divers SPIRITS *in shape of dogs and hounds, hunting them about;* PROSPERO *and* ARIEL *setting them on.*

PROSPERO. Hey, Mountain, hey!

ARIEL. Silver! there it goes, Silver!

224-25 *frippery:* old-clothes shop. 230 *luggage:* encumbering junk. 237 *by line and level:* according to rule. 241 *pass of pate:* thrust of wit. 243 *lime:* birdlime, which is sticky (hence, appropriate for thieves). 246 *barnacles:* geese.

PROSPERO. Fury, Fury! There, Tyrant, there! Hark, hark! 255
[CALIBAN, STEPHANO, *and* TRINCULO *are driven out.*]
Go, charge my goblins that they grind their joints
With dry convulsions, shorten up their sinews
With aged cramps, and more pinch-spotted make them
Than pard or cat o' mountain.
ARIEL. Hark, they roar!
PROSPERO. Let them be hunted soundly. At this hour 260
Lie at my mercy all mine enemies.
Shortly shall all my labors end, and thou
Shalt have the air at freedom. For a little,
Follow, and do me service. *Exeunt.*

Act V

SCENE I [*Before the cell of* PROSPERO]

Enter PROSPERO *in his magic robes, and* ARIEL.
PROSPERO. Now does my project gather to a head.
My charms crack not, my spirits obey, and time
Goes upright with his carriage. How's the day?
ARIEL. On the sixth hour, at which time, my lord,
You said our work should cease.
PROSPERO. I did say so 5
When first I raised the tempest. Say, my spirit,
How fares the King and 's followers?
ARIEL. Confined together
In the same fashion as you gave in charge,
Just as you left them—all prisoners, sir,
In the line-grove which weather-fends your cell. 10
They cannot budge till your release. The King,
His brother, and yours abide all three distracted,
And the remainder mourning over them,
Brimful of sorrow and dismay; but chiefly
Him that you termed, sir, "The good old Lord Gonzalo"; 15
His tears run down his beard like winter's drops
From eaves of reeds. Your charm so strongly works 'em,
That if you now beheld them, your affections
Would become tender.
PROSPERO. Dost thou think so, spirit?
ARIEL. Mine would, sir, were I human.

---

259 *pard:* leopard; *cat o' mountain:* catamount. V,i,2-3 *time . . . carriage:* time's burden is light. 10 *weather-fends:* protects from the weather. 11 *your release:* released by you. 17 *eaves of reeds:* i.e., a thatched roof.

PROSPERO. And mine shall. 20
Hast thou, which art but air, a touch, a feeling
Of their afflictions, and shall not myself,
One of their kind, that relish all as sharply
Passion as they, be kindlier moved than thou art?
Though with their high wrongs I am struck to th' quick, 25
Yet with my nobler reason 'gainst my fury
Do I take part. The rarer action is
In virtue than in vengeance. They being penitent,
The sole drift of my purpose doth extend
Not a frown further. Go, release them, Ariel. 30
My charms I'll break, their senses I'll restore,
And they shall be themselves.

ARIEL. I'll fetch them, sir. *Exit.*

PROSPERO. Ye elves of hills, brooks, standing lakes, and groves,
And ye that on the sands with printless foot
Do chase the ebbing Neptune, and do fly him 35
When he comes back; you demi-puppets that
By moonshine do the green sour ringlets make,
Whereof the ewe not bites; and you whose pastime
Is to make midnight mushrooms that rejoice
To hear the solemn curfew; by whose aid 40
(Weak masters though ye be) I have bedimmed
The noontide sun, called forth the mutinous winds,
And 'twixt the green sea and the azured vault
Set roaring war; to the dread rattling thunder
Have I given fire and rifted Jove's stout oak 45
With his own bolt; the strong-based promontory
Have I made shake and by the spurs plucked up
The pine and cedar; graves at my command
Have waked their sleepers, oped, and let 'em forth
By my so potent art. But this rough magic 50
I here abjure; and when I have required
Some heavenly music (which even now I do)
To work mine end upon their senses that
This airy charm is for, I'll break my staff,
Bury it certain fathoms in the earth, 55
And deeper than did ever plummet sound
I'll drown my book. *Solemn music.*

Here enters ARIEL *before; then* ALONSO, *with a frantic gesture, attended by* GONZALO; SEBASTIAN *and* ANTONIO *in like manner,*

---

23 *relish:* feel; *all:* quite. 36 *demi-puppets:* tiny elves. 45 *rifted:* split. 47 *spurs:* roots. 51 *required:* asked for.

attended by ADRIAN *and* FRANCISCO. *They all enter the circle which* PROSPERO *had made, and there stand charmed; which* PROSPERO *observing, speaks.*

A solemn air, and the best comforter
To an unsettled fancy, cure thy brains,
Now useless, boiled within thy skull! There stand, 60
For you are spell-stopped.
Holy Gonzalo, honorable man,
Mine eyes, ev'n sociable to the show of thine,
Fall fellowly drops. The charm dissolves apace;
And as the morning steals upon the night, 65
Melting the darkness, so their rising senses
Begin to chase the ignorant fumes that mantle
Their clearer reason. O good Gonzalo,
My true preserver, and a loyal sir
To him thou follow'st, I will pay thy graces 70
Home both in word and deed. Most cruelly
Didst thou, Alonso, use me and my daughter.
Thy brother was a furtherer in the act.
Thou art pinched for't now, Sebastian. Flesh and blood,
You, brother mine, that entertained ambition, 75
Expelled remorse and nature; whom, with Sebastian
(Whose inward pinches therefore are most strong),
Would here have killed your king; I do forgive thee,
Unnatural though thou art. Their understanding
Begins to swell, and the approaching tide 80
Will shortly fill the reasonable shore,
That now lies foul and muddy. Not one of them
That yet looks on me or would know me. Ariel,
Fetch me the hat and rapier in my cell.
I will discase me, and myself present 85
As I was sometime Milan. Quickly, spirit!
Thou shalt ere long be free.

ARIEL *sings and helps to attire him.*

Where the bee sucks, there suck I;
In a cowslip's bell I lie;
There I couch when owls do cry. 90
On the bat's back I do fly

---

58 *air:* musical air; *and:* i.e., which is. 63 *ev'n sociable to:* full of sympathy at. 64 *Fall:* let fall. 70-71 *pay . . . Home:* repay your past favors fully. 76 *remorse:* pity; *nature:* natural feeling. 81 *reasonable shore:* i.e., the mind. 85 *discase:* undress. 86 *sometime Milan:* when Duke of Milan.

After summer merrily.
Merrily, merrily shall I live now
Under the blossom that hangs on the bough.

PROSPERO. Why, that's my dainty Ariel! I shall miss thee, 95
But yet thou shalt have freedom; so, so, so.
To the King's ship, invisible as thou art!
There shalt thou find the mariners asleep
Under the hatches. The master and the boatswain
Being awake, enforce them to this place, 100
And presently, I prithee.
ARIEL. I drink the air before me, and return
Or ere your pulse twice beat. *Exit.*
GONZALO. All torment, trouble, wonder, and amazement
Inhabits here. Some heavenly power guide us 105
Out of this fearful country!
PROSPERO. Behold, sir King,
The wronged Duke of Milan, Prospero.
For more assurance that a living prince
Does now speak to thee, I embrace thy body,
And to thee and thy company I bid 110
A hearty welcome.
ALONSO. Whe'r thou be'st he or no,
Or some enchanted trifle to abuse me,
As late I have been, I not know. Thy pulse
Beats, as of flesh and blood; and, since I saw thee,
Th' affliction of my mind amends, with which, 115
I fear, a madness held me. This must crave
(An if this be at all) a most strange story.
Thy dukedom I resign and do entreat
Thou pardon me my wrongs. But how should Prospero
Be living and be here?
PROSPERO. First, noble friend, 120
Let me embrace thine age, whose honor cannot
Be measured or confined.
GONZALO. Whether this be
Or be not, I'll not swear.
PROSPERO. You do yet taste
Some subtleties o' th' isle, that will not let you

---

112 *trifle:* trick; *abuse:* deceive. 114 *as of:* as if composed of. 116 *crave:* require. 117 *An . . . all:* if this is actually happening. 118 *Thy . . . resign:* i.e., my right to tribute.

Believe things certain. Welcome, my friends all. 125
[*Aside to* SEBASTIAN *and* ANTONIO.] But you, my brace of lords,
were I so minded,
I here could pluck his Highness' frown upon you,
And justify you traitors. At this time
I will tell no tales.
SEBASTIAN. [*Aside.*] The devil speaks in him.
PROSPERO. No.
For you, most wicked sir, whom to call brother 130
Would even infect my mouth, I do forgive
Thy rankest fault—all of them; and require
My dukedom of thee, which perforce I know
Thou must restore.
ALONSO. If thou beest Prospero,
Give us particulars of thy preservation; 135
How thou has met us here, who three hours since
Were wrecked upon this shore; where I have lost
(How sharp the point of this remembrance is!)
My dear son Ferdinand.
PROSPERO. I am woe for't, sir.
ALONSO. Irreparable is the loss, and patience 140
Says it is past her cure.
PROSPERO. I rather think
You have not sought her help, of whose soft grace
For the like loss I have her sovereign aid
And rest myself content.
ALONSO. You the like loss?
PROSPERO. As great to me as late; and, supportable 145
To make the dear loss, have I means much weaker
Than you may call to comfort you; for I
Have lost my daughter.
ALONSO. A daughter?
O heavens, that they were living both in Naples,
The King and Queen there! That they were, I wish 150
Myself were mudded in that oozy bed
Where my son lies. When did you lose your daughter?
PROSPERO. In this last tempest. I perceive these lords
At this encounter do so much admire
That they devour their reason, and scarce think 155
Their eyes do offices of truth, their words
Are natural breath. But, howsoev'r you have

---

139 *woe:* sorry. 145 *late:* recent. 154 *admire:* wonder. 156 *Their . . . truth:* i.e., they can believe their eyes.

Been justled from your senses, know for certain
That I am Prospero, and that very duke
Which was thrust forth of Milan, who most strangely 160
Upon this shore, where you were wrecked, was landed
To be the lord on't. No more yet of this;
For 'tis a chronicle of day by day,
Not a relation for a breakfast, nor
Befitting this first meeting. Welcome, sir; 165
This cell's my court. Here have I few attendants,
And subjects none abroad. Pray you, look in.
My dukedom since you have given me again,
I will requite you with as good a thing,
At least bring forth a wonder to content ye 170
As much as me my dukedom.

Here PROSPERO *discovers* FERDINAND *and* MIRANDA *playing at chess.*

MIRANDA. Sweet lord, you play me false.

FERDINAND. No, my dearest love,
I would not for the world.

MIRANDA. Yes, for a score of kingdoms you should wrangle,
And I would call it fair play.

ALONSO. If this prove 175
A vision of the island, one dear son
Shall I twice lose.

SEBASTIAN. A most high miracle!

FERDINAND. Though the seas threaten, they are merciful.
I have cursed them without cause. [*Kneels.*]

ALONSO. Now all the blessings
Of a glad father compass thee about! 180
Arise, and say how thou cam'st here.

MIRANDA. O, wonder!
How many goodly creatures are there here!
How beauteous mankind is! O brave new world
That has such people in't!

PROSPERO. 'Tis new to thee.

ALONSO. What is this maid with whom thou wast at play? 185
Your eld'st acquaintance cannot be three hours.
Is she the goddess that hath severed us
And brought us thus together?

FERDINAND. Sir, she is mortal;
But by immortal providence she's mine.

---

171 S.D. *discovers:* reveals. 186 *eld'st:* i.e., longest period of.

I chose her when I could not ask my father 190
For his advice, nor thought I had one. She
Is daughter to this famous Duke of Milan,
Of whom so often I have heard renown
But never saw before; of whom I have
Received a second life; and second father 195
This lady makes him to me.

ALONSO. I am hers.
But, O, how oddly will it sound that I
Must ask my child forgiveness!

PROSPERO. There, sir, stop.
Let us not burden our remembrance with
A heaviness that's gone.

GONZALO. I have inly wept, 200
Or should have spoke ere this. Look down, you gods,
And on this couple drop a blessed crown!
For it is you that have chalked forth the way
Which brought us hither.

ALONSO. I say, Amen, Gonzalo.

GONZALO. Was Milan thrust from Milan that his issue 205
Should become kings of Naples? O, rejoice
Beyond a common joy, and set it down
With gold on lasting pillars: in one voyage
Did Claribel her husband find at Tunis,
And Ferdinand her brother found a wife 210
Where he himself was lost; Prospero his dukedom
In a poor isle; and all of us ourselves
When no man was his own.

ALONSO. [*To* FERDINAND *and* MIRANDA.] Give me your hands.
Let grief and sorrow still embrace his heart
That doth not wish you joy.

GONZALO. Be it so! Amen! 215

[*Re-*]*enter* ARIEL, *with the* MASTER *and* BOATSWAIN *amazedly following.*

Oh, look, sir; look, sir! Here is more of us!
I prophesied, if a gallows were on land,
This fellow could not drown. Now, blasphemy,
That swear'st grace o'erboard, not an oath on shore?
Hast thou no mouth by land? What is the news? 220

BOATSWAIN. The best news is that we have safely found
Our king and company; the next, our ship,

---

218 *blasphemy:* you blasphemer.

Which, but three glasses since, we gave out split,
Is tight and yare and bravely rigged as when
We first put out to sea.

ARIEL. [*Aside to* PROSPERO.] Sir, all this service 225
Have I done since I went.

PROSPERO. [*Aside to* ARIEL.] My tricksy spirit!

ALONSO. These are not natural events; they strengthen
From strange to stranger. Say, how came you hither?

BOATSWAIN. If I did think, sir, I were well awake,
I'ld strive to tell you. We were dead of sleep 230
And (how we know not) all clapped under hatches;
Where, but even now, with strange and several noises
Of roaring, shrieking, howling, jingling chains,
And mo diversity of sounds, all horrible,
We were awaked; straightway at liberty; 235
Where we, in all her trim, freshly beheld
Our royal, good, and gallant ship, our master
Cap'ring to eye her. On a trice, so please you,
Even in a dream, were we divided from them
And were brought moping hither.

ARIEL. [*Aside to* PROSPERO.] Was't well done? 240

PROSPERO. [*Aside to* ARIEL.] Bravely, my diligence. Thou shalt be free.

ALONSO. This is as strange a maze as e'er men trod;
And there is in this business more than nature
Was ever conduct of. Some oracle
Must rectify our knowledge.

PROSPERO. Sir, my liege, 245
Do not infest your mind with beating on
The strangeness of this business: at picked leisure,
Which shall be shortly single, I'll resolve you
(Which to you shall seem probable) of every
These happened accidents; till when, be cheerful
And think of each thing well. [*Aside to* ARIEL.] Come hit[illegible]
spirit.
Set Caliban and his companions free.
Untie the spell. [*Exit* ARIEL.] How fares my gracious [illegible]
There are yet missing of your company
Some few odd lads that you remember not.

---

224 *yare:* ready for sea. 226 *tricksy:* clever. 238 *Cap'ri*[illegible]
244 *conduct:* conductor. 246 *infest:* trouble. 248 *single*[illegible]
explain to you.

[*Re-*]*enter* ARIEL, *driving in* CALIBAN, STEPHANO, *and* TRINCULO, *in their stolen apparel.*

STEPHANO. Every man shift for all the rest, and let no man take care for himself; for all is but fortune. Coragio, bully-monster, coragio!

TRINCULO. If these be true spies which I wear in my head, here's a goodly sight. 260

CALIBAN. O Setebos, these be brave spirits indeed!
How fine my master is! I am afraid
He will chastise me.

SEBASTIAN. Ha, ha!
What things are these, my Lord Antonio?
Will money buy 'em?

ANTONIO. Very like. One of them 265
Is a plain fish and no doubt marketable.

PROSPERO. Mark but the badges of these men, my lords,
Then say if they be true. This misshapen knave,
His mother was a witch, and one so strong
That could control the moon, make flows and ebbs, 270
And deal in her command without her power.
These three have robbed me, and this demi-devil
(For he's a bastard one) had plotted with them
To take my life. Two of these fellows you
Must know and own; this thing of darkness I 275
Acknowledge mine.

CALIBAN. I shall be pinched to death.

ALONSO. Is not this Stephano, my drunken butler?

SEBASTIAN. He is drunk now: where had he wine?

ALONSO. And Trinculo is reeling ripe: where should they
Find this grand liquor that hath gilded 'em? 280
How cam'st thou in this pickle?

TRINCULO. I have been in such a pickle, since I saw you last, that I fear me will never out of my bones. I shall not fear fly-blowing.

SEBASTIAN. Why, how now, Stephano? 285

STEPHANO. O, touch me not! I am not Stephano, but a cramp.

PROSPERO. You'ld be king o' the isle, sirrah?

STEPHANO. I should have been a sore one then.

---

257 *Coragio:* courage. 259 *spies:* eyes. 267 *badges:* signs identifying them as servants. 271 *deal . . . command:* exercise the moon's power; *without . . . power:* beyond the moon's ability to control her. 284 *fly-blowing:* i.e., being pickled, he will not attract flies.

ALONSO. This is a strange thing as e'er I looked on. [*Pointing to* CALIBAN.]

PROSPERO. He is as disproportioned in his manners 290
As in his shape. Go, sirrah, to my cell;
Take with you your companions. As you look
To have my pardon, trim it handsomely.

CALIBAN. Ay, that I will; and I'll be wise hereafter,
And seek for grace. What a thrice-double ass 295
Was I to take this drunkard for a god
And worship this dull fool!

PROSPERO. Go to! Away!

ALONSO. Hence, and bestow your luggage where you found it.

SEBASTIAN. Or stole it rather.

[*Exeunt* CALIBAN, STEPHANO, *and* TRINCULO.]

PROSPERO. Sir, I invite your Highness and your train 300
To my poor cell, where you shall take your rest
For this one night; which, part of it, I'll waste
With such discourse as, I not doubt, shall make it
Go quick away—the story of my life,
And the particular accidents gone by 305
Since I came to this isle; and in the morn
I'll bring you to your ship, and so to Naples,
Where I have hope to see the nuptial
Of these our dear-beloved solemnized;
And thence retire me to my Milan, where 310
Every third thought shall be my grave.

ALONSO. I long
To hear the story of your life, which must
Take the ear strangely.

PROSPERO. I'll deliver all;
And promise you calm seas, auspicious gales,
And sail so expeditious that shall catch 315
Your royal fleet far off.—My Ariel, chick,
That is thy charge. Then to the elements
Be free, and fare thou well!—Please you, draw near.

Exeunt omnes.

Epilogue

Spoken by Prospero

Now my charms are all o'erthrown,
And what strength I have's mine own,

295 *grace:* favor. 313 *Take:* captivate. 315 *sail:* sailing.

Which is most faint. Now, 'tis true,
I must be here confined by you,
Or sent to Naples. Let me not,
Since I have my dukedom got,
And pardoned the deceiver, dwell
In this bare island by your spell;
But release me from my bands 10
With the help of your good hands.
Gentle breath of yours my sails
Must fill, or else my project fails,
Which was to please. Now I want
Spirits to enforce, art to enchant; 15
And my ending is despair
Unless I be relieved by prayer,
Which pierces so that it assaults
Mercy itself and frees all faults.
As you from crimes would pardoned be, 20
Let your indulgence set me free. *Exit.*

Epilogue 9 *bands:* bonds. 10 *hands:* i.e., applause to break the "spell" of silence. 13 *want:* lack.

Comus

JOHN MILTON

Milton, in his *Apology for Smectymnuus,* writes of discovering in fables and romances the lofty deeds of knighthood. "There I read it in the oath of every knight, that he should defend to the expense of his best blood, or of his life if it so befell him, the honor and chastity of virgin or matron; from whence even then I learned what a noble virtue chastity sure must be, to the defence of which so many worthies, by such a dear adventure of themselves, had sworn." Milton's relatively early work, *Comus,* is a presentation of chastity—the virtue which the youthful poet particularly prized—in conflict with sensuality.

It was apparently at the request of his friend, Henry Lawes, that Milton wrote *Comus,* and the famous seventeenth-century English composer himself wrote the music for the masque. Although masques, in general, are no longer performed today, they were extremely popular in England during the sixteenth and seventeenth centuries among the nobility. Early masques were musical entertainments that emphasized the spectacular, the amateur dancers usually wearing disguises. With the success of Ben Jonson's masques, the dramatic elements of plot and character increased in importance, and Milton's masque is in the Jonson tradition.

The text of *Comus,* which was originally titled simply, *A Maske,* is based upon that found in the 1645 edition of Milton's *Poems.* The spelling and punctuation have been modernized.

A Masque presented at Ludlow Castle, 1634, befor[illegible] of Bridgewater, then President of W[illegible]

The Persons

The ATTENDANT SPIRIT, *afterwards in the habit of* THYRSIS	FIRST BROTHER
COMUS, *with his crew*	SECOND BROTHER
The LADY	SABRINA, *the Nymph*

(*The first scene discovers a wild wood. The* ATTENDANT SPIRIT *descends or enters*)

Before the starry threshold of Jove's court
My mansion is, where those immortal shapes
Of bright aerial spirits live insphered
In regions mild of calm and serene air,
Above the smoke and stir of this dim spot 5
Which men call Earth, and with low-thoughted care,
Confined and pestered in this pinfold here,
Strive to keep up a frail and feverish being,
Unmindful of the crown that Virtue gives,
After this mortal change, to her true servants 10
Amongst the enthroned gods on sainted seats.
Yet some there be that by due steps aspire
To lay their just hands on that golden key
That opes the palace of Eternity.
To such my errand is, and but for such, 15
I would not soil these pure ambrosial weeds
With the rank vapors of this sin-worn mold.
But to my task. Neptune, besides the sway
Of every salt flood and each ebbing stream,
Took in by lot 'twixt high and nether Jove 20
Imperial rule of all the sea-girt isles
That like to rich and various gems inlay
The unadorned bosom of the deep,
Which he, to grace his tributary gods,
By course commits to several government, 25
And gives them leave to wear their sapphire crowns
And wield their little tridents. But this isle,
The greatest and the best of all the main,
He quarters to his blue-haired deities;
And all this tract that fronts the falling sun 30

---

3 *aerial spirits:* although Thyrsis (the Attendant Spirit) is an angel, Milton decks his Christian subject in pagan trappings throughout the masque. 7 *pinfold:* pound (a pen for animals). 16 *ambrosial weeds:* heavenly garments. 17 *mold:* the human body. 18-20 The universe, as represented by Homer in the *Iliad,* was divided among Poseidon (Neptune, the god of the sea), Zeus (Jove, the god of the sky), and Hades (Pluto, i.e., "nether Jove," the god of the underworld).

A noble Peer of mickle trust and power
Has in his charge, with tempered awe to guide
An old and haughty nation proud in arms;
Where his fair offspring, nursed in princely lore,
Are coming to attend their father's state 35
And new-entrusted scepter; but their way
Lies through the perplexed paths of this drear wood,
The nodding horror of whose shady brows
Threats the forlorn and wandering passenger.
And here their tender age might suffer peril, 40
But that by quick command from sovran Jove
I was despatched for their defence and guard;
And listen why, for I will tell ye now
What never yet was heard in tale or song
From old or modern bard in hall or bower. 45
  Bacchus, that first from out the purple grape
Crushed the sweet poison of misused wine,
After the Tuscan mariners transformed,
Coasting the Tyrrhene shore, as the winds listed,
On Circe's island fell. (Who knows not Circe, 50
The daughter of the Sun? whose charmed cup
Whoever tasted, lost his upright shape,
And downward fell into a groveling swine.)
This Nymph that gazed upon his clustering locks,
With ivy berries wreathed, and his blithe youth, 55
Had by him, ere he parted thence, a son
Much like his father, but his mother more,
Whom therefore she brought up and Comus named;
Who, ripe and frolic of his full-grown age,
Roving the Celtic and Iberian fields, 60
At last betakes him to this ominous wood,
And, in thick shelter of black shades imbowered,
Excels his mother at her mighty art,
Offering to every weary traveler
His orient liquor in a crystal glass, 65
To quench the drouth of Phoebus, which as they taste
(For most do taste through fond intemperate thirst),
Soon as the potion works, their human countenance,

---

31 *A noble Peer:* the Earl of Bridgewater, at whose castle in Wales the masque was first performed; *mickle:* great. 37 *perplexed:* confusing. 46 Bacchus, abducted by Tuscan pirates who wished to sell him into slavery, miraculously changes their ships into a grape arbor and them into dolphins. 60 *Celtic:* French; *Iberian:* Spanish. 65 *orient:* lustrous, like orient pearls. 66 *the drouth of Phoebus:* thirst caused by the sun.

The express resemblance of the gods, is changed
Into some brutish form of wolf, or bear, 70
Or ounce, or tiger, hog, or bearded goat,
All other parts remaining as they were.
And they, so perfect is their misery,
Not once perceive their foul disfigurement,
But boast themselves more comely than before 75
And all their friends, and native home forget
To roll with pleasure in a sensual sty.
Therefore when any favored of high Jove
Chances to pass through this adventurous glade,
Swift as the sparkle of a glancing star 80
I shoot from heaven to give him safe convoy,
As now I do. But first I must put off
These my sky-robes, spun out of Iris' woof,
And take the weeds and likeness of a swain
That to the service of this house belongs, 85
Who with his soft pipe and smooth-dittied song
Well knows to still the wild winds when they roar,
And hush the waving woods; nor of less faith,
And in this office of his mountain watch
Likeliest, and nearest to the present aid 90
Of this occasion. But I hear the tread
Of hateful steps; I must be viewless now.
(COMUS *enters, with a charming-rod in one hand, his glass in the other; with him a rout of monsters, headed like sundry sorts of wild beasts, but otherwise like men and women, their apparel glistening. They come in making a riotous and unruly noise, with torches in their hands*)

COMUS. The star that bids the shepherd fold
Now the top of heaven doth hold,
And the gilded car of day 95
His glowing axle doth allay
In the steep Atlantic stream;
And the slope sun his upward beam
Shoots against the dusky pole,
Pacing toward the other goal 100

---

71 *ounce:* lynx. 83 *Iris:* the goddess of the rainbow. 86 *smooth-dittied song:* probably a compliment to Henry Lawes, the great English composer, who had written the music for the songs of the masque and played the part of Thyrsis in the original presentation at Ludlow. 93 *star:* the evening star, Hesperus, a sign to shepherds to return their flocks to fold (i.e., enclosure). 95 the chariot of Phoebus, god of the sun. 96 *allay:* cool.

Of his chamber in the east.
Meanwhile welcome joy and feast,
Midnight shout and revelry,
Tipsy dance and jollity.
Braid your locks with rosy twine,
Dropping odors, dropping wine. 105
Rigor now is gone to bed,
And Advice with scrupulous head,
Strict Age, and sour Severity,
With their grave saws in slumber lie.
We that are of purer fire 110
Imitate the starry choir,
Who in their nightly watchful spheres
Lead in swift round the months and years.
The sounds and seas with all their finny drove
Now to the moon in wavering morris move, 115
And on the tawny sands and shelves
Trip the pert fairies and the dapper elves;
By dimpled brook and fountain brim,
The wood-nymphs, decked with daisies trim,
Their merry wakes and pastimes keep: 120
What hath night to do with sleep?
Night hath better sweets to prove,
Venus now wakes, and wakens Love.
Come, let us our rites begin;
'Tis only daylight that makes sin, 125
Which these dun shades will ne'er report.
Hail, goddess of nocturnal sport,
Dark-veiled Cotytto, to whom the secret flame
Of midnight torches burns; mysterious dame,
That ne'er art called but when the dragon womb 130
Of Stygian darkness spets her thickest gloom,
And makes one blot of all the air,
Stay thy cloudy ebon chair
Wherein thou rid'st with Hecat', and befriend
Us thy vowed priests, till utmost end 135
Of all thy dues be done, and none left out,
Ere the blabbing eastern scout,
The nice Morn on the Indian steep,

---

116 *morris:* a mumming dance. 129 *Cotytto:* Thracian goddess who conducted orgiastic rites. 132 *Stygian:* characteristic of the infernal regions and of the river Styx which encircles the underworld. 135 *Hecat':* the underworld goddess Hecate, mistress of witches.

From her cabined loop-hole peep, 140
And to the tell-tale Sun descry
Our concealed solemnity.
Come, knit hands, and beat the ground,
In a light fantastic round.

(*The Measure*)

Break off, break off, I feel the different pace 145
Of some chaste footing near about this ground.
Run to your shrouds within these brakes and trees;
Our number may affright. Some virgin sure
(For so I can distinguish by mine art)
Benighted in these woods. Now to my charms, 150
And to my wily trains; I shall ere long
Be well stocked with as fair a herd as grazed
About my mother Circe. Thus I hurl
My dazzling spells into the spongy air,
Of power to cheat the eye with blear illusion, 155
And give it false presentments, lest the place
And my quaint habits breed astonishment,
And put the damsel to suspicious flight,
Which must not be, for that's against my course;
I, under fair pretence of friendly ends, 160
And well-placed words of glozing courtesy,
Baited with reasons not unplausible,
Wind me into the easy-hearted man,
And hug him into snares. When once her eye
Hath met the virtue of this magic dust, 165
I shall appear some harmless villager
Whom thrift keeps up about his country gear.
But here she comes; I fairly step aside,
And hearken, if I may, her business here.

(*The* LADY *enters*)

LADY. This way the noise was, if mine ear be true, 170
My best guide now. Methought it was the sound
Of riot and ill-managed merriment,
Such as the jocund flute or gamesome pipe
Stirs up among the loose unlettered hinds,
When for their teeming flocks and granges full 175

---

144 *round:* a dance in which circular figures predominate. *The Measure:* here the dance is performed by Comus and his crew. 147 *shrouds:* hiding places, shelters; *brakes:* thickets. 151 *trains:* lures. 154 *spongy:* absorbing. 157 *quaint habits:* odd dress. 161 *glozing:* flattering. 165 *virtue:* power. 174 *hinds:* peasants. 175 *granges:* barns.

In wanton dance they praise the bounteous Pan,
And thank the gods amiss. I should be loth
To meet the rudeness and swilled insolence
Of such late wassailers; yet O where else
Shall I inform my unacquainted feet 180
In the blind mazes of this tangled wood?
My brothers, when they saw me wearied out
With this long way, resolving here to lodge
Under the spreading favor of these pines,
Stepped as they said to the next thicket side 185
To bring me berries, or such cooling fruit
As the kind hospitable woods provide.
They left me then when the gray-hooded Even,
Like a sad votarist in palmer's weed,
Rose from the hindmost wheels of Phoebus' wain. 190
But where they are, and why they came not back,
Is now the labor of my thoughts; 'tis likeliest
They had engaged their wandering steps too far,
And envious darkness, ere they could return,
Had stole them from me. Else, O thievish Night, 195
Why shouldst thou, but for some felonious end,
In thy dark lantern thus close up the stars
That Nature hung in heaven, and filled their lamps
With everlasting oil, to give due light
To the misled and lonely traveler? 200
This is the place, as well as I may guess,
Whence even now the tumult of loud mirth
Was rife, and perfect in my listening ear,
Yet nought but single darkness do I find.
What might this be? A thousand fantasies 205
Begin to throng into my memory,
Of calling shapes, and beckoning shadows dire,
And airy tongues that syllable men's names
On sands and shores and desert wildernesses.
These thoughts may startle well, but not astound 210
The virtuous mind, that ever walks attended
By a strong siding champion, Conscience.
O welcome, pure-eyed Faith, white-handed Hope,
Thou hovering angel girt with golden wings,
And thou unblemished form of Chastity, 215

---

176 *Pan:* the Greek god of shepherds and flocks. 178 *swilled:* drunken. 179 *wassailers:* revelers. 189 *votarist . . . weed:* one who has undertaken a vow and is garbed in pilgrim's dress. 204 *single:* total.

I see ye visibly, and now believe
That He, the Supreme Good, to whom all things ill
Are but as slavish officers of vengeance.
Would send a glistening guardian, if need were,
To keep my life and honor unassailed. 220
Was I deceived, or did a sable cloud
Turn forth her silver lining on the night?
I did not err, there does a sable cloud
Turn forth her silver lining on the night,
And casts a gleam over this tufted grove. 225
I cannot hallo to my brothers, but
Such noise as I can make to be heard farthest
I'll venture, for my new-enlivened spirits
Prompt me; and they perhaps are not far off.

Song

Sweet Echo, sweetest nymph, that liv'st unseen 230
Within thy airy shell
By slow Meander's margent green,
And in the violet-embroidered vale
Where the love-lorn nightingale
Nightly to thee her sad song mourneth well: 235
Canst thou not tell me of a gentle pair
That likest thy Narcissus are?
O if thou have
Hid them in some flowery cave,
Tell me but where, 240
Sweet queen of parley, daughter of the sphere;
So may'st thou be translated to the skies,
And give resounding grace to all heaven's harmonies.

COMUS. Can any mortal mixture of earth's mold
Breathe such divine enchanting ravishment? 245
Sure something holy lodges in that breast,
And with these raptures moves the vocal air
To testify his hidden residence;
How sweetly did they float upon the wings
Of silence, through the empty-vaulted night, 250
At every fall smoothing the raven down
Of darkness till it smiled. I have oft heard

---

230 *Echo:* a nymph in love with Narcissus; her unrequited love caused her to pine away until only her voice was left. 251 *fall:* cadence.

My mother Circe with the Sirens three,
Amidst the flowery-kirtled Naiades,
Culling their potent herbs and baleful drugs, 255
Who, as they sung, would take the prisoned soul
And lap it in Elysium; Scylla wept,
And chid her barking waves into attention,
And fell Charybdis murmured soft applause.
Yet they in pleasing slumber lulled the sense, 260
And in sweet madness robbed it of itself;
But such a sacred and home-felt delight,
Such sober certainty of waking bliss,
I never heard till now. I'll speak to her,
And she shall be my queen. Hail, foreign wonder, 265
Whom certain these rough shades did never breed,
Unless the goddess that in rural shrine
Dwell'st here with Pan or Sylvan, by blest song
Forbidding every bleak unkindly fog
To touch the prosperous growth of this tall wood. 270
LADY. Nay, gentle shepherd, ill is lost that praise
That is addressed to unattending ears.
Not any boast of skill, but extreme shift
How to regain my severed company
Compelled me to awake the courteous Echo 275
To give me answer from her mossy couch.
COMUS. What chance, good lady, hath bereft you thus?
LADY. Dim darkness and this leavy labyrinth.
COMUS. Could that divide you from near-ushering guides?
LADY. They left me weary on a grassy turf. 280
COMUS. By falsehood, or discourtesy, or why?
LADY. To seek in the valley some cool friendly spring.
COMUS. And left your fair side all unguarded, lady?
LADY. They were but twain, and purposed quick return.
COMUS. Perhaps forestalling night prevented them. 285
LADY. How easy my misfortune is to hit!
COMUS. Imports their loss, beside the present need?
LADY. No less than if I should my brothers lose.
COMUS. Were they of manly prime, or youthful bloom?
LADY. As smooth as Hebe's their unrazored lips. 290

---

253 *Sirens:* as described by Homer in the *Odyssey* their sweet songs lured sailors to detruction. 254 *Naiades:* water nymphs. 257-59 *Scylla . . . Charybdis:* monsters associated with the rocks and whirlpool on opposite sides of the Straits of Messina. 268 *Sylvan:* Sylvanus, god of the woods and fields. 290 *Hebe:* goddess of youth.

COMUS. Two such I saw, what time the labored ox
In his loose traces from the furrow came,
And the swinked hedger at his supper sat;
I saw them under a green mantling vine
That crawls along the side of yon small hill, 295
Plucking ripe clusters from the tender shoots;
Their port was more than human, as they stood.
I took it for a fairy vision
Of some gay creatures of the element,
That in the colors of the rainbow live, 300
And play in the plighted clouds. I was awe-strook,
And as I passed, I worshiped; if those you seek,
It were a journey like the path to Heaven
To help you find them.
LADY. Gentle villager,
What readiest way would bring me to that place? 305
COMUS. Due west it rises from this shrubby point.
LADY. To find out that, good shepherd, I suppose,
In such a scant allowance of star-light,
Would overtask the best land-pilot's art,
Without the sure guess of well-practised feet. 310
COMUS. I know each lane and every alley green,
Dingle or bushy dell, of this wild wood,
And every bosky bourn from side to side,
My daily walks and ancient neighborhood,
And if your stray attendance be yet lodged, 315
Or shroud within these limits, I shall know
Ere morrow wake or the low-roosted lark
From her thatched pallet rouse; if otherwise,
I can conduct you, lady, to a low
But loyal cottage, where you may be safe 320
Till further quest.
LADY. Shepherd, I take thy word,
And trust thy honest-offered courtesy,
Which oft is sooner found in lowly sheds
With smoky rafters, than in tapestry halls
And courts of princes, where it first was named, 325
And yet is most pretended. In a place
Less warranted than this, or less secure,
I cannot be, that I should fear to change it.

---

293 *swinked hedger:* weary hedgemaker. 297 *port:* bearing. 299 *element:* air. 301 *plighted:* folded. 312 *Dingle:* small wooded valley. 313 *bosky bourn:* bush-lined stream.

Eye me, blest Providence, and square my trial
To my proportioned strength. Shepherd, lead on. (*Exeunt*) 330
(*Enter the two* BROTHERS)
ELDER BROTHER. Unmuffle, ye faint stars, and thou, fair moon,
That wont'st to love the traveler's benison,
Stoop thy pale visage through an amber cloud,
And disinherit Chaos, that reigns here
In double night of darkness and of shades; 335
Or if your influence be quite dammed up
With black usurping mists, some gentle taper,
Though a rush-candle from the wicker hole
Of some clay habitation, visit us
With thy long leveled rule of streaming light, 340
And thou shalt be our star of Arcady,
Or Tyrian Cynosure.
SECOND BROTHER. Or if our eyes
Be barred that happiness, might we but hear
The folded flocks penned in their wattled cotes,
Or sound of pastoral reed with oaten stops, 345
Or whistle from the lodge, or village cock
Count the night-watches to his feathery dames,
'Twould be some solace yet, some little cheering,
In this close dungeon of innumerous boughs.
But O that hapless virgin, our lost sister, 350
Where may she wander now, whither betake her
From the chill dew, amongst rude burs and thistles?
Perhaps some cold bank is her bolster now,
Or 'gainst the rugged bark of some broad elm
Leans her unpillowed head, fraught with sad fears. 355
What if in wild amazement and affright,
Or, while we speak, within the direful grasp
Of savage hunger or of savage heat?
ELDER BROTHER. Peace, brother, be not over-exquisite
To cast the fashion of uncertain evils; 360

---

332 *benison:* blessing. 334 *disinherit:* dispossess. 341-42 *star . . . Cynosure:* the Arcadian princess Callisto was metamorphosed into the Great Bear constellation (Ursa Major) which Greek seamen navigated by; her son was changed into the Little Bear or Cynosura (Ursa Minor) used by Phoenician (Tyrian) navigators. 344 *wattled cotes:* sheepfolds of woven branches. 345 *pastoral reed with oaten stops:* traditional shepherd's pipe made of an oat stalk with small openings (stops). 349 *innumerous:* innumerable. 358 *heat:* lust. 359 *over-exquisite:* too curious or speculative.

For grant they be so, while they rest unknown,
What need a man forestall his date of grief,
And run to meet what he would most avoid?
Or if they be but false alarms of fear,
How bitter is such self-delusion? 365
I do not think my sister so to seek,
Or so unprincipled in virtue's book,
And the sweet peace that goodness bosoms ever,
As that the single want of light and noise
(Not being in danger, as I trust she is not) 370
Could stir the constant mood of her calm thoughts,
And put them into misbecoming plight.
Virtue could see to do what Virtue would
By her own radiant light, though sun and moon
Were in the flat sea sunk. And Wisdom's self 375
Oft seeks to sweet retired solitude,
Where with her best nurse, Contemplation,
She plumes her feathers, and lets grow her wings,
That in the various bustle of resort
Were all to-ruffled, and sometimes impaired. 380
He that has light within his own clear breast
May sit in the center, and enjoy bright day,
But he that hides a dark soul and foul thoughts
Benighted walks under the mid-day sun;
Himself is his own dungeon.
SECOND BROTHER. 'Tis most true 385
That musing meditation most affects
The pensive secrecy of desert cell,
Far from the cheerful haunt of men and herds,
And sits as safe as in a senate-house;
For who would rob a hermit of his weeds, 390
His few books, or his beads, or maple dish,
Or do his gray hairs any violence?
But Beauty, like the fair Hesperian tree
Laden with blooming gold, had need the guard
Of dragon-watch with unenchanted eye, 395
To save her blossoms, and defend her fruit
From the rash hand of bold Incontinence.
You may as well spread out the unsunned heaps
Of miser's treasure by an outlaw's den,

---

366 *so to seek:* so much at a loss. 380 *to-ruffled:* very badly ruffled (*to-* an intensive prefix). 393 *Hesperian tree:* the tree which bore the golden apples in the Garden of the Hesperides; it was guarded by a dragon.

And tell me it is safe, as bid me hope 400
Danger will wink on opportunity,
And let a single helpless maiden pass
Uninjured in this wild surrounding waste.
Of night or loneliness it recks me not;
I fear the dread events that dog them both, 405
Lest some ill-greeting touch attempt the person
Of our unowned sister.

ELDER BROTHER. I do not, brother,
Infer as if I thought my sister's state
Secure without all doubt or controversy;
Yet where an equal poise of hope and fear 410
Does arbitrate the event, my nature is
That I incline to hope, rather than fear,
And gladly banish squint suspicion.
My sister is not so defenceless left
As you imagine; she has a hidden strength 415
Which you remember not.

SECOND BROTHER. What hidden strength,
Unless the strength of Heaven, if you mean that?

ELDER BROTHER. I mean that too, but yet a hidden strength
Which, if Heaven gave it, may be termed her own:
'Tis chastity, my brother, chastity. 420
She that has that is clad in complete steel,
And, like a quivered nymph with arrows keen,
May trace huge forests and unharbored heaths,
Infamous hills and sandy perilous wilds,
Where, through the sacred rays of chastity, 425
No savage fierce, bandit, or mountaineer
Will dare to soil her virgin purity.
Yea, there where very desolation dwells,
By grots and caverns shagged with horrid shades,
She may pass on with unblenched majesty, 430
Be it not done in pride or in presumption.
Some say no evil thing that walks by night,
In fog or fire, by lake or moorish fen,
Blue meager hag, or stubborn unlaid ghost,
That breaks his magic chains at curfew time, 435
No goblin or swart fairy of the mine,

---

404 *it recks me not:* i.e., I make no distinction between them. 407 *unowned:* unprotected. 422 *a quivered nymph:* one who is a follower of Diana, goddess of chastity. 423 *unharbored:* shelterless. 430 *unblenched:* undismayed. 436 *swart:* black.

Hath hurtful power o'er true virginity.
Do ye believe me yet, or shall I call
Antiquity from the old schools of Greece
To testify the arms of chastity? 440
Hence had the huntress Dian her dread bow,
Fair silver-shafted queen for ever chaste,
Wherewith she tamed the brinded lioness
And spotted mountain-pard, but set at nought
The frivolous bolt of Cupid; gods and men 445
Feared her stern frown, and she was queen o' the woods.
What was that snaky-headed Gorgon shield
That wise Minerva wore, unconquered virgin,
Wherewith she freezed her foes to congealed stone,
But rigid looks of chaste austerity, 450
And noble grace that dashed brute violence
With sudden adoration and blank awe?
So dear to Heaven is saintly chastity
That when a soul is found sincerely so,
A thousand liveried angels lackey her, 455
Driving far off each thing of sin and guilt,
And in clear dream and solemn vision
Tell her of things that no gross ear can hear,
Till oft converse with heavenly habitants
Begin to cast a beam on the outward shape, 460
The unpolluted temple of the mind,
And turns it by degrees to the soul's essence,
Till all be made immortal. But when lust,
By unchaste looks, loose gestures, and foul talk,
But most by lewd and lavish act of sin, 465
Lets in defilement to the inward parts,
The soul grows clotted by contagion,
Imbodies and imbrutes, till she quite lose
The divine property of her first being.
Such are those thick and gloomy shadows damp 470
Oft seen in charnel vaults and sepulchres,
Lingering, and sitting by a new-made grave,
As loth to leave the body that it loved,
And linked itself by carnal sensualty
To a degenerate and degraded state. 475

---

439 *old schools of Greece:* the elder brother supports his case by citing the authority of mythology. 445 *bolt:* arrow. 448 *Minerva:* the goddess of wisdom who carried on her shield the head of the Gorgon, Medusa; but Milton here alters the old myth to suggest that chastity is the goddess's true strength.

SECOND BROTHER. How charming is divine philosophy!
Not harsh and crabbed, as dull fools suppose,
But musical as is Apollo's lute,
And a perpetual feast of nectared sweets,
Where no crude surfeit reigns.
ELDER BROTHER. List, list, I hear 480
Some far-off hallo break the silent air.
SECOND BROTHER. Methought so too; what should it be?
ELDER BROTHER. For certain,
Either some one, like us, night-foundered here,
Or else some neighbor woodman, or at worst,
Some roving robber calling to his fellows. 485
SECOND BROTHER. Heaven keep my sister! Again, again, and near!
Best draw, and stand upon our guard.
ELDER BROTHER. I'll hallo;
If he be friendly, he comes well; if not,
Defence is a good cause, and Heaven be for us.
(*Enter the* ATTENDANT SPIRIT, *habited like a shepherd*)
That hallo I should know; what are you? speak. 490
Come not too near, you fall on iron stakes else.
SPIRIT. What voice is that? my young lord? speak again.
SECOND BROTHER. O brother, 'tis my father's shepherd, sure.
ELDER BROTHER. Thyrsis, whose artful strains have oft delayed
The huddling brook to hear his madrigal, 495
And sweetened every musk-rose of the dale,
How cam'st thou here, good swain? Hath any ram
Slipped from the fold, or young kid lost his dam,
Or straggling wether the pent flock forsook?
How couldst thou find this dark sequestered nook? 500
SPIRIT. O my loved master's heir, and his next joy,
I came not here on such a trivial toy
As a strayed ewe, or to pursue the stealth
Of pilfering wolf; not all the fleecy wealth
That doth enrich these downs is worth a thought 505
To this my errand, and the care it brought.
But O my virgin lady, where is she?
How chance she is not in your company?
ELDER BROTHER. To tell thee sadly, shepherd, without blame
Or our neglect, we lost her as we came. 510

---

491 *iron stakes:* swords. 494 *Thyrsis:* a traditional name in pastoral poetry.

SPIRIT. Ay me unhappy, then my fears are true.
ELDER BROTHER. What fears, good Thyrsis? Prithee briefly shew.
SPIRIT. I'll tell ye. 'Tis not vain or fabulous
(Though so esteemed by shallow ignorance)
What the sage poets, taught by the heavenly Muse, 515
Storied of old in high immortal verse
Of dire Chimeras and enchanted isles,
And rifted rocks whose entrance leads to hell;
For such there be, but unbelief is blind.
Within the navel of this hideous wood, 520
Immured in cypress shades, a sorcerer dwells,
Of Bacchus and of Circe born, great Comus,
Deep skilled in all his mother's witcheries,
And here to every thirsty wanderer
By sly enticement gives his baneful cup, 525
With many murmurs mixed, whose pleasing poison
The visage quite transforms of him that drinks,
And the inglorious likeness of a beast
Fixes instead, unmolding reason's mintage
Charactered in the face; this have I learnt 530
Tending my flocks hard by in the hilly crofts
That brow this bottom glade, whence night by night
He and his monstrous rout are heard to howl
Like stabled wolves, or tigers at their prey,
Doing abhorred rites to Hecate 535
In their obscured haunts of inmost bowers.
Yet have they many baits and guileful spells
To inveigle and invite the unwary sense
Of them that pass unweeting by the way.
This evening late, by then the chewing flocks 540
Had ta'en their supper on the savory herb
Of knot-grass dew-besprent, and were in fold,
I sat me down to watch upon a bank
With ivy canopied, and interwove
With flaunting honeysuckle, and began, 545
Wrapped in a pleasing fit of melancholy,
To meditate my rural minstrelsy,
Till fancy had her fill. But ere a close

---

517 *Chimeras:* fire-breathing monsters having a lion's head, a goat's body, and a serpent's tail. 520 *navel:* center. 526 *murmurs:* incantations. 531 *crofts:* small enclosed fields. 532 *brow:* overlook. 539 *unweeting:* unaware. 547 *mediate . . . minstrelsy:* i.e., to play my shepherd's pipe.

The wonted roar was up amidst the woods,
And filled the air with barbarous dissonance, 550
At which I ceased, and listened them a while,
Till an unusual stop of sudden silence
Gave respite to the drowsy-flighted steeds
That draw the litter of close-curtained Sleep.
At last a soft and solemn-breathing sound 555
Rose like a steam of rich distilled perfumes,
And stole upon the air, that even Silence
Was took ere she was ware, and wished she might
Deny her nature and be never more,
Still to be so displaced. I was all ear, 560
And took in strains that might create a soul
Under the ribs of Death, but O ere long
Too well I did perceive it was the voice
Of my most honored lady, your dear sister.
Amazed I stood, harrowed with grief and fear, 565
And "O poor hapless nightingale," thought I,
"How sweet thou sing'st, how near the deadly snare!"
Then down the lawns I ran with headlong haste
Through paths and turnings often trod by day,
Till guided by mine ear I found the place 570
Where that damned wizard, hid in sly disguise
(For so by certain signs I knew), had met
Already, ere my best speed could prevent,
The aidless innocent lady, his wished prey,
Who gently asked if he had seen such two, 575
Supposing him some neighbor villager;
Longer I durst not stay, but soon I guessed
Ye were the two she meant; with that I sprung
Into swift flight, till I had found you here;
But further know I not.

SECOND BROTHER. O night and shades, 580
How are ye joined with hell in triple knot
Against the unarmed weakness of one virgin,
Alone and helpless! Is this the confidence
You gave me, brother?

ELDER BROTHER. Yes, and keep it still,
Lean on it safely; not a period 585
Shall be unsaid for me. Against the threats
Of malice or of sorcery, or that power

---

560 *still:* always. 585 *period:* sentence. 586 *for me:* on my part.

Which erring men call Chance, this I hold firm:
Virtue may be assailed, but never hurt,
Surprised by unjust force, but not enthralled; 590
Yea, even that which Mischief meant most harm
Shall in the happy trial prove most glory.
But evil on itself shall back recoil,
And mix no more with goodness, when at last,
Gathered like scum, and settled to itself, 595
It shall be in eternal restless change
Self-fed and self-consumed; if this fail,
The pillared firmament is rottenness,
And earth's base built on stubble. But come, let's on.
Against the opposing will and arm of Heaven 600
May never this just sword be lifted up;
But for that damned magician, let him be girt
With all the grisly legions that troop
Under the sooty flag of Acheron,
Harpies and Hydras, or all the monstrous forms 605
'Twixt Africa and Ind, I'll find him out,
And force him to return his purchase back,
Or drag him by the curls to a foul death,
Cursed as his life.

SPIRIT. Alas, good venturous youth,
I love thy courage yet, and bold emprise, 610
But here thy sword can do thee little stead;
Far other arms and other weapons must
Be those that quell the might of hellish charms.
He with his bare wand can unthread thy joints,
And crumble all thy sinews.

ELDER BROTHER. Why, prithee, shepherd, 615
How durst thou then thyself approach so near
As to make this relation?

SPIRIT. Care and utmost shifts
How to secure the lady from surprisal
Brought to my mind a certain shepherd lad,
Of small regard to see to, yet well skilled 620
In every virtuous plant and healing herb
That spreads her verdant leaf to the morning ray.
He loved me well, and oft would beg me sing;
Which when I did, he on the tender grass

---

604 *Acheron:* one of the four rivers of Hades, but here it stands for Hell itself. 605 *Harpies:* ravenous monsters, half-woman and half-bird; *Hydras:* many-headed serpents. 607 *purchase:* prey.

Would sit, and hearken even to ecstasy, 625
And in requital ope his leathern scrip,
And show me simples of a thousand names,
Telling their strange and vigorous faculties;
Amongst the rest a small unsightly root,
But of divine effect, he culled me out; 630
The leaf was darkish, and had prickles on it,
But in another country, as he said,
Bore a bright golden flower, but not in this soil;
Unknown, and like esteemed, and the dull swain
Treads on it daily with his clouted shoon; 635
And yet more med'cinal is it than that moly
That Hermes once to wise Ulysses gave;
He called it haemony, and gave it me,
And bade me keep it as of sovran use
'Gainst all enchantments, mildew blast, or damp, 640
Or ghastly Furies' apparition;
I pursed it up, but little reckoning made,
Till now that this extremity compelled,
But now I find it true; for by this means
I knew the foul enchanter though disguised, 645
Entered the very lime-twigs of his spells,
And yet came off. If you have this about you
(As I will give you when we go), you may
Boldly assault the necromancer's hall;
Where if he be, with dauntless hardihood 650
And brandished blade rush on him, break his glass,
And shed the luscious liquor on the ground,
But seize his wand. Though he and his curst crew
Fierce sign of battle make, and menace high,
Or like the sons of Vulcan vomit smoke, 655
Yet will they soon retire, if he but shrink.

ELDER BROTHER. Thyrsis, lead on apace, I'll follow thee,
And some good angel bear a shield before us.

(*The scene changes to a stately palace, set out with all manner of deliciousness: soft music, tables spread with all dainties.* COMUS *appears with his rabble, and the* LADY *set in an enchanted chair, to whom he offers his glass, which she puts by, and goes about to rise*)

COMUS. Nay, lady, sit; if I but wave this wand,

---

626 *scrip:* bag. 627 *simples:* herbs or plants to be used medicinally. 634 *like esteemed:* i.e., unvalued. 636 *moly:* the herb given by Hermes to Ulysses as a protection against the charms of Comus's mother, Circe. 646 *lime-twigs:* snares. 655 *Vulcan:* the god of fire.

Your nerves are all chained up in alabaster, 660
And you a statue, or as Daphne was,
Root-bound, that fled Apollo.
LADY. Fool, do not boast;
Thou canst not touch the freedom of my mind
With all thy charms, although this corporal rind
Thou hast immanacled, while Heaven sees good. 665
COMUS. Why are you vexed, lady? why do you frown?
Here dwell no frowns, nor anger; from these gates
Sorrow flies far. See, here be all the pleasures
That fancy can beget on youthful thoughts,
When the fresh blood grows lively, and returns 670
Brisk as the April buds in primrose season.
And first behold this cordial julep here
That flames and dances in his crystal bounds,
With spirits of balm and fragrant syrups mixed.
Not that nepenthes which the wife of Thone 675
In Egypt gave to Jove-born Helena
Is of such power to stir up joy as this,
To life so friendly, or so cool to thirst.
Why should you be so cruel to yourself,
And to those dainty limbs which Nature lent 680
For gentle usage and soft delicacy?
But you invert the covenants of her trust,
And harshly deal like an ill borrower
With that which you received on other terms,
Scorning the unexempt condition 685
By which all mortal frailty must subsist,
Refreshment after toil, ease after pain,
That have been tired all day without repast,
And timely rest have wanted; but, fair virgin,
This will restore all soon.
LADY. 'Twill not, false traitor, 690
'Twill not restore the truth and honesty
That thou hast banished from thy tongue with lies.
Was this the cottage and the safe abode
Thou told'st me of? What grim aspects are these,
These ugly-headed monsters? Mercy guard me! 695
Hence with thy brewed enchantments, foul deceiver;
Hast thou betrayed my credulous innocence

---

661 *Daphne:* a nymph who, in order to escape the pursuit of Apollo, was changed into a laurel tree. 675 *nepenthes:* a drug capable of banishing sorrow, mentioned by Homer in the *Odyssey*.

With vizored falsehood and base forgery,
And wouldst thou seek again to trap me here
With lickerish baits fit to ensnare a brute? 700
Were it a draught for Juno when she banquets,
I would not taste thy treasonous offer; none
But such as are good men can give good things,
And that which is not good is not delicious
To a well-governed and wise appetite. 705
COMUS. O foolishness of men! that lend their ears
To those budge doctors of the Stoic fur,
And fetch their precepts from the Cynic tub,
Praising the lean and sallow Abstinence.
Wherefore did Nature pour her bounties forth 710
With such a full and unwithdrawing hand,
Covering the earth with odors, fruits, and flocks,
Thronging the seas with spawn innumerable,
But all to please and sate the curious taste?
And set to work millions of spinning worms, 715
That in their green shops weave the smooth-haired silk
To deck her sons; and that no corner might
Be vacant of her plenty, in her own loins
She hutched the all-worshiped ore and precious gems
To store her children with. If all the world 720
Should in a pet of temperance feed on pulse,
Drink the clear stream, and nothing wear but frieze,
The All-giver would be unthanked, would be unpraised,
Not half his riches known, and yet despised,
And we should serve him as a grudging master, 725
As a penurious niggard of his wealth,
And live like Nature's bastards, not her sons,
Who would be quite surcharged with her own weight,
And strangled with her waste fertility:
The earth cumbered, and the winged air darked
with plumes, 730
The herds would over-multitude their lords,
The sea o'erfraught would swell, and the unsought diamonds
Would so emblaze the forehead of the deep,
And so bestud with stars, that they below
Would grow inured to light, and come at last 735

---

707 *budge . . . fur:* the professors of Stoicism identified by the fur trim on their academic gowns. 708 *Cynic tub:* Diogenes, the Cynic, is reputed to have lived in a tub. Like the Stoics, the Cynics were also associated with asceticism. 721 *pulse:* edible seeds. 722 *frieze:* coarse woolen cloth.

To gaze upon the sun with shameless brows.
List, lady, be not coy, and be not cozened
With that same vaunted name Virginity;
Beauty is Nature's coin, must not be hoarded,
But must be current, and the good thereof 740
Consists in mutual and partaken bliss,
Unsavory in the enjoyment of itself.
If you let slip time, like a neglected rose
It withers on the stalk with languished head.
Beauty is Nature's brag, and must be shown 745
In courts, at feasts, and high solemnities
Where most may wonder at the workmanship;
It is for homely features to keep home,
They had their name thence; coarse complexions
And cheeks of sorry grain will serve to ply 750
The sampler, and to tease the housewife's wool.
What need a vermeil-tinctured lip for that,
Love-darting eyes, or tresses like the morn?
There was another meaning in these gifts,
Think what, and be advised; you are but young yet. 755

LADY. I had not thought to have unlocked my lips
In this unhallowed air, but that this juggler
Would think to charm my judgment, as mine eyes,
Obtruding false rules pranked in reason's garb.
I hate when vice can bolt her arguments, 760
And virtue has no tongue to check her pride.
Impostor, do not charge most innocent Nature,
As if she would her children should be riotous
With her abundance; she, good cateress,
Means her provision only to the good, 765
That live according to her sober laws
And holy dictate of spare Temperance.
If every just man that now pines with want
Had but a moderate and beseeming share
Of that which lewdly-pampered luxury 770
Now heaps upon some few with vast excess,
Nature's full blessings would be well dispensed
In unsuperfluous even proportion,
And she no whit encumbered with her store;
And then the Giver would be better thanked, 775
His praise due paid, for swinish gluttony

---

737 *cozened:* deluded. 750 *sorry grain:* unattractive color. 751 *tease:* comb. 757 *juggler:* magician. 759 *pranked:* dressed up. 760 *bolt:* i.e., articulate.

Ne'er looks to Heaven amidst his gorgeous feast,
But with besotted base ingratitude
Crams, and blasphemes his Feeder. Shall I go on?
Or have I said enough? To him that dares 780
Arm his profane tongue with contemptuous words
Against the sun-clad power of Chastity,
Fain would I something say, yet to what end?
Thou hast nor ear nor soul to apprehend
The sublime notion and high mystery 785
That must be uttered to unfold the sage
And serious doctrine of Virginity,
And thou art worthy that thou shouldst not know
More happiness than this thy present lot.
Enjoy your dear wit and gay rhetoric 790
That hath so well been taught her dazzling fence,
Thou art not fit to hear thyself convinced;
Yet should I try, the uncontrolled worth
Of this pure cause would kindle my rapt spirits
To such a flame of sacred vehemence 795
That dumb things would be moved to sympathize,
And the brute Earth would lend her nerves, and shake,
Till all thy magic structures, reared so high,
Were shattered into heaps o'er thy false head.

COMUS. She fables not. I feel that I do fear 800
Her words set off by some superior power;
And though not mortal, yet a cold shuddering dew
Dips me all o'er, as when the wrath of Jove
Speaks thunder and the chains of Erebus
To some of Saturn's crew. I must dissemble, 805
And try her yet more strongly. Come, no more,
This is mere moral babble, and direct
Against the canon laws of our foundation;
I must not suffer this, yet 'tis but the lees
And settlings of a melancholy blood; 810
But this will cure all straight; one sip of this
Will bathe the drooping spirits in delight
Beyond the bliss of dreams. Be wise, and taste.

(*The* BROTHERS *rush in with swords drawn, wrest his glass out of his hand, and break it against the ground; his rout make sign of resistance, but are all driven in; the* ATTENDANT SPIRIT *comes in*)

SPIRIT. What, have you let the false enchanter scape?

---

785 *mystery:* supernatural doctrine. 803-5 *Jove . . . crew:* i.e., Jove thundered and sentenced the Titans, who were Saturn's allies, to Hell (Erebus).

O ye mistook, ye should have snatched his wand 815
And bound him fast; without his rod reversed,
And backward mutters of dissevering power,
We cannot free the lady that sits here
In stony fetters fixed and motionless;
Yet stay, be not disturbed; now I bethink me, 820
Some other means I have which may be used,
Which once of Meliboeus old I learnt,
The soothest shepherd that e'er piped on plains.
  There is a gentle Nymph not far from hence,
That with moist curb sways the smooth Severn stream; 825
Sabrina is her name, a virgin pure;
Whilom she was the daughter of Locrine,
That had the scepter from his father Brute.
She, guiltless damsel, flying the mad pursuit
Of her enraged stepdame Guendolen, 830
Commended her fair innocence to the flood
That stayed her flight with his cross-flowing course;
The water-nymphs that in the bottom played
Held up their pearled wrists and took her in,
Bearing her straight to aged Nereus' hall, 835
Who, piteous of her woes, reared her lank head,
And gave her to his daughters to imbathe
In nectared lavers strewed with asphodel,
And through the porch and inlet of each sense
Dropped in ambrosial oils, till she revived 840
And underwent a quick immortal change,
Made goddess of the river. Still she retains
Her maiden gentleness, and oft at eve
Visits the herds along the twilight meadows,
Helping all urchin blasts, and ill-luck signs 845
That the shrewd meddling elf delights to make,
Which she with precious vialed liquors heals;
For which the shepherds at their festivals
Carol her goodness loud in rustic lays,
And throw sweet garland wreaths into her stream 850
Of pansies, pinks, and gaudy daffodils.

---

822 *Meliboeus:* a typical pastoral name and an allusion to Spenser who tells the tale of Sabrina in his *Faerie Queene.* 823 *soothest:* truest. 825 *Severn:* a river which flows on the border between Wales and England. 827 *Whilom:* formerly. 828 *Brute:* the mythical founder of Britain. 835 *Nereus:* a sea-god, father of the water-nymphs or Nereids. 838 *lavers:* basins; *asphodel:* the flower of immortality. 845 *urchin blasts:* blights caused by evil spirits.

And, as the old swain said, she can unlock
The clasping charm and thaw the numbing spell,
If she be right invoked in warbled song;
For maidenhood she loves, and will be swift 855
To aid a virgin such as was herself
In hard-besetting need. This will I try,
And add the power of some adjuring verse.

Song

Sabrina fair,
  Listen where thou art sitting 860
Under the glassy, cool, translucent wave,
  In twisted braids of lilies knitting
The loose train of thy amber-dropping hair;
  Listen for dear honor's sake,
  Goddess of the silver lake, 865
    Listen and save.
Listen and appear to us
In name of great Oceanus,
By the earth-shaking Neptune's mace,
And Tethys' grave majestic pace, 870
By hoary Nereus' wrinkled look,
And the Carpathian wizard's hook,
By scaly Triton's winding shell,
And old soothsaying Glaucus' spell,
By Leucothea's lovely hands, 875
And her son that rules the strands,
By Thetis' tinsel-slippered feet,
And the songs of Sirens sweet,
By dead Parthenope's dear tomb,
And fair Ligea's golden comb, 880
Wherewith she sits on diamond rocks
Sleeking her soft alluring locks;
By all the nymphs that nightly dance
Upon thy streams with wily glance,

---

869 *Neptune's mace:* his trident. 870 *Tethys:* a Titaness, wife of the god Oceanus and, according to Hesiod, mother of rivers. 872 *Carpathian wizard:* Proteus; with the aid of his shepherd's hook, he looked after the "flocks of the sea." 873 *Triton:* regarded as Neptune's herald; he used a conch shell to proclaim his decrees. 874 *Glaucus:* a sea-wizard. 875 *Leucothea:* a sea goddess known for her whiteness; her son was Palaemon. 877 *Thetis:* one of the Nereids whom Homer called "silver-footed." 879 *Parthenope:* a Siren whose tomb was supposedly at Naples. 880 *Ligea:* another of the Sirens.

Rise, rise, and heave thy rosy head 885
From thy coral-paven bed,
And bridle in thy headlong wave,
Till thou our summons answered have.
Listen and save.
(SABRINA *rises, attended by water-nymphs, and sings*)
By the rushy-fringed bank, 890
Where grows the willow and the osier dank,
My sliding chariot stays,
Thick set with agate, and the azurn sheen
Of turquoise blue, and emerald green,
That in the channel strays, 895
Whilst from off the waters fleet
Thus I set my printless feet
O'er the cowslip's velvet head,
That bends not as I tread.
Gentle swain, at thy request 900
I am here.
SPIRIT. Goddess dear,
We implore thy powerful hand
To undo the charmed band
Of true virgin here distressed, 905
Through the force and through the wile
Of unblest enchanter vile.
SABRINA. Shepherd, 'tis my office best
To help ensnared chastity.
Brightest lady, look on me; 910
Thus I sprinkle on thy breast
Drops that from my fountain pure
I have kept of precious cure,
Thrice upon thy finger's tip,
Thrice upon thy rubied lip; 915
Next this marble venomed seat,
Smeared with gums of glutinous heat,
I touch with chaste palms moist and cold.
Now the spell hath lost his hold;
And I must haste ere morning hour 920
To wait in Amphitrite's bower.
(SABRINA *descends, and the* LADY *rises out of her seat*)
SPIRIT. Virgin, daughter of Locrine,
Sprung of old Anchises' line,

921 *Amphitrite:* Neptune's wife. 923 *Anchises:* the father of Aeneas who was the ancestor of Brute, grandfather of Sabrina.

May thy brimmed waves for this
Their full tribute never miss 925
From a thousand petty rills,
That tumble down the snowy hills;
Summer drouth or singed air
Never scorch thy tresses fair,
Nor wet October's torrent flood 930
Thy molten crystal fill with mud;
May thy billows roll ashore
The beryl and the golden ore;
May thy lofty head be crowned
With many a tower and terrace round, 935
And here and there thy banks upon
With groves of myrrh and cinnamon.
  Come, lady, while Heaven lends us grace,
Let us fly this cursed place,
Lest the sorcerer us entice 940
With some other new device.
Not a waste or needless sound
Till we come to holier ground;
I shall be your faithful guide
Through this gloomy covert wide, 945
And not many furlongs thence
Is your father's residence,
Where this night are met in state
Many a friend to gratulate
His wished presence, and beside 950
All the swains that there abide
With jigs and rural dance resort;
We shall catch them at their sport,
And our sudden coming there
Will double all their mirth and cheer. 955
Come, let us haste, the stars grow high,
But Night sits monarch yet in the mid sky.

(*The scene changes, presenting Ludlow Town, and the President's Castle; then come in* COUNTRY DANCERS, *after them the* ATTENDANT SPIRIT, *with the two* BROTHERS *and the* LADY)

Song

SPIRIT. Back, shepherds, back, enough your play
Till next sunshine holiday;

Here be without duck or nod 960
Other trippings to be trod
Of lighter toes, and such court guise
As Mercury did first devise
With the mincing Dryades
On the lawns and on the leas. 965
(*This second Song presents them to their father and mother*)
Noble Lord, and Lady bright,
I have brought ye new delight.
Here behold so goodly grown
Three fair branches of your own;
Heaven hath timely tried their youth, 970
Their faith, their patience, and their truth,
And sent them here through hard assays
With a crown of deathless praise,
To triumph in victorious dance
O'er sensual folly, and intemperance. 975
(*The dances ended, the* SPIRIT *epiloguizes*)
SPIRIT. To the ocean now I fly,
And those happy climes that lie
Where day never shuts his eye,
Up in the broad fields of the sky.
There I suck the liquid air 980
All amidst the gardens fair
Of Hesperus, and his daughters three
That sing about the golden tree.
Along the crisped shades and bowers
Revels the spruce and jocund Spring; 985
The Graces and the rosy-bosomed Hours
Thither all their bounties bring,
That there eternal summer dwells,
And west winds with musky wing
About the cedarn alleys fling 990
Nard and cassia's balmy smells.
Iris there with humid bow
Waters the odorous banks that blow
Flowers of more mingled hue
Than her purfled scarf can shew, 995
And drenches with Elysian dew

---

960 *without . . . nod:* free of exaggerated motions. 970 *timely:* early. 980 *liquid:* clear. 986 *Graces:* the three sister goddesses (Aglaia, Euphrosyne, Thalia), who dispensed pleasure, elegance, charm, and beauty. 993 *blow:* cause to blossom. 995 *purfled:* trimmed.

(List, mortals, if your ears be true)
Beds of hyacinth and roses,
Where young Adonis oft reposes,
Waxing well of his deep wound 1000
In slumber soft, and on the ground
Sadly sits the Assyrian queen;
But far above in spangled sheen
Celestial Cupid, her famed son, advanced,
Holds his dear Psyche, sweet entranced 1005
After her wandering labors long,
Till free consent the gods among
Make her his eternal bride,
And from her fair unspotted side
Two blissful twins are to be born, 1010
Youth and Joy; so Jove hath sworn.
  But now my task is smoothly done,
I can fly, or I can run
Quickly to the green earth's end,
Where the bowed welkin slow doth bend, 1015
And from thence can soar as soon
To the corners of the moon.
  Mortals that would follow me,
Love Virtue, she alone is free;
She can teach ye how to climb 1020
Higher than the sphery chime;
Or if Virtue feeble were,
Heaven itself would stoop to her.

999-1002 *Adonis . . . queen:* The death of the beautiful youth Adonis, killed while boar hunting, elicited such grief from Venus (the Assyrian queen) that the gods of the underworld allowed him to return to earth every year for a period of six months. 1004-5 *Cupid . . . Psyche:* The tale of the love of Cupid, son of Venus, for the mortal Psyche is told by Apuleius. 1015 *welkin:* sky. 1021 *Higher . . . chime:* i.e., even beyond the music of the spheres (redolent of perfect harmony) to bliss.

Songs of Innocence and of Experience

Shewing the Two Contrary States of the Human Soul

WILLIAM BLAKE

Poet, painter, mystic, the remarkable William Blake was born in London in 1757 and early trained as an engraver. His knowledge of the art of engraving is evident in his *Songs of Innocence* (1789) and *Songs of Experience* (1794), both printed by Blake himself from copper plates on which the texts and illustrated designs were etched in relief. After printing, each page was colored by hand, the completed manuscript evidencing a wholeness of conception characteristic of the poet's quest for a unified vision in his work. Swinburne has described these original illuminated pages as reflecting "the pure sweetness and singleness of design" of Blake's *Songs,* where "All the tremulous and tender splendour of spring is mixed into the written word and coloured draught. . . ." *

In his *Songs of Innocence,* Blake reveals a boundless world similar to that found in Thomas Traherne's poem, "Innocence," the seventeenth-century metaphysical poet presenting a Pisgah view of Paradise that is ravishing in its uncircumscribed freedom. If Blake's *Innocence* contains soot-black children locked in their coffins, it also provides the key by which they may escape all naked and white to "rise upon clouds and sport in the wind." In the world of *Experience,* however, the inhabitants are lost, hemmed in by wild animals, bound fast with briars, manacled. Frequently, in the literature that treats the subject of innocence, the dominant tension in the work arises out of the attempts to limit the physical action of the innocent. The restraints placed upon him in art, in a sense, parallel the civilizing process in life, but whereas the latter development is judged sympathetically, any encroachment on the literary innocent is generally condemned, as in these *Songs* of William Blake.

The text of Blake's *Songs of Innocence and of Experience* reprinted here has been taken from the Nonesuch Press edition of Blake's work edited by Geoffrey Keynes. The sequence of the individual poems varied considerably in early groupings, and it was not until 1815 that a more or less definite order was established, an order which this text follows.

---

* *William Blake* (London, 1925), p. 113.

Songs of Innocence

Introduction

Piping down the valleys wild,
Piping songs of pleasant glee,
On a cloud I saw a child,
And he laughing said to me:

"Pipe a song about a Lamb!"
So I piped with merry chear.
"Piper, pipe that song again;'
So I piped: he wept to hear.

"Drop thy pipe, thy happy pipe;
Sing thy songs of happy chear:"
So I sung the same again,
While he wept with joy to hear.

"Piper, sit thee down and write
In a book, that all may read."
So he vanish'd from my sight,
And I pluck'd a hollow reed,

And I made a rural pen,
And I stain'd the water clear,
And I wrote my happy songs
Every child may joy to hear.

The Shepherd

How sweet is the Shepherd's sweet lot!
From the morn to the evening he strays;
He shall follow his sheep all the day,
And his tongue shall be filled with praise.

For he hears the lamb's innocent call,
And he hears the ewe's tender reply;
He is watchful while they are in peace,
For they know when their Shepherd is nigh.

The Ecchoing Green

The Sun does arise,
And make happy the skies;
The merry bells ring
To welcome the Spring;

The skylark and thrush,
The birds of the bush,
Sing louder around
To the bells' chearful sound,
While our sports shall be seen
On the Ecchoing Green.

Old John, with white hair,
Does laugh away care,
Sitting under the oak,
Among the old folk.
They laugh at our play,
And soon they all say:
"Such, such were the joys
When we all, girls & boys,
In our youth time were seen
On the Ecchoing Green."

Till the little ones, weary,
No more can be merry;
The sun does descend,
And our sports have an end.
Round the laps of their mothers
Many sisters and brothers,
Like birds in their nest,
Are ready for rest,
And sport no more seen
On the darkening Green.

The Lamb

Little Lamb, who made thee?
Dost thou know who made thee?
Gave thee life, & bid thee feed
By the stream & o'er the mead;
Gave thee clothing of delight,
Softest clothing, wooly, bright;
Gave thee such a tender voice,
Making all the vales rejoice?
Little Lamb, who made thee?
Dost thou know who made thee?

Little Lamb, I'll tell thee,
Little Lamb, I'll tell thee:
He is called by thy name,

For he calls himself a Lamb.
He is meek, & he is mild;
He became a little child.
I a child, & thou a lamb,
We are called by his name.
Little Lamb, God bless thee!
Little Lamb, God bless thee!

The Little Black Boy

My mother bore me in the southern wild,
And I am black, but O! my soul is white;
White as an angel is the English child,
But I am black, as if bereav'd of light.

My mother taught me underneath a tree,
And sitting down before the heat of day,
She took me on her lap and kissed me,
And pointing to the east, began to say:

"Look on the rising sun: there God does live,
And gives his light, and gives his heat away;
And flowers and trees and beasts and man receive
Comfort in morning, joy in the noonday.

"And we are put on earth a little space,
That we may learn to bear the beams of love;
And these black bodies and this sunburnt face
Is but a cloud, and like a shady grove.

"For when our souls have learn'd that heat to bear,
The cloud will vanish; we shall hear his voice,
Saying: 'Come out from the grove, my love & care,
And round my golden tent like lambs rejoice.' "

Thus did my mother say, and kissed me;
And thus I say to little English boy:
When I from black and he from white cloud free,
And round the tent of God like lambs we joy,

I'll shade him from the heat, till he can bear
To lean in joy upon our father's knee;
And then I'll stand and stroke his silver hair,
And be like him, and he will then love me.

The Blossom

Merry, Merry Sparrow!
Under leaves so green
A happy Blossom
Sees you swift as arrow
Seek your cradle narrow
Near my Bosom.

Pretty, Pretty Robin!
Under leaves so green
A happy Blossom
Hears you sobbing, sobbing,
Pretty, Pretty Robin,
Near my Bosom.

The Chimney Sweeper

When my mother died I was very young,
And my father sold me while yet my tongue
Could scarcely cry " 'weep! 'weep! 'weep! 'weep!"
So your chimneys I sweep, & in soot I sleep.

There's little Tom Dacre, who cried when his head,
That curl'd like a lamb's back, was shav'd: so I said
"Hush, Tom! never mind it, for when your head's bare
You know that the soot cannot spoil your white hair."

And so he was quiet, & that very night,
As Tom was a-sleeping, he had such a sight!
That thousands of sweepers, Dick, Joe, Ned, & Jack,
Were all of them lock'd up in coffins of black.

And by came an Angel who had a bright key,
And he open'd the coffins & set them all free;
Then down a green plain leaping, laughing, they run,
And wash in a river, and shine in the Sun.

Then naked & white, all their bags left behind,
They rise upon clouds and sport in the wind;
And the Angel told Tom, if he'd be a good boy,
He'd have God for his father, & never want joy.

And so Tom awoke; and we rose in the dark,
And got with our bags & our brushes to work.
Tho' the morning was cold, Tom was happy & warm;
So if all do their duty they need not fear harm.

The Little Boy Lost

"Father! father! where are you going?
O do not walk so fast.
Speak, father, speak to your little boy,
Or else I shall be lost."

The night was dark, no father was there;
The child was wet with dew;
The mire was deep, & the child did weep,
And away the vapour flew.

The Little Boy Found

The little boy lost in the lonely fen,
Led by the wand'ring light,
Began to cry; but God, ever nigh,
Appear'd like his father in white.

He kissed the child & by the hand led
And to his mother brought,
Who in sorrow pale, thro' the lonely dale,
Her little boy weeping sought.

Laughing Song

When the green woods laugh with the voice of joy,
And the dimpling stream runs laughing by;
When the air does laugh with our merry wit,
And the green hill laughs with the noise of it;

When the meadows laugh with lively green,
And the grasshopper laughs in the merry scene,
When Mary and Susan and Emily
With their sweet round mouths sing "Ha, Ha, He!"

When the painted birds laugh in the shade,
Where our table with cherries and nuts is spread,
Come live & be merry, and join with me,
To sing the sweet chorus of "Ha, Ha, He!"

A Cradle Song

Sweet dreams, form a shade
O'er my lovely infant's head;
Sweet dreams of pleasant streams
By happy, silent, moony beams.

Sweet sleep, with soft down
Weave they brows an infant crown.
Sweet sleep, Angel mild,
Hover o'er my happy child.

Sweet smiles, in the night
Hover over my delight;
Sweet smiles, Mother's smiles,
All the livelong night beguiles.

Sweet moans, dovelike sighs,
Chase not slumber from thy eyes.
Sweet moans, sweeter smiles,
All the dovelike moans beguiles.

Sleep, sleep, happy child,
All creation slept and smil'd;
Sleep, sleep, happy sleep,
While o'er thee thy mother weep.

Sweet babe, in thy face
Holy image I can trace.
Sweet babe, once like thee,
Thy maker lay and wept for me,

Wept for me, for thee, for all,
When he was an infant small
Thou his image ever see,
Heavenly face that smiles on thee,

Smiles on thee, on me, on all;
Who became an infant small.
Infant smiles are his own smiles;
Heaven & earth to peace beguiles.

The Divine Image

To Mercy, Pity, Peace, and Love
All pray in their distress;
And to these virtues of delight
Return their thankfulness.

For Mercy, Pity, Peace, and Love
Is God, our father dear,
And Mercy, Pity, Peace, and Love
Is Man, his child and care.

For Mercy has a human heart,
Pity a human face,
And Love, the human form divine,
And Peace, the human dress.

Then every man, of every clime,
That prays in his distress,
Prays to the human form divine,
Love, Mercy, Pity, Peace.

And all must love the human form,
In heathen, turk, or jew;
Where Mercy, Love, & Pity dwell
There God is dwelling too.

Holy Thursday

'Twas on a Holy Thursday,[1] their innocent faces clean,
The children walking two & two, in red & blue & green,
Grey-headed beadles[2] walk'd before, with wands as white as snow,
Till into the high dome of Paul's[3] they like Thames' waters flow.

O what a multitude they seem'd, these flowers of London town!
Seated in companies they sit with radiance all their own.
The hum of multitudes was there, but multitudes of lambs,
Thousands of little boys & girls raising their innocent hands.

Now like a mighty wind they raise to heaven the voice of song,
Or like harmonious thunderings the seats of Heaven among.
Beneath them sit the aged men, wise guardians of the poor;
Then cherish pity, lest you drive an angel from your door.

Night

The sun descending in the west,
The evening star does shine;
The birds are silent in their nest,
And I must seek for mine.
The moon like a flower
In heaven's high bower,
With silent delight
Sits and smiles on the night.

---

[1] Ascension Day in the English church.
[2] A lower parish officer, one of whose duties it is to keep order.
[3] St. Paul's in London, the cathedral designed by the famous English architect, Sir Christopher Wren.

Farewell, green fields and happy groves,
Where flocks have took delight.
Where lambs have nibbled, silent moves
The feet of angels bright;
Unseen they pour blessing
And joy without ceasing,
On each bud and blossom,
And each sleeping bosom.

They look in every thoughtless nest,
Where birds are cover'd warm;
They visit caves of every beast,
To keep them all from harm.
If they see any weeping
That should have been sleeping,
They pour sleep on their head,
And sit down by their bed.

When wolves and tygers howl for prey,
They pitying stand and weep;
Seeking to drive their thirst away,
And keep them from the sheep;
But if they rush dreadful,
The angels, most heedful,
Receive each mild spirit,
New worlds to inherit.

And there the lion's ruddy eyes
Shall flow with tears of gold,
And pitying the tender cries,
And walking round the fold,
Saying "Wrath, by his meekness,
And by his health, sickness
Is driven away
From our immortal day.

"And now beside thee, bleating lamb,
I can lie down and sleep;
Or think on him who bore thy name,
Graze after thee and weep.
For, wash'd in life's river,
My bright mane for ever
Shall shine like the gold
As I guard o'er the fold."

Spring

Sound the Flute!
Now it's mute.
Birds delight
Day and Night;
Nightingale
In the dale,
Lark in Sky,
Merrily,
Merrily, Merrily, to welcome in the Year.

Little Boy,
Full of joy;
Little Girl,
Sweet and small;
Cock does crow,
So do you;
Merry voice,
Infant noise,
Merrily, Merrily, to welcome in the Year.

Little Lamb,
Here I am;
Come and lick
My white neck;
Let me pull
Your soft Wool;
Let me kiss
Your soft face:
Merrily, Merrily, we welcome in the Year.

Nurse's Song

When the voices of children are heard on the green
And laughing is heard on the hill,
My heart is at rest within my breast
And everything else is still.

"Then come home, my children, the sun is gone down
And the dews of night arise;
Come, come, leave off play, and let us away
Till the morning appears in the skies."

"No, no, let us play, for it is yet day
And we cannot go to sleep;

Besides, in the sky the little birds fly
And the hills are all cover'd with sheep."

"Well, well, go & play till the light fades away
And then go home to bed."
The little ones leaped & shouted & laugh'd
And all the hills ecchoed.

Infant Joy

"I have no name:
I am but two days old."
What shall I call thee?
"I happy am,
Joy is my name."
Sweet joy befall thee!

Pretty joy!
Sweet joy but two days old,
Sweet joy I call thee:
Thou dost smile,
I sing the while,
Sweet joy befall thee!

A Dream

Once a dream did weave a shade
O'er my Angel-guarded bed,
That an Emmet[4] lost its way
Where on grass methought I lay.

Troubled, 'wilder'd, and forlorn,
Dark, benighted, travel-worn,
Over many a tangled spray,
All heart-broke I heard her say:

"O, my children! do they cry?
Do they hear their father sigh?
Now they look abroad to see:
Now return and weep for me."

Pitying, I drop'd a tear;
But I saw a glow-worm near,
Who replied: "What wailing wight[5]
Calls the watchman of the night?

---

[4] Ant.
[5] Creature.

"I am set to light the ground,
While the beetle goes his round:
Follow now the beetle's hum;
Little wanderer, hie thee home."

On Another's Sorrow

Can I see another's woe,
And not be in sorrow too?
Can I see another's grief,
And not seek for kind relief?

Can I see a falling tear,
And not feel my sorrow's share?
Can a father see his child
Weep, nor be with sorrow fill'd?

Can a mother sit and hear
An infant groan an infant fear?
No, no! never can it be!
Never, never can it be!

And can he who smiles on all
Hear the wren with sorrows small,
Hear the small bird's grief & care,
Hear the woes that infants bear,

And not sit beside the nest,
Pouring pity in their breast;
And not sit the cradle near,
Weeping tear on infant's tear;

And not sit both night & day,
Wiping all our tears away?
O, no! never can it be!
Never, never can it be!

He doth give his joy to all;
He becomes an infant small;
He becomes a man of woe;
He doth feel the sorrow too.

Think not thou canst sigh a sigh
And thy maker is not by;
Think not thou canst weep a tear
And thy maker is not near.

O! he gives to us his joy
That our grief he may destroy;
Till our grief is fled & gone
He doth sit by us and moan.

Songs of Experience

Introduction

Hear the voice of the Bard!
Who Present, Past, & Future, sees;
Whose ears have heard
The Holy Word
That walk'd among the ancient trees,

Calling the lapsed Soul,
And weeping in the evening dew;
That might controll
The starry pole,
And fallen, fallen light renew!

"O Earth, O Earth, return!
Arise from out the dewy grass;
Night is worn,
And the morn
Rises from the slumberous mass.

"Turn away no more;
Why wilt thou turn away?
The starry floor,
The wat'ry shore,
Is giv'n thee till the break of day."

Earth's Answer

Earth rais'd up her head
From the darkness dread & drear
Her light fled,
Stony dread!
And her locks cover'd with grey despair.

"Prison'd on wat'ry shore,
Starry Jealousy does keep my den:
Cold and hoar,
Weeping o'er,
I hear the father of the ancient men.

"Selfish father of men!
Cruel, jealous, selfish fear!
Can delight,
Chain'd in night,
The virgins of youth and morning bear?

"Does spring hide its joy
When buds and blossoms grow?
Does the sower
Sow by night,
Or the plowman in darkness plow?

"Break this heavy chain
That does freeze my bones around.
Selfish! vain!
Eternal bane!
That free Love with bondage bound."

The Clod and the Pebble

"Love seeketh not Itself to please,
Nor for itself hath any care,
But for another gives its ease,
And builds a Heaven in Hell's despair."

So sung a little Clod of Clay
Trodden with the cattle's feet,
But a Pebble of the brook
Warbled out these metres meet:

"Love seeketh only Self to please,
To bind another to Its delight,
Joys in another's loss of ease,
And builds a Hell in Heaven's despite."

Holy Thursday

Is this a holy thing to see
In a rich and fruitful land,
Babes reduc'd to misery,
Fed with cold and usurous hand?

Is that trembling cry a song?
Can it be a song of joy?
And so many children poor?
It is a land of poverty!

And their sun does never shine,
And their fields are bleak & bare,
And their ways are fill'd with thorns:
It is eternal winter there.

For where-e'er the sun does shine,
And where-e'er the rain does fall,
Babe can never hunger there,
Nor poverty the mind appall.

The Little Girl Lost

In futurity
I prophetic see
That the earth from sleep
(Grave the sentence deep)

Shall arise and seek
For her maker meek;
And the desart wild
Become a garden mild.

* * *

In the southern clime,
Where the summer's prime
Never fades away,
Lovely Lyca lay.

Seven summers old
Lovely Lyca told;
She had wander'd long
Hearing wild birds' song.

"Sweet sleep, come to me
Underneath this tree.
Do father, mother weep,
Where can Lyca sleep?

"Lost in desart wild
Is your little child.
How can Lyca sleep

If her mother weep?
"If her heart does ake
Then let Lyca wake;
If my mother sleep,
Lyca shall not weep.

"Frowning, frowning night,
O'er this desart bright
Let thy moon arise
While I close my eyes."

Sleeping Lyca lay
While the beasts of prey,
Come from caverns deep,
View'd the maid asleep.

The kingly lion stood
And the virgin view'd,
Then he gamboll'd round
O'er the hallow'd ground.

Leopards, tygers, play
Round her as she lay,
While the lion old
Bow'd his mane of gold

And her bosom lick,
And upon her neck
From his eyes of flame
Ruby tears there came;

While the lioness
Loos'd her slender dress,
And naked they convey'd
To caves the sleeping maid.

The Little Girl Found

All the night in woe
Lyca's parents go
Over vallies deep,
While the desarts weep.

Tired and woe-begone,
Hoarse with making moan,
Arm in arm seven days
They trac'd the desart ways.

Seven nights they sleep
Among shadows deep,
And dream they see their child
Starv'd in desert wild.

Pale, thro' pathless ways
The fancied image strays
Famish'd, weeping, weak,
With hollow piteous shriek.

Rising from unrest,
The trembling woman prest
With feet of weary woe:
She could no further go.

In his arms he bore
Her, arm'd with sorrow sore;
Till before their way
A couching lion lay.

Turning back was vain:
Soon his heavy mane
Bore them to the ground.
Then he stalk'd around,

Smelling to his prey;
But their fears allay
When he licks their hands,
And silent by them stands.

They look upon his eyes
Fill'd with deep surprise,
And wondering behold
A spirit arm'd in gold.

On his head a crown,
On his shoulders down
Flow'd his golden hair.
Gone was all their care.

"Follow me," he said;
"Weep not for the maid;
In my palace deep
Lyca lies asleep."

Then they followed
Where the vision led,
And saw their sleeping child
Among tygers wild.

To this day they dwell
In a lonely dell;
Nor fear the wolvish howl
Nor the lions' growl.

The Chimney Sweeper

A little black thing among the snow,
Crying " 'weep! 'weep!" in notes of woe!
"Where are thy father & mother? say?"
"They are both gone up to the church to pray.

"Because I was happy upon the heath,
And smil'd among the winter's snow,
They clothed me in the clothes of death,
And taught me to sing the notes of woe.

"And because I am happy & dance & sing,
They think they have done me no injury,
And are gone to praise God & his Priest & King,
Who make up a heaven of our misery."

Nurse's Song

When the voices of children are heard on the green
And whisp'rings are in the dale,
The days of my youth rise fresh in my mind,
My face turns green and pale.

Then come home, my children, the sun is gone down,
And the dews of night arise;
Your spring & your day are wasted in play,
And your winter and night in disguise.

The Sick Rose

O rose, thou art sick!
The invisible worm
That flies in the night,
In the howling storm,

Has found out thy bed
Of crimson joy,
And his dark secret love
Does thy life destroy.

The Fly

Little Fly,
Thy summer's play
My thoughtless hand
Has brush'd away.

Am not I
A fly like thee?
Or art not thou
A man like me?

For I dance,
And drink, & sing,
Till some blind hand
Shall brush my wing.

If thought is life
And strength & breath,
And the want
Of thought is death;

Then am I
A happy fly,
If I live
Or if I die.

The Angel

I dreamt a Dream! what can it mean?
And that I was a maiden Queen,
Guarded by an Angel mild:
Witless woe was ne'er beguil'd!

And I wept both night and day,
And he wip'd my tears away,
And I wept both day and night,
And hid from him my heart's delight.

So he took his wings and fled;
Then the morn blush'd rosy red;
I dried my tears, & arm'd my fears
With ten thousand shields and spears.

Soon my Angel came again:
I was arm'd, he came in vain;
For the time of youth was fled,
And grey hairs were on my head.

The Tyger

Tyger! Tyger! burning bright
In the forests of the night,
What immortal hand or eye
Could frame thy fearful symmetry?

In what distant deeps or skies
Burnt the fire of thine eyes?
On what wings dare he aspire?
What the hand dare sieze the fire?

And what shoulder, & what art,
Could twist the sinews of thy heart?
And when thy heart began to beat,
What dread hand? & what dread feet? [6]

What the hammer? what the chain?
In what furnace was thy brain?
What the anvil? what dread grasp
Dare its deadly terrors clasp?

When the stars threw down their spears,
And water'd heaven with their tears,
Did he smile his work to see?
Did he who made the Lamb make thee?

Tyger! Tyger! burning bright
In the forests of the night,
What immortal hand or eye,
Dare frame thy fearful symmetry?

My Pretty Rose-Tree

A flower was offer'd to me,
Such a flower as May never bore;
But I said "I've a Pretty Rose-tree,"
And I passed the sweet flower o'er.

Then I went to my Pretty Rose-tree,
To tend her by day and by night;
But my Rose turn'd away with jealousy,
And her thorns were my only delight.

---

[6] This line was altered by Blake in one copy to read, "What dread hand Form'd thy dread feet?"

Ah! Sun-Flower

Ah, Sun-flower! weary of time,
Who countest the steps of the Sun,
Seeking after that sweet golden clime
Where the traveller's journey is done:

Where the Youth pined away with desire,
And the pale Virgin shrouded in snow
Arise from their graves, and aspire
Where my Sun-flower wishes to go.

The Lilly

The modest Rose puts forth a thorn,
The humble Sheep a threat'ning horn;
While the Lilly white shall in Love delight,
Nor a thorn, nor a threat, stain her beauty bright.

The Garden of Love

I went to the Garden of Love,
And saw what I never had seen:
A Chapel was built in the midst,
Where I used to play on the green.

And the gates of this Chapel were shut,
And "Thou shalt not" writ over the door;
So I turn'd to the Garden of Love
That so many sweet flowers bore;

And I saw it was filled with graves,
And tomb-stones where flowers should be:
And Priests in black gowns were walking their rounds,
And binding with briars my joys & desires.

The Little Vagabond

Dear Mother, dear Mother, the Church is cold,
But the Ale-house is healthy & pleasant & warm;
Besides I can tell where I am used well,
Such usage in Heaven will never do well.

But if at the Church they would give us some Ale,
And a pleasant fire our souls to regale,
We'd sing and we'd pray all the live-long day,
Nor ever once wish from the Church to stray.

Then the Parson might preach, & drink, & sing,
And we'd be as happy as birds in the spring;
And modest Dame Lurch, who is always at Church,
Would not have bandy children, nor fasting, nor birch.

And God, like a father rejoicing to see
His children as pleasant and happy as he,
Would have no more quarrel with the Devil or the Barrel,
But kiss him, & give him both drink and apparel.

London

I wander thro' each charter'd street,
Near where the charter'd Thames does flow,
And mark in every face I meet
Marks of weakness, marks of woe.

In every cry of every Man,
In every Infant's cry of fear,
In every voice, in every ban,[7]
The mind-forg'd manacles I hear.

How the Chimney-sweeper's cry
Every black'ning Church appalls;
And the hapless Soldier's sigh
Runs in blood down Palace walls.

But most thro' midnight streets I hear
How the youthful Harlot's curse
Blasts the new born Infant's tear,
And blights with plagues the Marriage hearse.

The Human Abstract

Pity would be no more
If we did not make somebody Poor;
And Mercy no more could be
If all were as happy as we.

And mutual fear brings peace,
Till the selfish loves increase:
Then Cruelty knits a snare,
And spreads his baits with care.

---

[7] Curse, public denunciation, marriage proclamation ("banns"); all of these definitions seem relevant here.

He sits down with holy fears,
And waters the ground with tears;
Then Humility takes its root
Underneath his foot.

Soon spreads the dismal shade
Of Mystery over his head;
And the Catterpiller and Fly
Feed on the Mystery.

And it bears the fruit of Deceit,
Ruddy and sweet to eat;
And the Raven his nest has made
In its thickest shade.

The Gods of the earth and sea
Sought thro' Nature to find this Tree;
But their search was all in vain:
There grows one in the Human Brain.

Infant Sorrow

My mother groan'd! my father wept.
Into the dangerous world I leapt:
Helpless, naked, piping loud:
Like a fiend hid in a cloud.

Struggling in my father's hands,
Striving against my swadling bands,
Bound and weary I thought best
To sulk upon my mother's breast.

A Poison Tree

I was angry with my friend:
I told my wrath, my wrath did end.
I was angry with my foe:
I told it not, my wrath did grow.

And I water'd it in fears,
Night & morning with my tears;
And I sunned it with smiles,
And with soft deceitful wiles.

And it grew both day and night,
Till it bore an apple bright;

And my foe beheld it shine,
And he knew that it was mine,

And into my garden stole
When the night had veil'd the pole:
In the morning glad I see
My foe outstretch'd beneath the tree.

A Little Boy Lost

'Nought loves another as itself,
Nor venerates another so,
Nor is it possible to Thought
A greater than itself to know:

"And Father, how can I love you
Or any of my brothers more?
I love you like the little bird
That picks up crumbs around the door."

The Priest sat by and heard the child,
In trembling zeal he siez'd his hair:
He led him by his little coat,
And all admir'd the Priestly care.

And standing on the altar high,
"Lo! what a fiend is here!" said he,
"One who sets reason up for judge
Of our most holy Mystery."

The weeping child could not be heard,
The weeping parents wept in vain;
They strip'd him to his little shirt,
And bound him in an iron chain;

And burn'd him in a holy place,
Where many had been burn'd before:
The weeping parents wept in vain.
Are such things done on Albion's[8] shore?

A Little Girl Lost

Children of the future Age
Reading this indignant page,
Know that in a former time
Love! sweet Love! was thought a crime.

[8] England's.

In the Age of Gold,
Free from winter's cold,
Youth and maiden bright
To the holy light,
Naked in the sunny beams delight.

Once a youthful pair,
Fill'd with softest care,
Met in garden bright
Where the holy light
Had just remov'd the curtains of the night.

There, in rising day,
On the grass they play;
Parents were afar,
Strangers came not near,
And the maiden soon forgot her fear.

Tired with kisses sweet,
They agree to meet
When the silent sleep
Waves o'er heaven's deep,
And the weary tired wanderers weep.

To her father white
Came the maiden bright;
But his loving look,
Like the holy book,
All her tender limbs with terror shook.

"Ona! pale and weak!
To thy father speak:
O, the trembling fear!
O, the dismal care!
That shakes the blossoms of my hoary hair."

To Tirzah

Whate'er is Born of Mortal Birth
Must be consumed with the Earth
To rise from Generation free:
Then what have I to do with thee?

The Sexes sprung from Shame & Pride,
Blow'd [9] in the morn; in evening died;

---

[9] Blossomed.

But Mercy chang'd Death into Sleep;
The Sexes rose to work & weep.

Thou, Mother of my Mortal part,
With cruelty didst mould my Heart,
And with false self-decieving tears
Didst bind my Nostrils, Eyes, & Ears:

Didst close my Tongue in senseless clay,
And me to Mortal Life betray.
The Death of Jesus set me free:
Then what have I to do with thee?

The Schoolboy

I love to rise in a summer morn
When the birds sing on every tree;
The distant huntsman winds his horn,
And the sky-lark sings with me.
O! what sweet company.

But to go to school in a summer morn,
O! it drives all joy away;
Under a cruel eye outworn,
The little ones spend the day
In sighing and dismay.

Ah! then at times I drooping sit,
And spend many an anxious hour,
Nor in my book can I take delight,
Nor sit in learning's bower,
Worn thro' with the dreary shower.

How can the bird that is born for joy
Sit in a cage and sing?
How can a child, when fears annoy,
But droop his tender wing,
And forget his youthful spring?

O! father & mother, if buds are nip'd
And blossoms blown away,
And if the tender plants are strip'd
Of their joy in the springing day,
By sorrow and care's dismay,

How shall the summer arise in joy,
Or the summer fruits appear?

Or how shall we gather what griefs destroy,
Or bless the mellowing year,
When the blasts of winter appear?

The Voice of the Ancient Bard

Youth of delight, come hither,
And see the opening morn,
Image of truth new born.
Doubt is fled, & clouds of reason,
Dark disputes & artful teazing.
Folly is an endless maze,
Tangled roots perplex her ways.
How many have fallen there!
They stumble all night over bones of the dead,
And feel they know not what but care,
And wish to lead others, when they should be led.

Additional Poem

A Divine Image[10]

Cruelty has a Human Heart,
And Jealousy a Human Face;
Terror the Human Form Divine,
And Secrecy the Human Dress.

The Human Dress is forged Iron,
The Human Form a fiery Forge,
The Human Face a Furnace seal'd,
The Human Heart its hungry Gorge.

---

[10] Although this poem was etched in 1794, it was not included by Blake.

Daisy Miller: A Study

HENRY JAMES

Although *Daisy Miller* was initially refused publication in the United States, its appearance in England in *The Cornhill Magazine* reflects the shrewd critical judgment of its editor—the father of the well-known novelist Virginia Woolf—Sir Leslie Stephen. The subsequent success of this story of an independent, pretty, and ingenuous American girl who meets a grim fate in Europe was so impressive that even Henry James, in his preface to the New York edition of the work, marvels at the "sweet tribute" of Boston producing a pirated edition. If some early critics celebrated James for his patriotism in warning unwary American girls of the pitfalls of travel abroad, we can today more accurately appreciate the "pure poetry" of his heroine and the artistry of her creator in presenting the social implications of innocence.

The text of *Daisy Miller* reprinted here is from the first publication of the manuscript in *The Cornhill Magazine* (1878). In his New York edition (1909), James made changes in his work that are relevant to the nature of Daisy's innocence, and an illuminating comparison can be made between the two versions of the story.

Part I

At the little town of Vevey,[1] in Switzerland, there is a particularly comfortable hotel. There are, indeed, many hotels; for the entertainment of tourists is the business of the place, which, as many travellers will remember, is seated upon the edge of a remarkably

---

[1] A resort on Lake Geneva.

blue lake—a lake that it behoves every tourist to visit. The shore of the lake presents an unbroken array of establishments of this order, of every category, from the "grand hotel" of the newest fashion, with a chalk-white front, a hundred balconies, and a dozen flags flying from its roof, to the little Swiss *pension* of an elder day, with its name inscribed in German-looking lettering upon a pink or yellow wall, and an awkward summerhouse in the angle of the garden. One of the hotels at Vevey, however, is famous, even classical, being distinguished from many of its upstart neighbours by an air both of luxury and of maturity. In this region, in the month of June, American travellers are extremely numerous; it may be said, indeed, that Vevey assumes at this period some of the characteristics of an American watering-place. There are sights and sounds which evoke a vision, an echo, of Newport and Saratoga.[2] There is a flitting hither and thither of "stylish" young girls, a rustling of muslin flounces, a rattle of dance-music in the morning hours, a sound of high-pitched voices at all times. You receive an impression of these things at the excellent inn of the "Trois Couronnes," and are transported in fancy to the Ocean House or to Congress Hall. But at the "Trois Couronnes," it must be added, there are other features that are much at variance with these suggestions: neat German waiters, who look like secretaries of legation; Russian princesses sitting in the garden; little Polish boys walking about, held by the hand, with their governors; a view of the sunny crest of the Dent du Midi[3] and the picturesque towers of the Castle of Chillon.[4]

I hardly know whether it was the analogies or the differences that were uppermost in the mind of a young American, who, two or three years ago, sat in the garden of the "Trois Couronnes," looking about him, rather idly, at some of the graceful objects I have mentioned. It was a beautiful summer morning, and in whatever fashion the young American looked at things, they must have seemed to him charming. He had come from Geneva the day before, by the little steamer, to see his aunt, who was staying at the hotel—Geneva having been for a long time his place of residence. But his aunt had a headache—his aunt had almost always a headache—and now she was shut up in her room, smelling camphor, so that he was at liberty to wander about. He was some seven-and-twenty years of age; when his friends spoke of him, they usually said that he was at Geneva, "studying." When his enemies spoke of him they said—but, after

[2] Fashionable spas of the nineteenth century in Rhode Island and New York.

[3] A high peak of the Swiss Alps.

[4] The castle on Lake Geneva celebrated in Byron's poem, "The Prisoner of Chillon."

all, he had no enemies; he was an extremely amiable fellow, and universally liked. What I should say is, simply, that when certain persons spoke of him they affirmed that the reason of his spending so much time at Geneva was that he was extremely devoted to a lady who lived there—a foreign lady—a person older than himself. Very few Americans—indeed I think none—had ever seen this lady, about whom there were some singular stories. But Winterbourne had an old attachment for the little metropolis of Calvinism;[5] he had been put to school there as a boy, and he had afterwards gone to college there—circumstances which had led to his forming a great many youthful friendships. Many of these he had kept, and they were a source of great satisfaction to him.

After knocking at his aunt's door and learning that she was indisposed, he had taken a walk about the town, and then he had come in to his breakfast. He had now finished his breakfast; but he was drinking a small cup of coffee, which had been served to him on a little table in the garden by one of the waiters who looked like an *attaché*. At last he finished his coffee and lit a cigarette. Presently a small boy came walking along the path—an urchin of nine or ten. The child, who was diminutive for his years, had an aged expression of countenance, a pale complexion, and sharp little features. He was dressed in knickerbockers, with red stockings, which displayed his poor little spindleshanks; he also wore a brilliant red cravat. He carried in his hand a long alpenstock, the sharp point of which he thrust into everything that he approached—the flower-beds, the garden-benches, the trains of the ladies' dresses. In front of Winterbourne he paused, looking at him with a pair of bright, penetrating little eyes.

"Will you give me a lump of sugar?" he asked, in a sharp, hard little voice—a voice immature, and yet, somehow, not young.

Winterbourne glanced at the small table near him, on which his coffee-service rested, and saw that several morsels of sugar remained. "Yes, you may take one," he answered; "but I don't think sugar is good for little boys."

This little boy stepped forward and carefully selected three of the coveted fragments, two of which he buried in the pocket of his knickerbockers, depositing the other as promptly in another place. He poked his alpenstock, lance-fashion, into Winterbourne's bench, and tried to crack the lump of sugar with his teeth.

"Oh, blazes; it's har-r-d!" he exclaimed, pronouncing the adjective in a peculiar manner.

Winterbourne had immediately perceived that he might have the

[5] The Protestant theologian, John Calvin (1509-1564), lived in Geneva.

honour of claiming him as a fellow-countryman. "Take care you don't hurt your teeth," he said, paternally.

"I haven't got any teeth to hurt. They have all come out. I have only got seven teeth. My mother counted them last night, and one came out right afterwards. She said she'd slap me if any more came out. I can't help it. It's this old Europe. It's the climate that makes them come out. In America they didn't come out. It's these hotels."

Winterbourne was much amused. "If you eat three lumps of sugar, your mother will certainly slap you," he said.

"She's got to give me some candy, then," rejoined his young interlocutor. "I can't get any candy here—any American candy. American candy's the best candy."

"And are American little boys the best little boys?" asked Winterbourne.

"I don't know. I'm an American boy," said the child.

"I see you are one of the best!" laughed Winterbourne.

"Are you an American man?" pursued this vivacious infant. And then, on Winterbourne's affirmative reply—"American men are the best," he declared.

His companion thanked him for the compliment; and the child, who had now got astride of his alpenstock, stood looking about him, while he attacked a second lump of sugar. Winterbourne wondered if he himself had been like this in his infancy, for he had been brought to Europe at about this age.

"Here comes my sister!" cried the child, in a moment. "She's an American girl."

Winterbourne looked along the path and saw a beautiful young lady advancing. "American girls are the best girls," he said, cheerfully, to his young companion.

"My sister ain't the best!" the child declared. "She's always blowing at me."

"I imagine that is your fault, not hers," said Winterbourne. The young lady meanwhile had drawn near. She was dressed in white muslin, with a hundred frills and flounces, and knots of pale-coloured ribbon. She was bare-headed; but she balanced in her hand a large parasol, with a deep border of embroidery; and she was strikingly, admirably pretty. "How pretty they are!" thought Winterbourne, straightening himself in his seat, as if he were prepared to rise.

The young lady paused in front of his bench, near the parapet of the garden, which overlooked the lake. The little boy had now converted his alpenstock into a vaulting-pole, by the aid of which he was springing about in the gravel, and kicking it up not a little.

"Randolph," said the young lady, "what *are* you doing?"

"I'm going up the Alps," replied Randolph. "This is the way!" And he gave another little jump, scattering the pebbles about Winterbourne's ears.

"That's the way they come down," said Winterbourne.

"He's an American man!" cried Randolph, in his little hard voice.

The young lady gave no heed to this announcement, but looked straight at her brother. "Well, I guess you had better be quiet," she simply observed.

It seemed to Winterbourne that he had been in a manner presented. He got up and stepped slowly towards the young girl, throwing away his cigarette. "This little boy and I have made acquaintance," he said, with great civility. In Geneva, as he had been perfectly aware, a young man was not at liberty to speak to a young unmarried lady except under certain rarely-occurring conditions; but here at Vevey, what conditions could be better than these?—a pretty American girl coming and standing in front of you in a garden. This pretty American girl, however, on hearing Winterbourne's observation, simply glanced at him; she then turned her head and looked over the parapet, at the lake and the opposite mountains. He wondered whether he had gone too far; but he decided that he must advance farther, rather then retreat. While he was thinking of something else to say, the young lady turned to the little boy again.

"I should like to know where you got that pole," she said.

"I bought it!" responded Randolph.

"You don't mean to say you're going to take it to Italy."

"Yes, I am going to take it to Italy!" the child declared.

The young girl glanced over the front of her dress, and smoothed out a knot or two of ribbon. Then she rested her eyes upon the prospect again. "Well, I guess you had better leave it somewhere," she said, after a moment.

"Are you going to Italy?" Winterbourne inquired, in a tone of great respect.

The young lady glanced at him again. "Yes, sir," she replied. And she said nothing more.

"Are you—a—going over the Simplon?" [6] Winterbourne pursued, a little embarrassed.

"I don't know," she said. "I suppose it's some mountain. Randolph, what mountain are we going over?"

"Going where?" the child demanded.

"To Italy," Winterbourne explained.

[6] A mountain pass through the Swiss Alps.

"I don't know," said Randolph. "I don't want to go to Italy. I want to go to America."

"Oh, Italy is a beautiful place!" rejoined the young man.

"Can you get candy there?" Randolph loudly inquired.

"I hope not," said his sister. "I guess you have had enough candy, and mother thinks so too."

"I haven't had any for ever so long—for a hundred weeks!" cried the boy, still jumping about.

The young lady inspected her flounces and smoothed her ribbons again; and Winterbourne presently risked an observation upon the beauty of the view. He was ceasing to be embarrassed, for he had begun to perceive that she was not in the least embarrassed herself. There had not been the slightest alteration in her charming complexion; she was evidently neither offended nor fluttered. If she looked another way when he spoke to her, and seemed not particularly to hear him, this was simply her habit, her manner. Yet, as he talked a little more, and pointed out some of the objects of interest in the view, with which she appeared quite unacquainted, she gradually gave him more of the benefit of her glance; and then he saw that this glance was perfectly direct and unshrinking. It was not, however, what would have been called an immodest glance, for the young girl's eyes were singularly honest and fresh. They were wonderfully pretty eyes; and, indeed, Winterbourne had not seen for a long time anything prettier than his fair countrywoman's various features—her complexion, her nose, her ears, her teeth. He had a great relish for feminine beauty; he was addicted to observing and analysing it; and as regards this young lady's face he made several observations. It was not at all insipid, but it was not exactly expressive; and though it was eminently delicate Winterbourne mentally accused it—very forgivingly—of a want of finish. He thought it very possible that Master Randolph's sister was a coquette; he was sure she had a spirit of her own; but in her bright, sweet, superficial little visage there was no mockery, no irony. Before long it became obvious that she was much disposed towards conversation. She told him that they were going to Rome for the winter—she and her mother and Randolph. She asked him if he was a "real American"; she shouldn't have taken him for one; he seemed more like a German —this was said after a little hesitation, especially when he spoke. Winterbourne, laughing, answered that he had met Germans who spoke like Americans; but that he had not, so far as he remembered, met an American who spoke like a German. Then he asked if she should not be more comfortable in sitting upon the bench which he just quitted. She answered that she liked standing up and walking about; but she presently sat down. She told him she was from New York State—"if you know where that is." Winterbourne learned more about her by catching hold of her small, slippery brother and making him stand a few minutes by his side.

"Tell me your name, my boy," he said.

"Randolph C. Miller," said the boy, sharply. "And I'll tell you her name"; and he levelled his alpenstock at his sister.

"You had better wait till you are asked!" said this young lady, calmly.

"I should like very much to know your name," said Winterbourne.

"Her name is Daisy Miller!" cried the child. "But that isn't her real name; that isn't her name on her cards."

"It's a pity you haven't got one of my cards!" said Miss Miller.

"Her real name is Annie P. Miller," the boy went on.

"Ask him *his* name," said his sister, indicating Winterbourne.

But on this point Randolph seemed perfectly indifferent; he continued to supply information with regard to his own family. "My father's name is Ezra B. Miller," he announced. "My father ain't in Europe; my father's in a better place than Europe."

Winterbourne imagined for a moment that this was the manner in which the child had been taught to intimate that Mr. Miller had been removed to the sphere of celestial rewards. But Randolph immediately added, "My father's in Schenectady. He's got a big business. My father's rich, you bet."

"Well!" ejaculated Miss Miller, lowering her parasol and looking at the embroidered border. Winterbourne presently released the child, who departed, dragging his alpenstock along the path. "He doesn't like Europe," said the young girl. "He wants to go back."

"To Schenectady, you mean?"

"Yes; he wants to go right home. He hasn't got any boys here. There is one boy here, but he always goes round with a teacher; they won't let him play."

"And your brother hasn't any teacher?" Winterbourne inquired.

"Mother thought of getting him one, to travel round with us. There was a lady told her of a very good teacher; an American lady —perhaps you know her—Mrs. Sanders. I think she came from Boston. She told her of this teacher, and we thought of getting him to travel round with us. But Randolph said he didn't want a teacher travelling round with us. He said he wouldn't have lessons when he was in the cars. And we *are* in the cars about half the time. There was an English lady we met in the cars—I think her name was Miss Featherstone; perhaps you know her. She wanted to know why I didn't give Randolph lessons—give him 'instruction,' she called it. I guess he could give me more instruction than I could give him. He's very smart."

"Yes," said Winterbourne; "he seems very smart."

"Mother's going to get a teacher for him as soon as we get to Italy. Can you get good teachers in Italy?"

"Very good, I should think," said Winterbourne.

"Or else she's going to find some school. He ought to learn some more. He's only nine. He's going to college." And in this way Miss Miller continued to converse upon the affairs of her family, and upon other topics. She sat there with her extremely pretty hands, ornamented with very brilliant rings, folded in her lap, and with her pretty eyes now resting upon those of Winterbourne, now wandering over the garden, the people who passed by, and the beautiful view. She talked to Winterbourne as if she had known him a long time. He found it very pleasant. It was many years since he had heard a young girl talk so much. It might have been said of this unknown young lady, who had come and sat down beside him upon a bench, that she chattered. She was very quiet; she sat in a charming tranquil attitude, but her lips and her eyes were constantly moving. She had a soft, slender, agreeable voice, and her tone was decidedly sociable. She gave Winterbourne a history of her movements and intentions, and those of her mother and brother, in Europe, and enumerated, in particular, the various hotels at which they had stopped. "That English lady, in the cars," she said—"Miss Featherstone—asked me if we didn't all live in hotels in America. I told her I had never been in so many hotels in my life as since I came to Europe. I have never seen so many—it's nothing but hotels." But Miss Miller did not make this remark with a querulous accent; she appeared to be in the best humour with everything. She declared that the hotels were very good, when once you got used to their ways, and that Europe was perfectly sweet. She was not disappointed—not a bit. Perhaps it was because she had heard so much about it before. She had ever so many intimate friends that had been there ever so many times. And then she had had ever so many dresses and things from Paris. Whenever she put on a Paris dress she felt as if she were in Europe.

"It was a kind of a wishing-cap," said Winterbourne.

"Yes," said Miss Miller, without examining this analogy; "it always made me wish I was here. But I needn't have done that for dresses. I am sure they send all the pretty ones to America; you see the most frightful things here. The only thing I don't like," she proceeded, "is the society. There isn't any society; or, if there is, I don't know where it keeps itself. Do you? I suppose there is some society somewhere, but I haven't seen anything of it. I'm very fond of society, and I have always had a great deal of it. I don't mean only in Schenectady, but in New York. I used to go to New York every winter. In New York I had lots of society. Last winter I had seventeen dinners given me; and three of them were by gentlemen," added Daisy Miller. "I have more friends in New York than in Schenectady—more gentleman friends; and more young lady friends too," she resumed in a moment. She paused again for an instant; she was looking at Winterbourne with all her prettiness in her lively eyes and in her light, slightly monotonous smile. "I have always had," she said, "a great deal of gentlemen's society."

Poor Winterbourne was amused, perplexed, and decidedly charmed. He had never yet heard a young girl express herself in just this fashion; never, at least, save in cases where to say such things seemed a kind of demonstrative evidence of a certain laxity of deportment. And yet was he to accuse Miss Daisy Miller of actual or potential *inconduite*,[7] as they said at Geneva? He felt that he had lived at Geneva so long that he had lost a good deal; he had become dishabituated to the American tone. Never, indeed, since he had grown old enough to appreciate things, had he encountered a young American girl of so pronounced a type as this. Certainly she was very charming, but how deucedly sociable! Was she simply a pretty girl from New York State—were they all like that, the pretty girls who had a good deal of gentlemen's society? Or was she also a designing, an audacious, an unscrupulous young person? Winterbourne had lost his instinct in this matter, and his reason could not help him. Miss Daisy Miller looked extremely innocent. Some people had told him that, after all, American girls were exceedingly innocent; and others had told him that, after all, they were not. He was inclined to think Miss Daisy Miller was a flirt—a pretty American flirt. He had never, as yet, had any relations with young ladies of this category. He had known, here in Europe, two or three women—persons older than Miss Daisy Miller, and provided, for respectability's sake, with husbands—who were great coquettes—dangerous, terrible women, with whom one's relations were liable to take a serious turn. But this young girl was not a coquette in that sense; she was very unsophisticated; she was only a pretty American flirt. Winterbourne was almost grateful for having found the formula that applied to Miss Daisy Miller. He leaned back in his seat; he remarked to him-

[7] Misconduct.

self that she had the most charming nose he had ever seen; he wondered what were the regular conditions and limitations of one's intercourse with a pretty American flirt. It presently became apparent that he was on the way to learn.

"Have you been to that old castle?" asked the young girl, pointing with her parasol to the far-gleaming walls of the Château de Chillon.

"Yes, formerly, more than once," said Winterbourne. "You too, I suppose, have seen it?"

"No; we haven't been there. I want to go there dreadfully. Of course I mean to go there. I wouldn't go away from here without having seen that old castle."

"It's a very pretty excursion," said Winterbourne, "and very easy to make. You can drive, you know, or you can go by the little steamer."

"You can go in the cars," said Miss Miller.

"Yes; you can go in the cars," Winterbourne assented.

"Our courier says they take you right up to the castle," the young girl continued. "We were going last week; but my mother gave out. She suffers dreadfully from dyspepsia. She said she couldn't go. Randolph wouldn't go either; he says he doesn't think much of old castles. But I guess we'll go this week, if we can get Randolph."

"Your brother is not interested in ancient monuments?" Winterbourne inquired, smiling.

"He says he don't care much about old castles. He's only nine. He wants to stay at the hotel. Mother's afraid to leave him alone, and the courier won't stay with him; so we haven't been to many places. But it will be too bad if we don't go up there." And Miss Miller pointed again at the Château de Chillon.

"I should think it might be arranged," said Winterbourne. "Couldn't you get some one to stay—for the afternoon—with Randolph?"

Miss Miller looked at him a moment; and then, very placidly—"I wish *you* would stay with him!" she said.

Winterbourne hesitated a moment. "I should much rather go to Chillon with you."

"With me?" asked the young girl, with the same placidity.

She didn't rise, blushing, as a young girl at Geneva would have done; and yet Winterbourne, conscious that he had been very bold, thought it possible she was offended. "With your mother," he answered very respectfully.

But it seemed that both his audacity and his respect were lost upon Miss Daisy Miller. "I guess my mother won't go after all," she said. "She don't like to ride round in the afternoon. But did you really mean what you said just now; that you would like to go up there?"

"Most earnestly," Winterbourne declared.

"Then we may arrange it. If mother will stay with Randolph, I guess Eugenio will."

"Eugenio?" the young man inquired.

"Eugenio's our courier. He doesn't like to stay with Randolph; he's the most fastidious man I ever saw. But he's a splendid courier. I guess he'll stay at home with Randolph if mother does, and then we can go to the castle."

Winterbourne reflected for an instant as lucidly as possible—"we" could only mean Miss Daisy Miller and himself. This programme seemed almost too agreeable for credence; he felt as if he ought to kiss the young lady's hand. Possibly he would have done so—and quite spoiled the project; but at this moment another person—presumably Eugenio—appeared. A tall, handsome man, with superb whiskers, wearing a velvet morning-coat and a brilliant watch-chain, approached Miss Miller, looking sharply at her companion. "Oh, Eugenio!" said Miss Miller, with the friendliest accent.

Eugenio had looked at Winterbourne from head to foot; he now bowed gravely to the young lady. "I have the honour to inform mademoiselle that luncheon is upon the table."

Miss Miller slowly rose. "See here, Eugenio," she said. "I'm going to that old castle, any way."

"To the Château de Chillon, mademoiselle?" the courier inquired. "Mademoiselle has made arrangements?" he added, in a tone which struck Winterbourne as very impertinent.

Eugenio's tone apparently threw, even to Miss Miller's own apprehension, a slightly ironical light upon the young girl's situation. She turned to Winterbourne, blushing a little—a very little. "You won't back out?" she said.

"I shall not be happy till we go!" he protested.

"And you are staying in this hotel?" she went on. "And you are really an American?"

The courier stood looking at Winterbourne, offensively. The young man, at least, thought his manner of looking an offence to Miss Miller; it conveyed an imputation that she "picked up" acquaintances. "I shall have the honour of presenting to you a person who will tell you all about me," he said smiling, and referring to his aunt.

"Oh, well, we'll go some day," said Miss Miller. And she gave him a smile and turned away. She put up her parasol and walked back to the inn beside Eugenio. Winterbourne stood looking after her; and as she moved away, drawing her muslin furbelows over the gravel, said to himself that she had the *tournure*[8] of a princess.

He had, however, engaged to do more than proved feasible, in promising to present his aunt, Mrs. Costello, to Miss Daisy Miller. As soon as the former lady had got better of her headache he waited upon her in her apartment; and, after the proper inquiries in regard to her health, he asked her if she had observed, in the hotel, an American family—a mamma, a daughter, and a little boy.

"And a courier?" said Mrs. Costello. "Oh, yes, I have observed them. Seen them—heard them—and kept out of their way." Mrs. Costello was a widow with a fortune; a person of much distinction, who frequently intimated that, if she were not so dreadfully liable to sick-headaches, she would probably have left a deeper impress upon her time. She had a long pale face, a high nose, and a great deal of very striking white hair, which she wore in large puffs and *rouleaux*[9] over the top of her head. She had two sons married in New York, and another who was now in Europe. This young man was amusing himself at Hombourg,[10] and, though he was on his travels, was rarely perceived to visit any particular city at the moment selected by his mother for her own appearance there. Her nephew, who had come up to Vevey expressly to see her, was therefore more attentive than those who, as she said, were nearer to her. He had imbibed at Geneva the idea that one must always be attentive to one's aunt. Mrs. Costello had not seen him for many years, and she was greatly pleased with him, manifesting her approbation by initiating him into many of the secrets of that social sway which, as she gave him to understand, she exerted in the American capital. She admitted that she was very exclusive; but, if he were acquainted with New York, he would see that one had to be. And her picture of the minutely hierarchical constitution of the society of that city, which she presented to him in many different lights, was, to Winterbourne's imagination, almost oppressively striking.

He immediately perceived, from her tone, that Miss Daisy Miller's place in the social scale was low. "I am afraid you don't approve of them," he said.

"They are very common," Mrs. Costello declared. "They are the sort of Americans that one does one's duty by not—not accepting."

"Ah, you don't accept them?" said the young man.

"I can't, my dear Frederick. I would if I could, but I can't."

"The young girl is very pretty," said Winterbourne, in a moment.

---

[8] Bearing.

[9] Little rolls.

[10] A resort in Prussia famous for its mineral springs.

"Of course she's pretty. But she is very common."

"I see what you mean of course," said Winterbourne, after another pause.

"She has that charming look that they all have," his aunt resumed. "I can't think where they pick it up; and she dresses in perfection—no, you don't know how well she dresses. I can't think where they get their taste."

"But, my dear aunt, she is not, after all, a Comanche savage."

"She is a young lady," said Mrs. Costello, "who has an intimacy with her mamma's courier."

"An intimacy with the courier?" the young man demanded.

"Oh, the mother is just as bad! They treat the courier like a familiar friend—like a gentleman. I shouldn't wonder if he dines with them. Very likely they have never seen a man with such good manners, such fine clothes, so like a gentleman. He probably corresponds to the young lady's idea of a Count. He sits with them in the garden, in the evening. I think he smokes."

Winterbourne listened with interest to these disclosures; they helped him to make up his mind about Miss Daisy. Evidently she was rather wild. "Well," he said, "I am not a courier, and yet she was very charming to me."

"You had better have said at first," said Mrs. Costello with dignity, "that you had made her acquaintance."

"We simply met in the garden, and we talked a bit."

"*Tout bonnement!*[11] And pray what did you say?"

"I said I should take the liberty of introducing her to my admirable aunt."

"I am much obliged to you."

"It was to guarantee my respectability," said Winterbourne.

"And pray who is to guarantee hers?"

"Ah, you are cruel!" said the young man. "She's a very nice young girl."

"You don't say that as if you believed it," Mrs. Costello observed.

"She is completely uncultivated," Winterbourne went on. "But she is wonderfully pretty, and, in short, she is very nice. To prove that I believe it, I am going to take her to the Château de Chillon."

"You two are going off there together? I should say it proved just the contrary. How long had you known her, may I ask, when this interesting project was formed? You haven't been twenty-four hours in the house."

"I had known her half an hour!" said Winterbourne, smiling.

---

[11] Simply!

"Dear me!" cried Mrs. Costello. "What a dreadful girl!"

Her nephew was silent for some moments. "You really think, then," he began, earnestly, and with a desire for trustworthy information—"you really think that——"But he paused again.

"Think what, sir?" said his aunt.

"That she is the sort of young lady who expects a man—sooner or later—to carry her off?"

"I haven't the least idea what such young ladies expect a man to do. But I really think that you had better not meddle with little American girls that are uncultivated, as you call them. You have lived too long out of the country. You will be sure to make some great mistake. You are too innocent."

"My dear aunt, I am not so innocent," said Winterbourne, smiling and curling his moustache.

"You are too guilty, then!"

Winterbourne continued to curl his moustache, meditatively. "You won't let the poor girl know you then?" he asked at last.

"Is it literally true that she is going to the Château de Chillon with you?"

"I think that she fully intends it."

"Then, my dear Frederick," said Mrs. Costello, "I must decline the honour of her acquaintance. I am an old woman, but I am not too old—thank Heaven—to be shocked!"

"But don't they all do these things—the young girls in America?" Winterbourne inquired.

Mrs. Costello stared a moment. "I should like to see my granddaughters do them!" she declared, grimly.

This seemed to throw some light upon the matter, for Winterbourne remembered to have heard that his pretty cousins in New York were "tremendous flirts." If, therefore, Miss Daisy Miller exceeded the liberal margin allowed to these young ladies, it was probable that anything might be expected of her. Winterbourne was impatient to see her again, and he was vexed with himself that, by instinct, he should not appreciate her justly.

Though he was impatient to see her, he hardly knew what he should say to her about his aunt's refusal to become acquainted with her; but he discovered, promptly enough, that with Miss Daisy Miller there was no great need of walking on tiptoe. He found her that evening in the garden, wandering about in the warm starlight, like an indolent sylph, and swinging to and fro the largest fan he had ever beheld. It was ten o'clock. He had dined with his aunt, had been sitting with her since dinner, and had just taken leave of her till the morrow. Miss Daisy Miller seemed very glad to see him; she declared it was the longest evening she had ever passed.

"Have you been all alone?" he asked.

"I have been walking round with mother. But mother gets tired walking round," she answered.

"Has she gone to bed?"

"No; she doesn't like to go to bed," said the young girl. "She doesn't sleep—not three hours. She says she doesn't know how she lives. She's dreadfully nervous. I guess she sleeps more than she thinks. She's gone somewhere after Randolph; she wants to try to get him to go to bed. He doesn't like to go to bed."

"Let us hope she will persuade him," observed Winterbourne.

"She will talk to him all she can; but he doesn't like her to talk to him," said Miss Daisy, opening her fan. "She's going to try to get Eugenio to talk to him. But he isn't afraid of Eugenio. Eugenio's a splendid courier, but he can't make much impression on Randolph! I don't believe he'll go to bed before eleven." It appeared that Randolph's vigil was in fact triumphantly prolonged, for Winterbourne strolled about with the young girl for some time without meeting her mother. "I have been looking round for that lady you want to introduce me to," his companion resumed. "She's your aunt." Then, on Winterbourne's admitting the fact, and expressing some curiosity as to how she had learned it, she said she had heard all about Mrs. Costello from the chambermaid. She was very quiet and very *comme il faut;*[12] she wore white puffs; she spoke to no one, and she never dined at the *table d'hôte.*[13] Every two days she had a headache. "I think that's a lovely description, headache and all!" said Miss Daisy, chattering along in her thin, gay voice. "I want to know her ever so much. I know just what *your* aunt would be; I know I should like her. She would be very exclusive. I like a lady to be exclusive; I'm dying to be exclusive myself. Well, we *are* exclusive, mother and I. We don't speak to every one—or they don't speak to us. I suppose it's about the same thing. Any way, I shall be ever so glad to know your aunt."

Winterbourne was embarrassed. "She would be most happy," he said; "but I am afraid those headaches will interfere."

The young girl looked at him through the dusk. "But I suppose she doesn't have a headache every day," she said, sympathetically.

Winterbourne was silent a moment. "She tells me she does," he answered at last—not knowing what to say.

---

[12] Correct.

[13] A common table for guests at a hotel.

Miss Daisy Miller stopped and stood looking at him. Her prettiness was still visible in the darkness; she was opening and closing her enormous fan. "She doesn't want to know me!" she said, suddenly. "Why don't you say so? You needn't be afraid. I'm not afraid!" And she gave a little laugh.

Winterbourne fancied there was a tremor in her voice; he was touched, shocked, mortified by it. "My dear young lady," he protested, "she knows no one. It's her wretched health."

The young girl walked on a few steps, laughing still. "You needn't be afraid," she repeated. "Why should she want to know me?" Then she paused again; she was close to the parapet of the garden, and in front of her was the starlit lake. There was a vague sheen upon its surface, and in the distance were dimly-seen mountain forms. Daisy Miller looked out upon the mysterious prospect, and then she gave another little laugh. "Gracious! she *is* exclusive!" she said. Winterbourne wondered whether she was seriously wounded, and for a moment almost wished that her sense of injury might be such as to make it becoming in him to attempt to reassure and comfort her. He had a pleasant sense that she would be very approachable for consolatory purposes. He felt then, for the instant, quite ready to sacrifice his aunt, conversationally; to admit that she was a proud, rude woman, and to declare that they needn't mind her. But before he had time to commit himself to this perilous mixture of gallantry and impiety, the young lady, resuming her walk, gave an exclamation in quite another tone. "Well; here's mother! I guess she hasn't got Randolph to go to bed." The figure of a lady appeared, at a distance, very indistinct in the darkness, and advancing with a slow and wavering movement. Suddenly it seemed to pause.

"Are you sure it is your mother? Can you distinguish her in this thick dusk?" Winterbourne asked.

"Well!" cried Miss Daisy Miller, with a laugh, "I guess I know my own mother. And when she has got on my shawl, too! She is always wearing my things."

The lady in question, ceasing to advance, hovered vaguely about the spot at which she had checked her steps.

"I am afraid your mother doesn't see you," said Winterbourne. "Or perhaps," he added—thinking, with Miss Miller, the joke permissible—"perhaps she feels guilty about your shawl."

"Oh, it's a fearful old thing!" the young girl replied, serenely. "I told her she could wear it. She won't come here, because she sees you."

"Ah, then," said Winterbourne, "I had better leave you."

"Oh, no; come on!" urged Miss Daisy Miller.

"I'm afraid your mother doesn't approve of my walking with you."

Miss Miller gave him a serious glance. "It isn't for me; it's for you—that is, it's for *her*. Well; I don't know who it's for! But mother doesn't like any of my gentlemen friends. She's right down timid. She always makes a fuss if I introduce a gentleman. But I *do* introduce them—almost always. If I didn't introduce my gentlemen friends to mother," the young girl added, in her little soft, flat monotone, "I shouldn't think I was natural."

"To introduce me," said Winterbourne, "you must know my name." And he proceeded to pronounce it.

"Oh, dear; I can't say all that!" said his companion, with a laugh. But by this time they had come up to Mrs. Miller, who, as they drew near, walked to the parapet of the garden and leaned upon it, looking intently at the lake, and turning her back to them. "Mother!" said the young girl, in a tone of decision. Upon this the elder lady turned round. "Mr. Winterbourne," said Miss Daisy Miller, introducing the young man very frankly and prettily. "Common" she was, as Mrs. Costello had pronounced her; yet it was a wonder to Winterbourne that, with her commonness, she had a singularly delicate grace.

Her mother was a small, spare, light person, with a wandering eye, a very exiguous nose, and a large forehead, decorated with a certain amount of thin, much-frizzled hair. Like her daughter, Mrs. Miller was dressed with extreme elegance; she had enormous diamonds in her ears. So far as Winterbourne could observe, she gave him no greeting—she certainly was not looking at him. Daisy was near her, pulling her shawl straight. "What are you doing, poking round here?" this young lady inquired; but by no means with that harshness of accent which her choice of words may imply.

"I don't know," said her mother, turning towards the lake again.

"I shouldn't think you'd want that shawl!" Daisy exclaimed.

"Well—I do!" her mother answered, with a little laugh.

"Did you get Randolph to go to bed?" asked the young girl.

"No; I couldn't induce him," said Mrs. Miller, very gently. "He wants to talk to the waiter. He likes to talk to that waiter."

"I was telling Mr. Winterbourne," the young girl went on; and to the young man's ear her tone might have indicated that she had been uttering his name all her life.

"Oh, yes!" said Winterbourne; "I have the pleasure of knowing your son."

Randolph's mamma was silent; she turned her attention to the lake. But at last she spoke. "Well, I don't see how he lives!"

"Anyhow, it isn't so bad as it was at Dover," said Daisy Miller.

"And what occurred at Dover?" Winterbourne asked.

"He wouldn't go to bed at all. I guess he sat up all night—in the public parlour. He wasn't in bed at twelve o'clock: I know that."

"It was half-past twelve," declared Mrs. Miller, with mild emphasis.

"Does he sleep much during the day?" Winterbourne demanded.

"I guess he doesn't sleep much," Daisy rejoined.

"I wish he would!" said her mother. "It seems as if he couldn't."

"I think he's real tiresome," Daisy pursued.

Then, for some moments, there was silence. "Well, Daisy Miller," said the elder lady, presently, "I shouldn't think you'd want to talk against your own brother!"

"Well, he *is* tiresome, mother," said Daisy, quite without the asperity of a retort.

"He's only nine," urged Mrs. Miller.

"Well, he wouldn't go to that castle," said the young girl. "I'm going there with Mr. Winterbourne."

To this announcement, very placidly made, Daisy's mamma offered no response. Winterbourne took for granted that she deeply disapproved of the projected excursion; but he said to himself that she was a simple, easily-managed person, and that a few deferential protestations would take the edge from her displeasure. "Yes," he began; "your daughter has kindly allowed me the honour of being her guide."

Mrs. Miller's wandering eyes attached themselves, with a sort of appealing air, to Daisy, who, however, strolled a few steps farther, gently humming to herself. "I presume you will go in the cars," said her mother.

"Yes; or in the boat," said Winterbourne.

"Well, of course, I don't know," Mrs. Miller rejoined. "I have never been to that castle."

"It is a pity you shouldn't go," said Winterbourne, beginning to feel reassured as to her opposition. And yet he was quite prepared to find that, as a matter of course, she meant to accompany her daughter.

"We've been thinking ever so much about going," she pursued; "but it seems as if we couldn't. Of course Daisy—she wants to go round. But there's a lady here—I don't know her name—she says she shouldn't think we'd want to go to see castles *here;* she should think we'd want to wait till we got to Italy. It seems as if there would be so many there," continued Mrs. Miller, with an air of increasing confidence. "Of course, we only want to see the principal ones. We visited several in England," she presently added.

"Ah, yes! in England there are beautiful castles," said Winterbourne. "But Chillon, here, is very well worth seeing."

"Well, if Daisy feels up to it——," said Mrs. Miller, in a tone impregnated with a sense of the magnitude of the enterprise. "It seems as if there was nothing she wouldn't undertake."

"Oh, I think she'll enjoy it!" Winterbourne declared. And he desired more and more to make it a certainty that he was to have the privilege of a *tête-à-tête*[14] with the young lady, who was still strolling along in front of them, softly vocalising. "You are not disposed, madam," he inquired, "to undertake it yourself?"

Daisy's mother looked at him, an instant, askance, and then walked forward in silence. Then—"I guess she had better go alone," she said, simply.

Winterbourne observed to himself that this was a very different type of maternity from that of the vigilant matrons who massed themselves in the forefront of social intercourse in the dark old city at the other end of the lake. But his meditations were interrupted by hearing his name very distinctly pronounced by Mrs. Miller's unprotected daughter.

"Mr. Winterbourne!" murmured Daisy.

"Mademoiselle!" said the young man.

"Don't you want to take me out in a boat?"

"At present?" he asked.

"Of course!" said Daisy.

"Well, Annie Miller!" exclaimed her mother.

"I beg you, madam, to let her go," said Winterbourne, ardently; for he had never yet enjoyed the sensation of guiding through the summer starlight a skiff freighted with a fresh and beautiful young girl.

"I shouldn't think she'd want to," said her mother. "I should think she'd rather go indoors."

"I'm sure Mr. Winterbourne wants to take me," Daisy declared. "He's so awfully devoted!"

"I will row you over to Chillon, in the starlight."

"I don't believe it!" said Daisy.

"Well!" ejaculated the elder lady again.

"You haven't spoken to me for half an hour," her daughter went on.

"I have been having some very pleasant conversation with your mother," said Winterbourne.

"Well; I want you to take me out in a boat!" Daisy repeated. They

---

[14] Private conversation.

had all stopped, and she had turned round and was looking at Winterbourne. Her face wore a charming smile, her pretty eyes were gleaming, she was swinging her great fan about. No; it's impossible to be prettier than that, thought Winterbourne.

"There are half a dozen boats moored at that landing-place," he said, pointing to certain steps which descended from the garden to the lake. "If you will do me the honour to accept my arm, we will go and select one of them."

Daisy stood there smiling; she threw back her head and gave a little, light laugh. "I like a gentleman to be formal!" she declared.

"I assure you it's a formal offer."

"I was bound I would make you say something," Daisy went on.

"You see it's not very difficult," said Winterbourne. "But I am afraid you are chaffing me."

"I think not, sir," remarked Mrs. Miller, very gently.

"Do, then, let me give you a row," he said to the young girl.

"It's quite lovely, the way you say that!" cried Daisy.

"It will be still more lovely to do it."

"Yes, it would be lovely!" said Daisy. But she made no movement to accompany him; she only stood there laughing.

"I should think you had better find out what time it is," interposed her mother.

"It is eleven o'clock, madam," said a voice, with a foreign accent, out of the neighbouring darkness; and Winterbourne, turning, perceived the florid personage who was in attendance upon the two ladies. He had apparently just approached.

"Oh, Eugenio," said Daisy, "I am going out in a boat!"

Eugenio bowed. "At eleven o'clock, mademoiselle?"

"I am going with Mr. Winterbourne. This very minute."

"Do tell her she can't," said Mrs. Miller to the courier.

"I think you had better not go out in a boat, mademoiselle," Eugenio declared.

Winterbourne wished to heaven this pretty girl were not so familiar with her courier; but he said nothing.

"I suppose you don't think it's proper!" Daisy exclaimed. "Eugenio doesn't think anything's proper."

"I am at your service," said Winterbourne.

"Does mademoiselle propose to go alone?" asked Eugenio of Mrs. Miller.

"Oh, no; with this gentleman!" answered Daisy's mamma.

The courier looked for a moment at Winterbourne—the latter thought he was smiling—and then, solemnly, with a bow, "As mademoiselle pleases!" he said.

"Oh, I hoped you would make a fuss!" said Daisy. "I don't care to go now."

"I myself shall make a fuss if you don't go," said Winterbourne.

"That's all I want—a little fuss!" And the young girl began to laugh again.

"Mr. Randolph has gone to bed!" the courier announced, frigidly.

"Oh, Daisy; now we can go!" said Mrs. Miller.

Daisy turned away from Winterbourne, looking at him, smiling, and fanning herself. "Good-night," she said; "I hope you are disappointed, or disgusted, or something!"

He looked at her, taking the hand she offered him. "I am puzzled," he answered.

"Well; I hope it won't keep you awake!" she said, very smartly; and, under the escort of the privileged Eugenio, the two ladies passed towards the house.

Winterbourne stood looking after them; he was indeed puzzled. He lingered beside the lake for a quarter of an hour, turning over the mystery of the young girl's sudden familiarities and caprices. But the only very definite conclusion he came to was that he should enjoy deucedly "going off" with her somewhere.

Two days afterwards he went off with her to the Castle of Chillon. He waited for her in the large hall of the hotel, where the couriers, the servants, the foreign tourists were lounging about and staring. It was not the place he should have chosen, but she had appointed it. She came tripping downstairs, buttoning her long gloves, squeezing her folded parasol against her pretty figure, dressed in the perfection of a soberly elegant travelling-costume. Winterbourne was a man of imagination and, as our ancestors used to say, sensibility; as he looked at her dress and, on the great staircase, her little rapid, confiding step, he felt as if there were something romantic going forward. He could have believed he was going to elope with her. He passed out with her among all the idle people that were assembled there; they were all looking at her very hard; she had begun to chatter as soon as she joined him. Winterbourne's preference had been that they should be conveyed to Chillon in a carriage; but she expressed a lively wish to go in the little steamer; she declared that she had a passion for steamboats. There was always such a lovely breeze upon the water, and you saw such lots of people. The sail was not long, but Winterbourne's companion found time to say a great many things. To the young man himself their little excursion was so much of an escapade—an adventure—that, even allowing for her habitual sense of freedom, he had some expectation of seeing her regard it in the same way. But it must be confessed that, in this particular, he was disappointed. Daisy Miller was extremely animated, she was in charming spirits; but she was apparently not at all excited; she was not fluttered; she avoided neither his eyes nor those of any one else; she blushed neither when she looked at him nor when she felt that people were looking at her. People continued to look at her a great deal, and Winterbourne took much satisfaction in his pretty companion's distinguished air. He had been a little afraid that she would talk loud, laugh overmuch, and even, perhaps, desire to move about the boat a good deal. But he quite forgot his fears; he sat smiling, with his eyes upon her face, while, without moving from her place, she delivered herself of a great number of original reflections. It was the most charming garrulity he had ever heard. He had assented to the idea that she was "common"; but was she so, after all, or was he simply getting used to her commonness? Her conversation was chiefly of what metaphysicians term the objective cast; but every now and then it took a subjective turn.

"What on *earth* are you so grave about?" she suddenly demanded, fixing her agreeable eyes upon Winterbourne's.

"Am I grave?" he asked. "I had an idea I was grinning from ear to ear."

"You look as if you were taking me to a funeral. If that's a grin, your ears are very near together."

"Should you like me to dance a hornpipe on the deck?"

"Pray do, and I'll carry round your hat. It will pay the expenses of our journey."

"I never was better pleased in my life," murmured Winterbourne.

She looked at him a moment, and then burst into a little laugh. "I like to make you say those things! You're a queer mixture!"

In the castle, after they had landed, the subjective element decidedly prevailed. Daisy tripped about the vaulted chambers, rustled her skirts in the corkscrew staircases, flirted back with a pretty little cry and a shudder from the edge of the *oubliettes,*[15] and turned a singularly well-shaped ear to everything that Winterbourne told her about the place. But he saw that she cared very little for feudal antiquities, and that the dusky traditions of Chillon made but a slight impression upon her. They had the good fortune to have been able to walk about without other companionship than that of the custodian; and Winterbourne arranged with this functionary that they should not be hurried—that they should linger and pause wherever they chose. The custodian interpreted the bargain gen-

---

[15] Dungeons whose only opening is at the top.

erously—Winterbourne, on his side, had been generous—and ended by leaving them quite to themselves. Miss Miller's observations were not remarkable for logical consistency; for anything she wanted to say she was sure to find a pretext. She found a great many pretexts in the rugged embrasures of Chillon for asking Winterbourne sudden questions about himself—his family, his previous history, his tastes, his habits, his intentions—and for supplying information upon corresponding points in her own personality. Of her own tastes, habits, and intentions Miss Miller was prepared to give the most definite, and indeed the most favourable, account.

"Well; I hope you know enough!" she said to her companion, after he had told her the history of the unhappy Bonnivard.[16] "I never saw a man that knew so much!" The history of Bonnivard had evidently, as they say, gone into one ear and out of the other. But Daisy went on to say that she wished Winterbourne would travel with them and "go round" with them; they might know something, in that case. "Don't you want to come and teach Randolph?" she asked. Winterbourne said that nothing could possibly please him so much; but that he had unfortunately other occupations. "Other occupations? I don't believe it!" said Miss Daisy. "What do you mean? You are not in business." The young man admitted that he was not in business; but he had engagements which, even within a day or two, would force him to go back to Geneva. "Oh, bother!" she said: "I don't believe it!" and she began to talk about something else. But a few moments later, when he was pointing out to her the pretty design of an antique fireplace, she broke out irrelevantly, "You don't mean to say you are going back to Geneva?"

"It is a melancholy fact that I shall have to return to Geneva tomorrow."

"Well, Mr. Winterbourne," said Daisy; "I think you're horrid!"

"Oh, don't say such dreadful things!" said Winterbourne—"Just at the last!"

"The last!" cried the young girl; "I call it the first. I have half a mind to leave you here and go straight back to the hotel alone." And for the next ten minutes she did nothing but call him horrid. Poor Winterbourne was fairly bewildered; no young lady had as yet done him the honour to be so agitated by the announcement of his movements. His companion, after this, ceased to pay any attention to the curiosities of Chillon or the beauties of the lake; she opened fire upon the mysterious charmer in Geneva whom she appeared to have

[16] François de Bonnivard (1496-1570), Swiss patriot whose imprisonment in the Castle of Chillon is the subject of Byron's poem.

instantly taken it for granted that he was hurrying back to see. How did Miss Daisy Miller know that there was a charmer in Geneva? Winterbourne, who denied the existence of such a person, was quite unable to discover; and he was divided between amazement at the rapidity of her induction and amusement at the frankness of her *persiflage*. She seemed to him, in all this, an extraordinary mixture of innocence and crudity. "Does she never allow you more than three days at a time?" asked Daisy, ironically. "Doesn't she give you a vacation in summer? There's no one so hard worked but they can get leave to go off somewhere at this season. I suppose, if you stay another day, she'll come after you in the boat. Do wait over till Friday, and I will go down to the landing to see her arrive!" Winterbourne began to think he had been wrong to feel disappointed in the temper in which the young lady had embarked. If he had missed the personal accent, the personal accent was now making its appearance. It sounded very distinctly, at last, in her telling him she would stop "teasing" him if he would promise her solemnly to come down to Rome in the winter.

"That's not a difficult promise to make," said Winterbourne. "My aunt has taken an apartment in Rome for the winter, and has already asked me to come and see her."

"I don't want you to come for your aunt," said Daisy; "I want you to come for me." And this was the only allusion that the young man was ever to hear her make to his invidious kinswoman. He declared that, at any rate, he would certainly come. After this Daisy stopped teasing. Winterbourne took a carriage, and they drove back to Vevey in the dusk; the young girl was very quiet.

In the evening Winterbourne mentioned to Mrs. Costello that he had spent the afternoon at Chillon, with Miss Daisy Miller.

"The Americans—of the courier?" asked this lady.

"Ah, happily," said Winterbourne, "the courier stayed at home."

"She went with you all alone?"

"All alone."

Mrs. Costello sniffed a little at her smelling-bottle. "And that," she explained, "is the young person whom you wanted me to know!"

Part II

Winterbourne, who had returned to Geneva the day after his excursion to Chillon, went to Rome towards the end of January. His aunt had been established there for several weeks, and he had received a couple of letters from her. "Those people you were so devoted to last summer at Vevey have turned up here, courier and all," she wrote. "They seem to have made several acquaintances, but the courier continues to be the most *intime*. The young lady, however, is also very intimate with some third-rate Italians, with whom she rackets about in a way that makes much talk. Bring me that pretty novel of Cherbuliez's[17]—'Paule Méré'—and don't come later than the 23rd."

In the natural course of events, Winterbourne, on arriving in Rome, would presently have ascertained Mrs. Miller's address at the American banker's, and have gone to pay his compliments to Miss Daisy. "After what happened at Vevey I think I may certainly call upon them," he said to Mrs. Costello.

"If, after what happens—at Vevey and everywhere—you desire to keep up the acquaintance, you are very welcome. Of course a man may know every one. Men are welcome to the privilege!"

"Pray what is it that happens—here, for instance?" Winterbourne demanded.

"The girl goes about alone with her foreigners. As to what happens further, you must apply elsewhere for information. She has picked up half-a-dozen of the regular Roman fortune-hunters, and she takes them about to people's houses. When she comes to a party she brings with her a gentleman with a good deal of manner and a wonderful moustache."

"And where is the mother?"

"I haven't the least idea. They are very dreadful people."

Winterbourne meditated a moment. "They are very ignorant—very innocent only. Depend upon it they are not bad."

"They are hopelessly vulgar," said Mrs. Costello. "Whether or no being hopelessly vulgar is being 'bad' is a question for the metaphysicians. They are bad enough to dislike, at any rate; and for this short life that is quite enough."

The news that Daisy Miller was surrounded by half-a-dozen wonderful moustaches checked Winterbourne's impulse to go straightway to see her. He had perhaps not definitely flattered himself that he had made an ineffaceable impression upon her heart, but he was annoyed at hearing of a state of affairs so little in harmony with an image that had lately flitted in and out of his own meditations; the image of a very pretty girl looking out of an old Roman window and asking herself urgently when Mr. Winterbourne would arrive. If, however, he determined to wait a little before reminding Miss Miller of his claims to her consideration, he went very soon to call upon two or three other friends. One of these friends was an Ameri-

---

[17] Victor Cherbuliez (1829-1899), French novelist of Swiss origin.

can lady who had spent several winters at Geneva, where she had placed her children at school. She was a very accomplished woman, and she lived in the Via Gregoriana. Winterbourne found her in a little crimson drawing-room, on a third floor; the room was filled with southern sunshine. He had not been there ten minutes when the servant came in, announcing "Madame Mila!" This announcement was presently followed by the entrance of little Randolph Miller, who stopped in the middle of the room and stood staring at Winterbourne. An instant later his pretty sister crossed the threshold; and then, after a considerable interval, Mrs. Miller slowly advanced.

"I know you!" said Randolph.

"I'm sure you know a great many things," exclaimed Winterbourne, taking him by the hand. "How is your education coming on?"

Daisy was exchanging greetings very prettily with her hostess; but when she heard Winterbourne's voice she quickly turned her head. "Well, I declare!" she said.

"I told you I should come, you know," Winterbourne rejoined, smiling.

"Well—I didn't believe it," said Miss Daisy.

"I am much obliged to you," laughed the young man.

"You might have come to see me!" said Daisy.

"I arrived only yesterday."

"I don't believe that!" the young girl declared.

Winterbourne turned with a protesting smile to her mother; but this lady evaded his glance, and, seating herself, fixed her eyes upon her son. "We've got a bigger place than this," said Randolph. "It's all gold on the walls."

Mrs. Miller turned uneasily in her chair. "I told you if I were to bring you, you would say something!" she murmured.

"I told *you!*" Randolph exclaimed. "I tell *you,* sir!" he added jocosely, giving Winterbourne a thump on the knee. "It *is* bigger, too!"

Daisy had entered upon a lively conversation with her hostess; Winterbourne judged it becoming to address a few words to her mother. "I hope you have been well since we parted at Vevey," he said.

Mrs. Miller now certainly looked at him—at his chin. "Not very well, sir," she answered.

"She's got the dyspepsia," said Randolph. "I've got it too. Father's got it. I've got it most!"

This announcement, instead of embarrassing Mrs. Miller, seemed to relieve her. "I suffer from the liver," she said. "I think it's this climate; it's less bracing than Schenectady, especially in the winter season. I don't know whether you know we reside at Schenectady. I was saying to Daisy that I certainly hadn't found any one like Dr. Davis, and I didn't believe I should. Oh, at Schenectady, he stands first; they think everything of him. He has so much to do, and yet there was nothing he wouldn't do for me. He said he never saw anything like my dyspepsia, but he was bound to cure it. I'm sure there was nothing he wouldn't try. He was just going to try something new when we came off. Mr. Miller wanted Daisy to see Europe for herself. But I wrote to Mr. Miller that it seems as if I couldn't get on without Dr. Davis. At Schenectady he stands at the very top; and there's a great deal of sickness there, too. It affects my sleep."

Winterbourne had a good deal of pathological gossip with Dr. Davis's patient, during which Daisy chattered unremittingly to her own companion. The young man asked Mrs. Miller how she was pleased with Rome. "Well, I must say I am disappointed," she answered. "We had heard so much about it; I suppose we had heard too much. But we couldn't help that. We had been led to expect something different."

"Ah, wait a little, and you will become very fond of it," said Winterbourne.

"I hate it worse and worse every day!" cried Randolph.

"You are like the infant Hannibal," [18] said Winterbourne.

"No, I ain't!" Randolph declared, at a venture.

"You are not much like an infant," said his mother. "But we have seen places," she resumed, "that I should put a long way before Rome." And in reply to Winterbourne's interrogation, "There's Zurich," she concluded; "I think Zurich is lovely; and we hadn't heard half so much about it."

"The best place we've seen is the City of Richmond!" said Randolph.

"He means the ship," his mother explained. "We crossed in that ship. Randolph had a good time on the City of Richmond."

"It's the best place I've seen," the child repeated. "Only it was turned the wrong way."

"Well, we've got to turn the right way some time," said Mrs. Miller, with a little laugh. Winterbourne expressed the hope that her daughter at least found some gratification in Rome, and she declared that Daisy was quite carried away. "It's on account of the society—the society's splendid. She goes round everywhere; she has

---

[18] Carthaginian general (247-183 B.C.), who as a child was dedicated by his father to unrelenting hatred of Rome.

made a great number of acquaintances. Of course she goes round more than I do. I must say they have been very sociable; they have taken her right in. And then she knows a great many gentlemen. Oh, she thinks there's nothing like Rome. Of course, it's a great deal pleasanter for a young lady if she knows plenty of gentlemen."

By this time Daisy had turned her attention again to Winterbourne. "I've been telling Mrs. Walker how mean you were!" the young girl announced.

"And what is the evidence you have offered?" asked Winterbourne, rather annoyed at Miss Miller's want of appreciation of the zeal of an admirer who on his way down to Rome had stopped neither at Bologna nor at Florence, simply because of a certain sentimental impatience. He remembered that a cynical compatriot had once told him that American women—the pretty ones, and this gave a largeness to the axiom—were at once the most exacting in the world and the least endowed with a sense of indebtedness.

"Why, you were awfully mean at Vevey," said Daisy. "You wouldn't do anything. You wouldn't stay there when I asked you."

"My dearest young lady," cried Winterbourne, with eloquence, "have I come all the way to Rome to encounter your reproaches?"

"Just hear him say that!" said Daisy to her hostess, giving a twist to a bow on this lady's dress. "Did you ever hear anything so quaint?"

"So quaint, my dear?" murmured Mrs. Walker, in the tone of a partisan of Winterbourne.

"Well, I don't know," said Daisy, fingering Mrs. Walker's ribbons. "Mrs. Walker, I want to tell you something."

"Mother-r," interposed Randolph, with his rough ends to his words, "I tell you you've got to go. Eugenio'll raise something!"

"I'm not afraid of Eugenio," said Daisy, with a toss of her head. "Look here, Mrs. Walker," she went on, "you know I'm coming to your party."

"I am delighted to hear it."

"I've got a lovely dress."

"I am very sure of that."

"But I want to ask a favour—permission to bring a friend."

"I shall be happy to see any of your friends," said Mrs. Walker, turning with a smile to Mrs. Miller.

"Oh, they are not my friends," answered Daisy's mamma, smiling shyly, in her own fashion. "I never spoke to them!"

"It's an intimate friend of mine—Mr. Giovanelli," said Daisy, without a tremor in her clear little voice or a shadow on her brilliant little face.

Mrs. Walker was silent a moment, she gave a rapid glance at

Winterbourne. "I shall be glad to see Mr. Giovanelli," she then said.

"He's an Italian," Daisy pursued, with the prettiest serenity. "He's a great friend of mine—he's the handsomest man in the world—except Mr. Winterbourne! He knows plenty of Italians, but he wants to know some Americans. He thinks ever so much of Americans. He's tremendously clever. He's perfectly lovely!"

It was settled that this brilliant personage should be brought to Mrs. Walker's party, and then Mrs. Miller prepared to take her leave. "I guess we'll go back to the hotel," she said.

"You may go back to the hotel, mother, but I'm going to take a walk," said Daisy.

"She's going to walk with Mr. Giovanelli," Randolph proclaimed.

"I am going to the Pincio," [19] said Daisy, smiling.

"Alone, my dear—at this hour?" Mrs. Walker asked. The afternoon was drawing to a close—it was the hour for the throng of carriages and of contemplative pedestrians. "I don't think it's safe, my dear," said Mrs. Walker.

"Neither do I," subjoined Mrs. Miller. "You'll get the fever as sure as you live. Remember what Dr. Davis told you!"

"Give her some medicine before she goes," said Randolph.

The company had risen to its feet; Daisy, still showing her pretty teeth, bent over and kissed her hostess. "Mrs. Walker, you are too perfect," she said. "I'm not going alone; I am going to meet a friend."

"Your friend won't keep you from getting the fever," Mrs. Miller observed.

"Is it Mr. Giovanelli?" asked the hostess.

Winterbourne was watching the young girl; at this question his attention quickened. She stood there smiling and smoothing her bonnet ribbons; she glanced at Winterbourne. Then, while she glanced and smiled, she answered without a shade of hesitation, "Mr. Giovanelli—the beautiful Giovanelli."

"My dear young friend," said Mrs. Walker, taking her hand, pleadingly, "don't walk off to the Pincio at this hour to meet a beautiful Italian."

"Well, he speaks English," said Mrs. Miller.

"Gracious me!" Daisy exclaimed, "I don't want to do anything improper. There's an easy way to settle it." She continued to glance at Winterbourne. "The Pincio is only a hundred yards distant, and if Mr. Winterbourne were as polite as he pretends he would offer to walk with me!"

Winterbourne's politeness hastened to affirm itself, and the young

---

[19] The name of a hill (Monte Pincio) and of a public garden in Rome.

girl gave him gracious leave to accompany her. They passed downstairs before her mother, and at the door Winterbourne perceived Mrs. Miller's carriage drawn up, with the ornamental courier whose acquaintance he had made at Vevey seated within. "Good-by, Eugenio!" cried Daisy, "I'm going to take a walk." The distance from the Via Gregoriana to the beautiful garden at the other end of the Pincian Hill is, in fact, rapidly traversed. As the day was splendid, however, and the concourse of vehicles, walkers, and loungers numerous, the young Americans found their progress much delayed. This fact was highly agreeable to Winterbourne, in spite of his consciousness of his singular situation. The slow-moving, idly-gazing Roman crowd bestowed much attention upon the extremely pretty young foreign lady who was passing through it upon his arm; and he wondered what on earth had been in Daisy's mind when she proposed to expose herself, unattended, to its appreciation. His own mission, to her sense, apparently, was to consign her to the hands of Mr. Giovanelli; but Winterbourne, at once annoyed and gratified, resolved that he would do no such thing.

"Why haven't you been to see me?" asked Daisy. "You can't get out of that."

"I have had the honour of telling you that I have only just stepped out of the train."

"You must have stayed in the train a good while after it stopped!" cried the young girl, with her little laugh. "I suppose you were asleep. You have had time to go to see Mrs. Walker."

"I knew Mrs. Walker—" Winterbourne began to explain.

"I knew where you knew her. You knew her at Geneva. She told me so. Well, you knew me at Vevey. That's just as good. So you ought to have come." She asked him no other question than this; she began to prattle about her own affairs. "We've got splendid rooms at the hotel; Eugenio says they're the best rooms in Rome. We are going to stay all winter—if we don't die of the fever; and I guess we'll stay then. It's a great deal nicer than I thought; I thought it would be fearfully quiet; I was sure it would be awfully poky. I was sure we should be going round all the time with one of those dreadful old men that explain about the pictures and things. But we only had about a week of that, and now I'm enjoying myself. I know ever so many people, and they are all so charming. The society's extremely select. There are all kinds—English, and Germans, and Italians. I think I like the English best. I like their style of conversation. But there are some lovely Americans. I never saw anything so hospitable. There's something or other every day. There's not much dancing; but I must say I never thought dancing was everything. I was always fond of conversation. I guess I shall have plenty at Mrs. Walker's —her rooms are so small." When they had passed the gate of the Pincian Gardens, Miss Miller began to wonder where Mr. Giovanelli might be. "We had better go straight to that place in front," she said, "where you look at the view."

"I certainly shall not help you to find him," Winterbourne declared.

"Then I shall find him without you," said Miss Daisy.

"You certainly won't leave me!" cried Winterbourne.

She burst into her little laugh. "Are you afraid you'll get lost—or run over? But there's Giovanelli, leaning against that tree. He's staring at the women in the carriages: did you ever see anything so cool?"

Winterbourne perceived at some distance a little man standing with folded arms, nursing his cane. He had a handsome face, an artfully poised hat, a glass in one eye and a nosegay in his buttonhole. Winterbourne looked at him a moment and then said, "Do you mean to speak to that man?"

"Do I mean to speak to him? Why, you don't suppose I mean to communicate by signs?"

"Pray understand, then," said Winterbourne, "that I intend to remain with you."

Daisy stopped and looked at him, without a sign of troubled consciousness in her face; with nothing but the presence of her charming eyes and her happy dimples. "Well, she's a cool one!" thought the young man.

"I don't like the way you say that," said Daisy. "It's too imperious."

"I beg your pardon if I say it wrong. The main point is to give you an idea of my meaning."

The young girl looked at him more gravely, but with eyes that were prettier than ever. "I have never allowed a gentleman to dictate to me, or to interfere with anything I do."

"I think you have made a mistake," said Winterbourne. "You should sometimes listen to a gentleman—the right one."

Daisy began to laugh again. "I do nothing but listen to gentlemen!" she exclaimed. "Tell me if Mr. Giovanelli is the right one?"

The gentleman with the nosegay in his bosom had now perceived our two friends, and was approaching the young girl with obsequious rapidity. He bowed to Winterbourne as well as to the latter's companion; he had a brilliant smile, an intelligent eye; Winterbourne thought him not a bad-looking fellow. But he nevertheless said to Daisy—"No, he's not the right one."

Daisy evidently had a natural talent for performing introductions; she mentioned the name of each of her companions to the other. She strolled along with one of them on each side of her; Mr. Giovanelli, who spoke English very cleverly—Winterbourne afterwards learned that he had practised the idiom upon a great many American heiresses—addressed her a great deal of very polite nonsense; he was extremely urbane, and the young American, who said nothing, reflected upon that profundity of Italian cleverness which enables people to appear more gracious in proportion as they are more acutely disappointed. Giovanelli, of course, had counted upon something more intimate; he had not bargained for a party of three. But he kept his temper in a manner which suggested far-stretching intentions. Winterbourne flattered himself that he had taken his measure. "He is not a gentleman," said the young American; "he is only a clever imitation of one. He is a music-master, or a penny-a-liner, or a third-rate artist. Damn his good looks!" Mr. Giovanelli had certainly a very pretty face; but Winterbourne felt a superior indignation at his own lovely fellow-countrywoman's not knowing the difference between a spurious gentleman and a real one. Giovanelli chattered and jested and made himself wonderfully agreeable. It was true that if he was an imitation the imitation was brilliant. "Nevertheless," Winterbourne said to himself, "a nice girl ought to know!" And then he came back to the question whether this was in fact a nice girl. Would a nice girl—even allowing for her being a little American flirt—make a rendezvous with a presumably low-lived foreigner? The rendezvous in this case, indeed, had been in broad daylight, and in the most crowded corner of Rome; but was it not impossible to regard the choice of these circumstances as a proof of extreme cynicism? Singular though it may seem, Winterbourne was vexed that the young girl, in joining her *amoroso*,[20] should not appear more impatient of his own company, and he was vexed because of his inclination. It was impossible to regard her as a perfectly well-conducted young lady; she was wanting in a certain indispensable delicacy. It would therefore simplify matters greatly to be able to treat her as the object of one of those sentiments which are called by romancers "lawless passions." That she should seem to wish to get rid of him would help him to think more lightly of her, and to be able to think more lightly of her would make her much less perplexing. But Daisy, on this occasion, continued to present herself as an inscrutable combination of audacity and innocence.

---

[20] Lover.

She had been walking some quarter of an hour, attended by her two cavaliers, and responding in a tone of very childish gaiety, as it seemed to Winterbourne, to the pretty speeches of Mr. Giovanelli, when a carriage that had detached itself from the revolving train drew up beside the path. At the same moment Winterbourne perceived that his friend Mrs. Walker—the lady whose house he had lately left—was seated in the vehicle and was beckoning to him. Leaving Miss Miller's side, he hastened to obey her summons. Mrs. Walker was flushed; she wore an excited air. "It is really too dreadful," she said. "That girl must not do this sort of thing. She must not walk here with you two men. Fifty people have noticed her."

Winterbourne raised his eyebrows. "I think it's a pity to make too much fuss about it."

"It's a pity to let the girl ruin herself!"

"She is very innocent," said Winterbourne.

"She's very crazy!" cried Mrs. Walker. "Did you ever see anything so imbecile as her mother? After you had all left me, just now, I could not sit still for thinking of it. It seemed too pitiful, not even to attempt to save her. I ordered the carriage and put on my bonnet, and came here as quickly as possible. Thank heaven, I have found you!"

"What do you propose to do with us?" asked Winterbourne, smiling.

"To ask her to get in, to drive her about here for half-an-hour, so that the world may see she is not running absolutely wild, and then to take her safely home."

"I don't think it's a very happy thought," said Winterbourne; "but you can try."

Mrs. Walker tried. The young man went in pursuit of Miss Miller, who had simply nodded and smiled at his interlocutor in the carriage, and had gone her way with her companion. Daisy, on learning that Mrs. Walker wished to speak to her, retraced her steps with a perfect good grace and with Mr. Giovanelli at her side. She declared that she was delighted to have a chance to present this gentleman to Mrs. Walker. She immediately achieved the introduction, and declared that she had never in her life seen anything so lovely as Mrs. Walker's carriage-rug.

"I am glad you admire it," said this lady, smiling sweetly. "Will you get in and let me put it over you?"

"Oh, no, thank you," said Daisy. "I shall admire it much more as I see you driving round with it."

"Do get in and drive with me," said Mrs. Walker.

"That would be charming, but it's so enchanting just as I am!"

and Daisy gave a brilliant glance at the gentlemen on either side of her.

"It may be enchanting, dear child, but it is not the custom here," urged Mrs. Walker, leaning forward in her victoria with her hands devoutly clasped.

"Well, it ought to be, then!" said Daisy. "If I didn't walk I should expire."

"You should walk with your mother, dear," cried the lady from Geneva, losing patience.

"With my mother dear!" exclaimed the young girl. Winterbourne saw that she scented interference. "My mother never walked ten steps in her life. And then, you know," she added with a laugh, "I am more than five years old."

"You are old enough to be more reasonable. You are old enough, dear Miss Miller, to be talked about."

Daisy looked at Mrs. Walker, smiling intensely. "Talked about? What do you mean?"

"Come into my carriage and I will tell you."

Daisy turned her quickened glance again from one of the gentlemen beside her to the other. Mr. Giovanelli was bowing to and fro, rubbing down his gloves and laughing very agreeably; Winterbourne thought it a most unpleasant scene. "I don't think I want to know what you mean," said Daisy presently. "I don't think I should like it."

Winterbourne wished that Mrs. Walker would tuck in her carriage-rug and drive away; but this lady did not enjoy being defied, as she afterwards told him. "Should you prefer being thought a very reckless girl?" she demanded.

"Gracious!" exclaimed Daisy. She looked again at Mr. Giovanelli, then she turned to Winterbourne. There was a little pink flush in her cheek; she was tremendously pretty. "Does Mr. Winterbourne think," she asked slowly, smiling, throwing back her head and glancing at him from head to foot, "that—to save my reputation—I ought to get into the carriage?"

Winterbourne coloured; for an instant he hesitated greatly. It seemed so strange to hear her speak that way of her "reputation." But he himself, in fact, must speak in accordance with gallantry. The finest gallantry, here, was simply to tell her the truth; and the truth, for Winterbourne, as the few indications I have been able to give have made him known to the reader, was that Daisy Miller should take Mrs. Walker's advice. He looked at her exquisite prettiness; and then he said very gently, "I think you should get into the carriage."

Daisy gave a violent laugh. "I never heard anything so stiff! If this is improper, Mrs. Walker," she pursued, "then I am all improper, and you must give me up. Good-by; I hope you'll have a lovely ride!" and, with Mr. Giovanelli, who made a triumphantly obsequious salute, she turned away.

Mrs. Walker sat looking after her, and there were tears in Mrs. Walker's eyes. "Get in here, sir," she said to Winterbourne, indicating the place beside her. The young man answered that he felt bound to accompany Miss Miller; whereupon Mrs. Walker declared that if he refused her this favour she would never speak to him again. She was evidently in earnest. Winterbourne overtook Daisy and her companion and, offering the young girl his hand, told her that Mrs. Walker had made an imperious claim upon his society. He expected that in answer she would say something rather free, something to commit herself still further to that "recklessness" from which Mrs. Walker had so charitably endeavoured to dissuade her. But she only shook his hand, hardly looking at him; while Mr. Giovanelli bade him farewell with a too-emphatic flourish of the hat.

Winterbourne was not in the best possible humour as he took his seat in Mrs. Walker's victoria. "That was not clever of you," he said candidly, while the vehicle mingled again with the throng of carriages.

"In such a case," his companion answered, "I don't wish to be clever, I wish to be *earnest!*"

"Well, your earnestness has only offended her and put her off."

"It has happened very well," said Mrs. Walker. "If she is so perfectly determined to compromise herself, the sooner one knows it the better; one can act accordingly."

"I suspect she meant no harm," Winterbourne rejoined.

"So I thought a month ago. But she has been going too far."

"What has she been doing?"

"Everything that is not done here. Flirting with any man she could pick up; sitting in corners with mysterious Italians; dancing all the evening with the same partners; receiving visits at eleven o'clock at night. Her mother goes away when visitors come."

"But her brother," said Winterbourne, laughing, "sits up till midnight."

"He must be edified by what he sees. I'm told that at their hotel every one is talking about her, and that a smile goes round among all the servants when a gentleman comes and asks for Miss Miller."

"The servants be hanged!" said Winterbourne angrily. "The poor girl's only fault," he presently added, "is that she is very uncultivated."

"She is naturally indelicate," Mrs. Walker declared. "Take that example this morning. How long had you known her at Vevey?"

"A couple of days."

"Fancy, then, her making it a personal matter that you should have left the place!"

Winterbourne was silent for some moments, then he said, "I suspect, Mrs. Walker, that you and I have lived too long at Geneva!" And he added a request that she should inform him with what particular design she had made him enter her carriage.

"I wish to beg you to cease your relations with Miss Miller—not to flirt with her—to give her no further opportunity to expose herself—to let her alone, in short."

"I'm afraid I can't do that," said Winterbourne. "I like her extremely."

"All the more reason that you shouldn't help her to make a scandal."

"There shall be nothing scandalous in my attentions to her."

"There certainly will be in the way she takes them. But I have said what I had on my conscience," Mrs. Walker pursued. "If you wish to rejoin the young lady I will put you down. Here, by-the-way, you have a chance."

The carriage was traversing that part of the Pincian Garden that overhangs the wall of Rome and overlooks the beautiful Villa Borghese. It is bordered by a large parapet, near which there are several seats. One of the seats, at a distance, was occupied by a gentleman and a lady, towards whom Mrs. Walker gave a toss of her head. At the same moment these persons rose and walked towards the parapet. Winterbourne had asked the coachman to stop; he now descended from the carriage. His companion looked at him a moment in silence; then, while he raised his hat, she drove majestically away. Winterbourne stood there; he had turned his eyes towards Daisy and her cavalier. They evidently saw no one; they were too deeply occupied with each other. When they reached the low garden-wall they stood a moment looking off at the great flat-topped pine-clusters of the Villa Borghese; then Giovanelli seated himself, familiarly, upon the broad ledge of the wall. The western sun in the opposite sky sent out a brilliant shaft through a couple of cloud-bars, whereupon Daisy's companion took her parasol out of her hands and opened it. She came a little nearer and he held the parasol over her; then, still holding it, he let it rest upon her shoulder, so that both of their heads were hidden from Winterbourne. This young man lingered a moment, then he began to walk. But he walked—not towards the couple with the parasol; towards the residence of his aunt, Mrs. Costello.

He flattered himself on the following day that there was no smiling among the servants when he, at least, asked for Mrs. Miller at her hotel. This lady and her daughter, however, were not at home; and on the next day after, repeating his visit, Winterbourne again had the misfortune not to find them. Mrs. Walker's party took place on the evening of the third day, and in spite of the frigidity of his last interview with the hostess Winterbourne was among the guests. Mrs. Walker was one of those American ladies who, while residing abroad, make a point, in their own phrase, of studying European society; and she had on this occasion collected several specimens of her diversely-born fellow-mortals to serve, as it were, as text-books. When Winterbourne arrived Daisy Miller was not there, but in a few moments he saw her mother come in alone, very shyly and ruefully. Mrs. Miller's hair above her exposed-looking temples was more frizzled than ever. As she approached Mrs. Walker, Winterbourne also drew near.

"You see I've come all alone," said poor Mrs. Miller. "I'm so frightened; I don't know what to do; it's the first time I've ever been to a party alone—especially in this country. I wanted to bring Randolph or Eugenio, or someone, but Daisy just pushed me off by myself. I ain't used to going round alone."

"And does not your daughter intend to favour us with her society?" demanded Mrs. Walker, impressively.

"Well, Daisy's all dressed," said Mrs. Miller, with that accent of the dispassionate, if not of the philosophic, historian with which she always recorded the current incidents of her daughter's career. "She got dressed on purpose before dinner. But she's got a friend of hers there; that gentleman—the Italian—that she wanted to bring. They've got going at the piano; it seems as if they couldn't leave off. Mr. Giovanelli sings splendidly. But I guess they'll come before very long," concluded Mrs. Miller hopefully.

"I'm sorry she should come—in that way," said Mrs. Walker.

"Well, I told her that there was no use in her getting dressed before dinner if she was going to wait three hours," responded Daisy's mamma. "I didn't see the use of her putting on such a dress as that to sit round with Mr. Giovanelli."

"This is most horrible!" said Mrs. Walker, turning away and addressing herself to Winterbourne. "*Elle s'affiche.*[21] It's her revenge for my having ventured to remonstrate with her. When she comes I shall not speak to her."

Daisy came after eleven o'clock, but she was not, on such an occasion, a young lady to wait to be spoken to. She rustled forward in radiant loveliness, smiling and chattering, carrying a large bouquet

[21] She's making a show of herself.

and attended by Mr. Giovanelli. Everyone stopped talking, and turned and looked at her. She came straight to Mrs. Walker. "I'm afraid you thought I never was coming, so I sent mother off to tell you. I wanted to make Mr. Giovanelli practise some things before he came; you know he sings beautifully, and I want you to ask him to sing. This is Mr. Giovanelli; you know I introduced him to you; he's got the most lovely voice and he knows the most charming set of songs. I made him go over them this evening, on purpose; we had the greatest time at the hotel." Of all this Daisy delivered herself with the sweetest, brightest audibleness, looking now at her hostess and now round the room, while she gave a series of little pats, round her shoulders, to the edges of her dress. "Is there anyone I know?" she asked.

"I think everyone knows you!" said Mrs. Walker pregnantly, and she gave a very cursory greeting to Mr. Giovanelli. This gentleman bore himself gallantly. He smiled and bowed and showed his white teeth, he curled his moustaches and rolled his eyes, and performed all the proper functions of a handsome Italian at an evening party. He sang, very prettily, half-a-dozen songs, though Mrs. Walker afterwards declared that she had been quite unable to find out who asked him. It was apparently not Daisy who had given him his orders. Daisy sat at a distance from the piano, and though she had publicly, as it were, professed a high admiration for his singing, talked, not inaudibly, while it was going on.

"It's a pity these rooms are so small; we can't dance," she said to Winterbourne as if she had seen him five minutes before.

"I am not sorry we can't dance," Winterbourne answered; "I don't dance."

"Of course you don't dance; you're too stiff," said Miss Daisy. "I hope you enjoyed your drive with Mrs. Walker."

"No, I didn't enjoy it; I preferred walking with you."

"We paired off, that was much better," said Daisy. "But did you ever hear anything so cool as Mrs. Walker's wanting me to get into her carriage and drop poor Mr. Giovanelli, and under the pretext that it was proper? People have different ideas! It would have been most unkind; he had been talking about that walk for ten days."

"He should not have talked about it at all," said Winterbourne; "he would never have proposed to a young lady of this country to walk about the streets with him."

"About the streets?" cried Daisy, with her pretty stare. "Where then would he have proposed to her to walk? The Pincio is not the streets, either; and I, thank goodness, am not a young lady of this country. The young ladies of this country have a dreadfully poky time of it, so far as I can learn; I don't see why I should change my habits for *them*."

"I am afraid your habits are those of a flirt," said Winterbourne gravely.

"Of course they are," she cried, giving him her little smiling stare again. "I'm a fearful, frightful flirt! Did you ever hear of a nice girl that was not? But I suppose you will tell me now that I am not a nice girl."

"You're a very nice girl, but I wish you would flirt with me and me only," said Winterbourne.

"Ah! thank you, thank you very much; you are the last man I should think of flirting with. As I have had the pleasure of informing you, you are too stiff."

"You say that too often," said Winterbourne.

Daisy gave a delighted laugh. "If I could have the sweet hope of making you angry, I should say it again."

"Don't do that; when I am angry I'm stiffer than ever. But if you won't flirt with me, do cease at least to flirt with your friend at the piano; they don't understand that sort of thing here."

"I thought they understood nothing else!" exclaimed Daisy.

"Not in young unmarried women."

"It seems to me much more proper in young unmarried women than in old married ones," Daisy declared.

"Well," said Winterbourne, "when you deal with natives you must go by the custom of the place. Flirting is a purely American custom; it doesn't exist here. So when you show yourself in public with Mr. Giovanelli and without your mother——"

"Gracious! poor mother!" interposed Daisy.

"Though you may be flirting, Mr. Giovanelli is not; he means something else."

"He isn't preaching, at any rate," said Daisy with vivacity. "And if you want very much to know, we are neither of us flirting; we are too good friends for that; we are very intimate friends."

"Ah!" rejoined Winterbourne, "if you are in love with each other it is another affair."

She had allowed him up to this point to talk so frankly that he had no expectation of shocking her by this ejaculation; but she immediately got up, blushing visibly, and leaving him to exclaim mentally that little American flirts were the queerest creatures in the world. "Mr. Giovanelli, at least," she said, giving her interlocutor a single glance, "never says such very disagreeable things to me."

Winterbourne was bewildered; he stood staring. Mr. Giovanelli had finished singing; he left the piano and came over to Daisy. "Won't you come into the other room and have some tea?" he asked, bending before her with his ornamental smile.

Daisy turned to Winterbourne, beginning to smile again. He was still more perplexed, for this inconsequent smile made nothing clear, though it seemed to prove, indeed, that she had a sweetness and softness that reverted instinctively to the pardon of offences. "It has never occurred to Mr. Winterbourne to offer me any tea," she said, with her little tormenting manner.

"I have offered you advice," Winterbourne rejoined.

"I prefer weak tea!" cried Daisy, and she went off with the brilliant Giovanelli. She sat with him in the adjoining room, in the embrasure of the window, for the rest of the evening. There was an interesting performance at the piano, but neither of these young people gave heed to it. When Daisy came to take leave of Mrs. Walker, this lady conscientiously repaired the weakness of which she had been guilty at the moment of the young girl's arrival. She turned her back straight upon Miss Miller and left her to depart with what grace she might. Winterbourne was standing near the door; he saw it all. Daisy turned very pale and looked at her mother, but Mrs. Miller was humbly unconscious of any violation of the usual social forms. She appeared, indeed, to have felt an incongruous impulse to draw attention to her own striking observance of them. "Good-night, Mrs. Walker," she said; "we've had a beautiful evening. You see if I let Daisy come to parties without me, I don't want her to go away without me." Daisy turned away, looking with a pale, grave face at the circle near the door; Winterbourne saw that, for the first moment, she was too much shocked and puzzled even for indignation. He on his side was greatly touched.

"That was very cruel," he said to Mrs. Walker.

"She never enters my drawing-room again," replied his hostess.

Since Winterbourne was not to meet her in Mrs. Walker's drawing-room, he went as often as possible to Mrs. Miller's hotel. The ladies were rarely at home, but when he found them the devoted Giovanelli was always present. Very often the brilliant little Roman was in the drawing-room with Daisy alone, Mrs. Miller being apparently constantly of the opinion that discretion is the better part of surveillance. Winterbourne noted, at first with surprise, that Daisy on these occasions was never embarrassed or annoyed by his own entrance; but he very presently began to feel that she had no more surprises for him; the unexpected in her behaviour was the only thing to expect. She showed no displeasure at her *tête-à-tête* with Giovanelli being interrupted; she could chatter as freshly and freely with two gentlemen as with one; there was always, in her conversation, the same odd mixture of audacity and puerility. Winterbourne remarked to himself that if she was seriously interested in Giovanelli it was very singular that she should not take more trouble to preserve the sanctity of their interviews, and he liked her the more for her innocent-looking indifference and her apparently inexhaustible good humour. He could hardly have said why, but she seemed to him a girl who would never be jealous. At the risk of exciting a somewhat derisive smile on the reader's part, I may affirm that with regard to the women who had hitherto interested him, it very often seemed to Winterbourne among the possibilities that, given certain contingencies, he should be afraid—literally afraid—of these ladies; he had a pleasant sense that he should never be afraid of Daisy Miller. It must be added that this sentiment was not altogether flattering to Daisy; it was part of his conviction, or rather of his apprehension, that she would prove a very light young person.

But she was evidently very much interested in Giovanelli. She looked at him whenever he spoke; she was perpetually telling him to do this and to do that; she was constantly "chaffing" and abusing him. She appeared completely to have forgotten that Winterbourne had said anything to displease her at Mrs. Walker's little party. One Sunday afternoon, having gone to St. Peter's with his aunt, Winterbourne perceived Daisy strolling about the great church in company with the inevitable Giovanelli. Presently he pointed out the young girl and her cavalier to Mrs. Costello. This lady looked at them a moment through her eyeglass, and then she said:

"That's what makes you so pensive in these days, eh?"

"I had not the least idea I was pensive," said the young man.

"You are very much pre-occupied; you are thinking of something."

"And what is it," he asked, "that you accuse me of thinking of?"

"Of that young lady's—Miss Baker's, Miss Chandler's—what's her name? Miss Miller's intrigue with that little barber's block."

"Do you call it an intrigue," Winterbourne asked—"an affair that goes on with such peculiar publicity?"

"That's their folly," said Mrs. Costello, "it's not their merit."

"No," rejoined Winterbourne, with something of that pensiveness to which his aunt had alluded. "I don't believe that there is anything to be called an intrigue."

"I have heard a dozen people speak of it; they say she is quite carried away by him."

"They are certainly very intimate," said Winterbourne.

Mrs. Costello inspected the young couple again with her optical instrument. "He is very handsome. One easily sees how it is. She thinks him the most elegant man in the world, the finest gentleman. She has never seen anything like him; he is better even than the courier. It was the courier probably who introduced him, and if he succeeds in marrying the young lady, the courier will come in for a magnificent commission."

"I don't believe she thinks of marrying him," said Winterbourne, "and I don't believe he hopes to marry her."

"You may be very sure she thinks of nothing. She goes on from day to day, from hour to hour, as they did in the Golden Age. I can imagine nothing more vulgar. And at the same time," added Mrs. Costello, "depend upon it that she may tell you any moment that she is 'engaged.' "

"I think that is more than Giovanelli expects," said Winterbourne.

"Who is Giovanelli?"

"The little Italian. I have asked questions about him and learned something. He is apparently a perfectly respectable little man. I believe he is in a small way, a *cavaliere avvocato*.[22] But he doesn't move in what are called the first circles. I think it is really not absolutely impossible that the courier introduced him. He is evidently immensely charmed with Miss Miller. If she thinks him the finest gentleman in the world, he, on his side, has never found himself in personal contact with such splendor, such opulence, such expensiveness, as this young lady's. And then she must seem to him wonderfully pretty and interesting. I rather doubt that he dreams of marrying her. That must appear to him too impossible a piece of luck. He has nothing but his handsome face to offer, and there is a substantial Mr. Miller in that mysterious land of dollars. Giovanelli knows that he hasn't a title to offer. If he were only a count or a *marchese!* [23] He must wonder at his luck at the way they have taken him up."

"He accounts for it by his handsome face, and thinks Miss Miller a young lady *qui se passe ses fantaisies!*" [24] said Mrs. Costello.

"It is very true," Winterbourne pursued, "that Daisy and her mamma have not yet risen to that stage of—what shall I call it?—of culture, at which the idea of catching a count or a *marchese* begins. I believe that they are intellectually incapable of that conception."

---

[22] Lawyer.

[23] In Italy, a noble above a count but below a prince in rank.

[24] Who is indulging her whims.

"Ah! but the *avvocato* can't believe it," said Mrs. Costello.

Of the observation excited by Daisy's "intrigue," Winterbourne gathered that day at St. Peter's[25] sufficient evidence. A dozen of the American colonists in Rome came to talk with Mrs. Costello, who sat on a little portable stool at the base of one of the great pilasters. The vesper service was going forward in splendid chants and organ-tones in the adjacent choir, and meanwhile, between Mrs. Costello and her friends, there was a great deal said about poor little Miss Miller's going really "too far." Winterbourne was not pleased with what he heard; but when, coming out upon the great steps of the church, he saw Daisy, who had emerged before him, get into an open cab with her accomplice and roll away through the cynical streets of Rome, he could not deny to himself that she was going very far indeed. He felt very sorry for her—not exactly that he believed that she had completely lost her head, but because it was painful to hear so much that was pretty, and undefended, and natural, assigned to a vulgar place among the categories of disorder. He made an attempt after this to give a hint to Mrs. Miller. He met one day in the Corso a friend—a tourist like himself—who had just come out of the Doria Palace,[26] where he had been walking through the beautiful gallery. His friend talked for a moment about the superb portrait of Innocent X, by Velasquez,[27] which hangs in one of the cabinets of the palace, and then said, "And in the same cabinet, by-the-way, I had the pleasure of contemplating a picture of a different kind—that pretty American girl whom you pointed out to me last week." In answer to Winterbourne's inquiries, his friend narrated that the pretty American girl—prettier than ever—was seated with a companion in the secluded nook in which the great papal portrait was enshrined.

"Who was her companion?" asked Winterbourne.

"A little Italian with a bouquet in his button-hole. The girl is delightfully pretty, but I thought I understood from you the other day that she was a young lady *du meilleur monde*." [28]

"So she is!" answered Winterbourne; and having assured himself that his informant had seen Daisy and her companion but five minutes before, he jumped into a cab and went to call on Mrs. Miller. She was at home; but she apologised to him for receiving him in Daisy's absence.

---

[25] The patriarchal basilica of St. Peter, designed by Michelangelo, which adjoins the Vatican palace.

[26] An imposing Roman structure built in the seventeenth century and containing a valuable collection of paintings.

[27] Diego Rodriguez de Silva y Velásquez (1599-1660), Spanish painter.

[28] Of the best society.

"She's gone out somewhere with Mr. Giovanelli," said Mrs. Miller. "She's always going round with Mr. Giovanelli."

"I have noticed that they are very intimate," Winterbourne observed.

"Oh! it seems as if they couldn't live without each other!" said Mrs. Miller. "Well, he's a real gentleman anyhow. I keep telling Daisy she's engaged!"

"And what does Daisy say?"

"Oh, she says she isn't engaged. But she might as well be!" this impartial parent resumed. "She goes on as if she was. But I've made Mr. Giovanelli promise to tell me, if *she* doesn't. I should want to write to Mr. Miller about it—shouldn't you?"

Winterbourne replied that he certainly should; and the state of mind of Daisy's mamma struck him as so unprecedented in the annals of parental vigilance that he gave up as utterly irrelevant the attempt to place her upon her guard.

After this Daisy was never at home, and Winterbourne ceased to meet her at the houses of their common acquaintance, because, as he perceived, these shrewd people had quite made up their minds that she was going too far. They ceased to invite her, and they intimated that they desired to express to observant Europeans the great truth that, though Miss Daisy Miller was a young American lady, her behaviour was not representative—was regarded by her compatriots as abnormal. Winterbourne wondered how she felt about all the cold shoulders that were turned towards her, and sometimes it annoyed him to suspect that she did not feel at all. He said to himself that she was too light and childish, too uncultivated and unreasoning, too provincial, to have reflected upon her ostracism or even to have perceived it. Then at other moments he believed that she carried about in her elegant and irresponsible little organism a defiant, passionate, perfectly observant consciousness of the impression she produced. He asked himself whether Daisy's defiance came from the consciousness of innocence or from her being, essentially, a young person of the reckless class. It must be admitted that holding oneself to a belief in Daisy's "innocence" came to seem to Winterbourne more and more a matter of fine-spun gallantry. As I have already had occasion to relate, he was angry at finding himself reduced to chopping logic about this young lady; he was vexed at his want of instinctive certitude as to how far her eccentricities were generic, national, and how far they were personal. From either view of them he had somehow missed her, and now it was too late. She was "carried away" by Mr. Giovanelli.

A few days after his brief interview with her mother, he encountered her in that beautiful abode of flowering desolation known as the Palace of the Cæsars. The early Roman spring had filled the air with bloom and perfume, and the rugged surface of the Palatine[29] was muffled with tender verdure. Daisy was strolling along the top of one of those great mounds of ruin that are embanked with mossy marble and paved with monumental inscriptions. It seemed to him that Rome had never been so lovely as just then. He stood looking off at the enchanting harmony of line and colour that remotely encircles the city, inhaling the softly humid odours and feeling the freshness of the year and the antiquity of the place reaffirm themselves in mysterious interfusion. It seemed to him also that Daisy had never looked so pretty; but this had been an observation of his whenever he met her. Giovanelli was at her side, and Giovanelli, too, wore an aspect of even unwonted brilliancy.

"Well," said Daisy, "I should think you would be lonesome!"

"Lonesome?" asked Winterbourne.

"You are always going round by yourself. Can't you get anyone to walk with you?"

"I am not so fortunate," said Winterbourne, "as your companion."

Giovanelli, from the first, had treated Winterbourne with distinguished politeness; he listened with a deferential air to his remarks; he laughed, punctiliously, at his pleasantries; he seemed disposed to testify to his belief that Winterbourne was a superior young man. He carried himself in no degree like a jealous wooer; he had obviously a great deal of tact; he had no objection to your expecting a little humility of him. It even seemed to Winterbourne at times that Giovanelli would find a certain mental relief in being able to have a private understanding with him—to say to him, as an intelligent man, that, bless you, *he* knew how extraordinary was this young lady, and didn't flatter himself with delusive—or at least *too* delusive—hopes of matrimony and dollars. On this occasion he strolled away from his companion to pluck a sprig of almond-blossom, which he carefully arranged in his button-hole.

"I know why you say that," said Daisy, watching Giovanelli. "Because you think I go round too much with *him!*" And she nodded at her attendant.

"Every one thinks so—if you care to know," said Winterbourne.

"Of course I care to know!" Daisy exclaimed seriously. "But I don't believe it. They are only pretending to be shocked. They don't really care a straw what I do. Besides, I don't go round so much."

"I think you will find they do care. They will show it—disagreeably."

[29] One of the Seven Hills of Rome.

Daisy looked at him a moment. "How—disagreeably?"

"Haven't you noticed anything?" Winterbourne asked.

"I have noticed you. But I noticed you were as stiff as an umbrella the first time I saw you."

"You will find I am not so stiff as several others," said Winterbourne, smiling.

"How shall I find it?"

"By going to see the others."

"What will they do to me?"

"They will give you the cold shoulder. Do you know what that means?"

Daisy was looking at him intently; she began to colour. "Do you mean as Mrs. Walker did the other night?"

"Exactly!" said Winterbourne.

She looked away at Giovanelli, who was decorating himself with his almond-blossom. Then looking back at Winterbourne—"I shouldn't think you would let people be so unkind!" she said.

"How can I help it?" he asked.

"I should think you would say something."

"I do say something;" and he paused a moment. "I say that your mother tells me that she believes you are engaged."

"Well, she does," said Diasy very simply.

Winterbourne began to laugh. "And does Randolph believe it?" he asked.

"I guess Randolph doesn't believe anything," said Daisy. Randolph's scepticism excited Winterbourne to further hilarity, and he observed that Giovanelli was coming back to them. Daisy, observing it too, addressed herself again to her countryman. "Since you have mentioned it," she said, "I *am* engaged." . . . Winterbourne looked at her; he had stopped laughing. "You don't believe it!" she added.

He was silent a moment; and then, "Yes, I believe it!" he said.

"Oh, no, you don't," she answered. "Well, then—I am not!"

The young girl and her cicerone were on their way to the gate of the enclosure, so that Winterbourne, who had but lately entered, presently took leave of them. A week afterwards he went to dine at a beautiful villa on the Cælian Hill, and, on arriving, dismissed his hired vehicle. The evening was charming, and he promised himself the satisfaction of walking home beneath the Arch of Constantine[30] and past the vaguely-lighted monuments of the Forum. There was a waning moon in the sky, and her radiance was not brilliant, but she was veiled in a thin cloud-curtain which seemed to diffuse and

---

[30] A memorial arch near the Colosseum built by the Emperor Constantine in 311 to celebrate his victory over Maxentius.

equalise it. When, on his return from the villa (it was eleven o'clock), Winterbourne approached the dusky circle of the Colosseum, it recurred to him, as a lover of the picturesque, that the interior, in the pale moonshine, would be well worth a glance. He turned aside and walked to one of the empty arches, near which, as he observed, an open carriage—one of the little Roman street-cabs—was stationed. Then he passed in, among the cavernous shadows of the great structure, and emerged upon the clear and silent arena. The place had never seemed to him more impressive. One-half of the gigantic circus was in deep shade; the other was sleeping in the luminous dusk. As he stood there he began to murmur Byron's famous lines, out of "Manfred;" [31] but before he had finished his quotation he remembered that if nocturnal meditations in the Colosseum are recommended by the poets, they are deprecated by the doctors. The historic atmosphere was there, certainly; but the historic atmosphere, scientifically considered, was no better than a villainous miasma. Winterbourne walked to the middle of the arena, to take a more general glance, intending thereafter to make a hasty retreat. The great cross in the centre was covered with shadow; it was only as he drew near it that he made it out distinctly. Then he saw that two persons were stationed upon the low steps which formed its base. One of these was a woman, seated; her companion was standing in front of her.

Presently the sound of the woman's voice came to him distinctly in the warm night-air. "Well, he looks at us as one of the old lions or tigers may have looked at the Christian martyrs!" These were the words he heard, in the familiar accent of Miss Daisy Miller.

"Let us hope he is not very hungry," responded the ingenious Giovanelli. "He will have to take me first; you will serve for dessert!"

Winterbourne stopped, with a sort of horror; and, it must be added, with a sort of relief. It was as if a sudden illumination had been flashed upon the ambiguity of Daisy's behaviour and the riddle had become easy to read. She was a young lady whom a gentleman need no longer be at pains to respect. He stood there looking at her —looking at her companion, and not reflecting that though he saw them vaguely, he himself must have been more brightly visible. He felt angry with himself that he had bothered so much about the right way of regarding Miss Daisy Miller. Then, as he was going to advance again, he checked himself; not from the fear that he was doing her injustice, but from a sense of the danger of appearing unbecomingly exhilarated by this sudden revulsion from cautious

[31] Act III, Scene iv.

criticism. He turned away towards the entrance of the place; but as he did so he heard Daisy speak again.

"Why, it was Mr. Winterbourne! He saw me—and he cuts me!"

What a clever little reprobate she was, and how smartly she played at injured innocence! But he wouldn't cut her. Winterbourne came forward again, and went towards the great cross. Daisy had got up; Giovanelli lifted his hat. Winterbourne had now begun to think simply of the craziness, from a sanitary point of view, of a delicate young girl lounging away the evening in this nest of malaria. What if she *were* a clever little reprobate? that was no reason for her dying of the *perniciosa*.[32] "How long have you been here?" he asked, almost brutally.

Daisy, lovely in the flattering moonlight, looked at him a moment. Then—"All the evening," she answered gently. . . . "I never saw anything so pretty."

"I am afraid," said Winterbourne, "that you will not think Roman fever very pretty. This is the way people catch it. I wonder," he added, turning to Giovanelli, "that you, a native Roman, should countenance such a terrible indiscretion."

"Ah," said the handsome native, "for myself, I am not afraid."

"Neither am I—for you! I am speaking for this young lady."

Giovanelli lifted his well-shaped eyebrows and showed his brilliant teeth. But he took Winterbourne's rebuke with docility. "I told the Signorina it was a grave indiscretion; but when was the Signorina ever prudent?"

"I never was sick, and I don't mean to be!" the Signorina declared. "I don't look like much, but I'm healthy! I was bound to see the Colosseum by moonlight; I shouldn't have wanted to go home without that; and we have had the most beautiful time, haven't we, Mr. Giovanelli? If there has been any danger, Eugenio can give me some pills. He has got some splendid pills."

"I should advise you," said Winterbourne, "to drive home as fast as possible and take one!"

"What you say is very wise," Giovanelli rejoined. "I will go and make sure the carriage is at hand." And he went forward rapidly.

Daisy followed with Winterbourne. He kept looking at her; she seemed not in the least embarrassed. Winterbourne said nothing; Daisy chattered about the beauty of the place. "Well, I *have* seen the Colosseum by moonlight!" she exclaimed. "That's one good thing." Then, noticing Winterbourne's silence, she asked him why he didn't speak. He made no answer; he only began to laugh. They

[32] A malignant fever, i.e., malaria.

passed under one of the dark archways; Giovanelli was in front with the carriage. Here Daisy stopped a moment, looking at the young American. "*Did* you believe I was engaged the other day?" she asked.

"It doesn't matter what I believed the other day," said Winterbourne, still laughing.

"Well, what do you believe now?"

"I believe that it makes very little difference whether you are engaged or not!"

He felt the young girl's pretty eyes fixed upon him through the thick gloom of the archway; she was apparently going to answer. But Giovanelli hurried her forward. "Quick, quick," he said; "if we get in by midnight we are quite safe."

Daisy took her seat in the carriage, and the fortunate Italian placed himself beside her. "Don't forget Eugenio's pills!" said Winterbourne, as he lifted his hat.

"I don't care," said Daisy, in a little strange tone, "whether I have Roman fever or not!" Upon this the cab-driver cracked his whip, and they rolled away over the desultory patches of the antique pavement.

Winterbourne—to do him justice, as it were—mentioned to no one that he had encountered Miss Miller, at midnight, in the Colosseum with a gentleman; but nevertheless, a couple of days later, the fact of her having been there under these circumstances was known to every member of the little American circle, and commented accordingly. Winterbourne reflected that they had of course known it at the hotel, and that, after Daisy's return, there had been an exchange of remarks between the porter and the cab-driver. But the young man was conscious at the same moment that it had ceased to be a matter of serious regret to him that the little American flirt should be "talked about" by low-minded menials. These people, a day or two later, had serious information to give: the little American flirt was alarmingly ill. Winterbourne, when the rumour came to him, immediately went to the hotel for more news. He found that two or three charitable friends had preceded him, and that they were being entertained in Mrs. Miller's salon by Randolph.

"It's going round at night," said Randolph—"that's what made her sick. She's always going round at night. I shouldn't think she'd want to—it's so plaguey dark. You can't see anything here at night, except when there's a moon. In America there's always a moon!" Mrs. Miller was invisible; she was now, at least, giving her daughter the advantage of her society. It was evident that Daisy was dangerously ill.

Winterbourne went often to ask for news of her, and once he saw Mrs. Miller, who, though deeply alarmed, was—rather to his surprise—perfectly composed, and, as it appeared, a most efficient and judicious nurse. She talked a good deal about Dr. Davis, but Winterbourne paid her the compliment of saying to himself that she was not, after all, such a monstrous goose. "Daisy spoke of you the other day," she said to him. "Half the time she doesn't know what she's saying, but that time I think she did. She gave me a message; she told me to tell you. She told me to tell you that she never was engaged to that handsome Italian. I am sure I am very glad; Mr. Giovanelli hasn't been near us since she was taken ill. I thought he was so much of a gentleman; but I don't call that very polite! A lady told me that he was afraid I was angry with him for taking Daisy round at night. Well, so I am; but I suppose he knows I'm a lady. I would scorn to scold him. Any way, she says she's not engaged. I don't know why she wanted you to know; but she said to me three times—'Mind you tell Mr. Winterbourne.' And then she told me to ask if you remembered the time you went to that castle, in Switzerland. But I said I wouldn't give any such messages as that. Only, if she is not engaged, I'm sure I'm glad to know it."

But, as Winterbourne had said, it mattered very little. A week after this the poor girl died; it had been a terrible case of the fever. Daisy's grave was in the little Protestant cemetery, in an angle of the wall of imperial Rome, beneath the cypresses and the thick springflowers. Winterbourne stood there beside it, with a number of other mourners; a number larger than the scandal excited by the young lady's career would have led you to expect. Near him stood Giovanelli, who came nearer still before Winterbourne turned away. Giovanelli was very pale; on this occasion he had no flower in his button-hole; he seemed to wish to say something. At last he said, "She was the most beautiful young lady I every saw, and the most amiable." And then he added in a moment, "And she was the most innocent."

Winterbourne looked at him, and presently repeated his words, "And the most innocent?"

"The most innocent!"

Winterbourne felt sore and angry. "Why the devil," he asked, "did you take her to that fatal place?"

Mr. Giovanelli's urbanity was apparently imperturbable. He looked on the ground a moment, and then he said, "For myself, I had no fear; and she wanted to go."

"That was no reason!" Winterbourne declared.

The subtle Roman again dropped his eyes. "If she had lived, I should have got nothing. She would never have married me, I am sure."

"She would never have married you?"

"For a moment I hoped so. But no. I am sure."

Winterbourne listened to him; he stood staring at the raw protuberance among the April daisies. When he turned away again Mr. Giovanelli, with his light slow step, had retired.

Winterbourne almost immediately left Rome; but the following summer he again met his aunt, Mrs. Costello, at Vevey. Mrs. Costello was fond of Vevey. In the interval Winterbourne had often thought of Daisy Miller and her mystifying manners. One day he spoke of her to his aunt—said it was on his conscience that he had done her injustice.

"I am sure I don't know," said Mrs. Costello. "How did your injustice affect her?"

"She sent me a message before her death which I didn't understand at the time. But I have understood it since. She would have appreciated one's esteem."

"Is that a modest way," asked Mrs. Costello, "of saying that she would have reciprocated one's affection?"

Winterbourne offered no answer to this question; but he presently said, "You were right in that remark that you made last summer. I was booked to make a mistake. I have lived too long in foreign parts."

Nevertheless, he went back to live at Geneva, whence there continue to come the most contradictory accounts of his motives of sojourn: a report that he is "studying" hard—an intimation that he is much interested in a very clever foreign lady.

Billy Budd, Sailor

(An Inside Narrative)

HERMAN MELVILLE

Billy Budd is the story of three men, a homicide, and a hanging, but it is this and much more. In Melville's work the principal characters are given a symbolic dimension, and we have here the epic confrontation of innocence and evil in the guileless Billy's encounter with the "natural depravity" of the master-at-arms, Claggart. Since its posthumous publication in 1924, *Billy Budd* has received a phenomenal amount of critical attention, and it has been called everything from Melville's "testament of acceptance" to his "testament of resistance." This diversity of opinion need not necessarily be alarming, for it attests not only to the popularity of the work but to the stimulating nature of its enigmatic meaning as well.

Upon his retirement in 1885 from his job as a customs inspector in New York City, Herman Melville took up his unfinished literary work. From 1885 to his death in 1891, he developed his tale of the luckless seaman, Billy Budd, leaving a manuscript that had been revised many times and containing numerous variant readings. The text of *Billy Budd* chosen for this book is that of Harrison Hayford and Merton M. Sealts, Jr., who, after consulting Melville's original manuscript, have attempted to determine as accurately as possible the author's final artistic intention.

Dedicated to Jack Chase, ENGLISHMAN
Wherever that great heart may now be
Here on Earth or harbored in Paradise
Captain of the Maintop in the year 1843
in the U.S. Frigate, *United States*

1

In the time before steamships, or then more frequently than now, a stroller along the docks of any considerable seaport would occasionally have his attention arrested by a group of bronzed mariners, man-of-war's men or merchant sailors in holiday attire, ashore on liberty. In certain instances they would flank, or like a bodyguard quite surround, some superior figure of their own class, moving along with them like Aldebaran[1] among the lesser lights of his constellation. That signal object was the "Handsome Sailor" of the less prosaic time alike of the military and merchant navies. With no perceptible trace of the vainglorious about him, rather with the offhand unaffectedness of natural regality, he seemed to accept the spontaneous homage of his shipmates.

A somewhat remarkable instance recurs to me. In Liverpool, now half a century ago, I saw under the shadow of the great dingy street-wall of Prince's Dock (an obstruction long since removed) a common sailor so intensely black that he must needs have been a native African of the unadulterate blood of Ham[2]—a symmetric figure much above the average height. The two ends of a gay silk handkerchief thrown loose about the neck danced upon the displayed ebony of his chest, in his ears were big hoops of gold, and a Highland bonnet with a tartan band set off his shapely head. It was a hot noon in July; and his face, lustrous with perspiration, beamed with barbaric good humor. In jovial sallies right and left, his white teeth flashing into view, he rollicked along, the center of a company of his shipmates. These were made up of such an assortment of tribes and complexions as would have well fitted them to be marched up by Anacharsis Cloots[3] before the bar of the first French Assembly as Representatives of the Human Race. At each spontaneous tribute rendered by the wayfarers to this black pagod of a fellow—the tribute of a pause and stare, and less frequently an exclamation—the motley retinue showed that they took that sort of pride in the evoker of it which the Assyrian priests doubtless showed for their grand sculptured Bull when the faithful prostrated themselves.

To return. If in some cases a bit of a nautical Murat[4] in setting

---

[1] The brightest star in the Hyades.

[2] The second son of Noah from whom the peoples of Africa were said to have descended.

[3] The Baron de Clootz (1755-1794), a Prussian, who migrated to Paris and adopted both the name "Anacharsis" and revolutionary views.

[4] Joachim Murat who became Marshal of France in 1804.

forth his person ashore, the Handsome Sailor of the period in question evinced nothing of the dandified Billy-be-Dam, an amusing character all but extinct now, but occasionally to be encountered, and in a form yet more amusing than the original, at the tiller of the boats on the tempestuous Erie Canal or, more likely, vaporing in the groggeries along the towpath. Invariably a proficient in his perilous calling, he was also more or less of a mighty boxer or wrestler. It was strength and beauty. Tales of his prowess were recited. Ashore he was the champion; afloat the spokesman; on every suitable occasion always foremost. Close-reefing topsails in a gale, there he was, astride the weather yardarm-end, foot in the Flemish horse[5] as stirrup, both hands tugging at the earing as at a bridle, in very much the attitude of young Alexander curbing the fiery Bucephalus.[6] A superb figure, tossed up as by the horns of Taurus against the thunderous sky, cheerily hallooing to the strenuous file along the spar.

The moral nature was seldom out of keeping with the physical make. Indeed, except as toned by the former, the comeliness and power, always attractive in masculine conjunction, hardly could have drawn the sort of honest homage the Handsome Sailor in some examples received from his less gifted asssociates.

Such a cynosure, at least in aspect, and something such too in nature, though with important variations made apparent as the story proceeds, was welkin-eyed Billy Budd—or Baby Budd, as more familiarly, under circumstances hereafter to be given, he at last came to be called—aged twenty-one, a foretopman of the British fleet toward the close of the last decade of the eighteenth century. It was not very long prior to the time of the narration that follows that he had entered the King's service, having been impressed on the Narrow Seas[7] from a homeward-bound English merchantman into a seventy-four[8] outward bound, H.M.S. *Bellipotent*; which ship, as was not unusual in those hurried days, having been obliged to put to sea short of her proper complement of men. Plump upon Billy at first sight in the gangway the boarding officer, Lieutenant Ratcliffe, pounced, even before the merchantman's crew was formally mustered on the quarter-deck for his deliberate inspection. And him only he elected. For whether it was because the other men when ranged before him showed to ill advantage after Billy, or whether he had some scruples in view of the merchantman's being rather

---

[5] A short footrope at the outer end of a yard.
[6] The war horse of Alexander the Great.
[7] The straits of the sea between England and France.
[8] A warship rated as carrying seventy-four guns.

short-handed, however it might be, the officer contented himself with his first spontaneous choice. To the surprise of the ship's company, though much to the lieutenant's satisfaction, Billy made no demur. But, indeed, any demur would have been as idle as the protest of a goldfinch popped into a cage.

Noting this uncomplaining acquiescence, all but cheerful, one might say, the shipmaster turned a surprised glance of silent reproach at the sailor. The shipmaster was one of those worthy mortals found in every vocation, even the humbler ones—the sort of person whom everybody agrees in calling "a respectable man." And —nor so strange to report as it may appear to be—though a ploughman of the troubled waters, lifelong contending with the intractable elements, there was nothing this honest soul at heart loved better than simple peace and quiet. For the rest, he was fifty or thereabouts, a little inclined to corpulence, a prepossessing face, unwhiskered, and of an agreeable color—a rather full face, humanely intelligent in expression. On a fair day with a fair wind and all going well, a certain musical chime in his voice seemed to be the veritable unobstructed outcome of the innermost man. He had much prudence, much conscientiousness, and there were occasions when these virtues were the cause of overmuch disquietude in him. On a passage, so long as his craft was in any proximity to land, no sleep for Captain Graveling. He took to heart those serious responsibilities not so heavily borne by some shipmasters.

Now while Billy Budd was down in the forecastle getting his kit together, the *Bellipotent*'s lieutenant, burly and bluff, nowise disconcerted by Captain Graveling's omitting to proffer the customary hospitalities on an occasion so unwelcome to him, an omission simply caused by preoccupation of thought, unceremoniously invited himself into the cabin, and also to a flask from the spirit locker, a receptacle which his experienced eye instantly discovered. In fact he was one of those sea dogs in whom all the hardship and peril of naval life in the great prolonged wars of his time never impaired the natural instinct for sensuous enjoyment. His duty he always faithfully did; but duty is sometimes a dry obligation, and he was for irrigating its aridity, whensoever possible, with a fertilizing decoction of strong waters. For the cabin's proprietor there was nothing left but to play the part of the enforced host with whatever grace and alacrity were practicable. As necessary adjuncts to the flask, he silently placed tumbler and water jug before the irrepressible guest. But excusing himself from partaking just then, he dismally watched the unembarrassed officer deliberately diluting his grog a little, then tossing it off in three swallows, pushing the empty tumbler away, yet not so far as to be beyond easy reach, at the same time settling himself in his seat and smacking his lips with high satisfaction, looking straight at the host.

These proceedings over, the master broke the silence; and there lurked a rueful reproach in the tone of his voice: "Lieutenant, you are going to take my best man from me, the jewel of 'em."

"Yes, I know," rejoined the other, immediately drawing back the tumbler preliminary to a replenishing. "Yes, I know. Sorry."

"Beg pardon, but you don't understand, Lieutenant. See here, now. Before I shipped that young fellow, my forecastle was a rat-pit of quarrels. It was black times, I tell you, aboard the *Rights* here. I was worried to that degree my pipe had no comfort for me. But Billy came; and it was like a Catholic priest striking peace in an Irish shindy. Not that he preached to them or said or did anything in particular; but a virtue went out of him, sugaring the sour ones. They took to him like hornets to treacle; all but the buffer of the gang, the big shaggy chap with the fire-red whiskers. He indeed, out of envy, perhaps, of the newcomer, and thinking such a "sweet and pleasant fellow," as he mockingly designated him to the others, could hardly have the spirit of a gamecock, must needs bestir himself in trying to get up an ugly row with him. Billy forebore with him and reasoned with him in a pleasant way—he is something like myself, Lieutenant, to whom aught like a quarrel is hateful—but nothing served. So, in the second dogwatch one day, the Red Whiskers in presence of the others, under pretense of showing Billy just whence a sirloin steak was cut—for the fellow had once been a butcher—insultingly gave him a dig under the ribs. Quick as lightning Billy let fly his arm. I dare say he never meant to do quite as much as he did, but anyhow he gave the burly fool a terrible drubbing. It took about half a minute, I should think. And, lord bless you, the lubber was astonished at the celerity. And will you believe it, Lieutenant, the Red Whiskers now really loves Billy—loves him, or is the biggest hypocrite that ever I heard of. But they all love him. Some of 'em do his washing, darn his old trousers for him; the carpenter is at odd times making a pretty little chest of drawers for him. Anybody will do anything for Billy Budd; and it's the happy family here. But now, Lieutenant, if that young fellow goes—I know how it will be aboard the *Rights*. Not again very soon shall I, coming up from dinner, lean over the capstan smoking a quiet pipe—no, not very soon again, I think. Ay, Lieutenant, you are going to take away the jewel of 'em; you are going to take away my peacemaker!" And with that the good soul had really some ado in checking a rising sob.

"Well," said the lieutenant, who had listened with amused interest to all this and now was waxing merry with his tipple; "well, blessed are the peacemakers, especially the fighting peacemakers. And such are the seventy-four beauties some of which you see poking their noses out of the portholes of yonder warship lying to for me," pointing through the cabin window at the *Bellipotent.* "But courage! Don't look so downhearted, man. Why, I pledge you in advance the royal approbation. Rest assured that His Majesty will be delighted to know that in a time when his hardtack is not sought for by sailors with such avidity as should be, a time also when some shipmasters privily resent the borrowing from them a tar or two for the service; His Majesty, I say, will be delighted to learn that *one* shipmaster at least cheerfully surrenders to the King the flower of his flock, a sailor who with equal loyalty makes no dissent.—But where's my beauty? Ah," looking through the cabin's open door, "here he comes; and, by Jove, lugging along his chest—Apollo with his portmanteau!—My man," stepping out to him, "you can't take that big box aboard a warship. The boxes there are mostly shot boxes. Put your duds in a bag, lad. Boot and saddle for the cavalryman, bag and hammock for the man-of-war's man."

The transfer from chest to bag was made. And, after seeing his man into the cutter and then following him down, the lieutenant pushed off from the *Rights-of-Man.* That was the merchant ship's name, though by her master and crew abbreviated in sailor fashion into the *Rights.* The hardheaded Dundee owner was a staunch admirer of Thomas Paine, whose book in rejoinder to Burke's arraignment of the French Revolution had then been published for some time and had gone everywhere. In christening his vessel after the title of Paine's volume the man of Dundee was something like his contemporary shipowner, Stephen Girard [9] of Philadelphia, whose sympathies, alike with his native land and its liberal philosophers, he evinced by naming his ships after Voltaire, Diderot, and so forth.

But now, when the boat swept under the merchantman's stern, and officer and oarsmen were noting—some bitterly and others with a grin—the name emblazoned there; just then it was that the new recruit jumped up from the bow where the coxswain had directed him to sit, and waving hat to his silent shipmates sorrowfully looking over at him from the taffrail, bade the lads a genial good-bye. Then, making a salutation as to the ship herself, "And good-bye to you too, old *Rights-of-Man.*"

[9] American banker and shipowner of French birth (1750-1831), who also named ships after Montesquieu and Rousseau.

"Down, sir!" roared the lieutenant, instantly assuming all the rigor of his rank, though with difficulty repressing a smile.

To be sure, Billy's action was a terrible breach of naval decorum. But in that decorum he had never been instructed; in consideration of which the lieutenant would hardly have been so energetic in reproof but for the concluding farewell to the ship. This he rather took as meant to convey a covert sally on the new recruit's part, a sly slur at impressment in general, and that of himself in especial. And yet, more likely, if satire it was in effect, it was hardly so by intention, for Billy, though happily endowed with the gaiety of high health, youth, and a free heart, was yet by no means of a satirical turn. The will to it and the sinister dexterity were alike wanting. To deal in double meanings and insinuations of any sort was quite foreign to his nature.

As to his enforced enlistment, that he seemed to take pretty much as he was wont to take any vicissitude of weather. Like the animals, though no philosopher, he was, without knowing it, practically a fatalist. And it may be that he rather liked this adventurous turn in his affairs, which promised an opening into novel scenes and martial excitements.

Aboard the *Bellipotent* our merchant sailor was forthwith rated as an able seaman and assigned to the starboard watch of the foretop. He was soon at home in the service, not at all disliked for his unpretentious good looks and a sort of genial happy-go-lucky air. No merrier man in his mess: in marked contrast to certain other individuals included like himself among the impressed portion of the ship's company; for these when not actively employed were sometimes, and more particularly in the last dogwatch[10] when the drawing near of twilight induced revery, apt to fall into a saddish mood which in some partook of sullenness. But they were not so young as our foretopman, and no few of them must have known a hearth of some sort, others may have had wives and children left, too probably, in uncertain circumstances, and hardly any but must have had acknowledged kith and kin, while for Billy, as will shortly be seen, his entire family was practically invested in himself.

2

Though our new-made foretopman was well received in the top and on the gun decks, hardly here was he that cynosure he had previously been among those minor ship's companies of the mer-

---

[10] A watch of two hours on shipboard; there are two, from 4:00 to 6:00 P.M. and from 6:00 to 8:00 P.M. respectively.

chant marine, with which companies only had he hitherto consorted.

He was young; and despite his all but fully developed frame, in aspect looked even younger than he really was, owing to a lingering adolescent expression in the as yet smooth face all but feminine in purity of natural complexion but where, thanks to his seagoing, the lily was quite suppressed and the rose had some ado visibly to flush through the tan.

To one essentially such a novice in the complexities of factitious life, the abrupt transition from his former and simpler sphere to the ampler and more knowing world of a great warship; this might well have abashed him had there been any conceit or vanity in his composition. Among her miscellaneous multitude, the *Bellipotent* mustered several individuals who however inferior in grade were of no common natural stamp, sailors more signally susceptive of that air which continuous martial discipline and repeated presence in battle can in some degree impart even to the average man. As the Handsome Sailor, Billy Budd's position aboard the seventy-four was something analogous to that of a rustic beauty transplanted from the provinces and brought into competition with the highborn dames of the court. But this change of circumstances he scarce noted. As little did he observe that something about him provoked an ambiguous smile in one or two harder faces among the bluejackets. Nor less unaware was he of the peculiar favorable effect his person and demeanor had upon the more intelligent gentlemen of the quarter-deck. Nor could this well have been otherwise. Cast in a mold peculiar to the finest physical examples of those Englishmen in whom the Saxon strain would seem not at all to partake of any Norman or other admixture, he showed in face that humane look of reposeful good nature which the Greek sculptor in some instances gave to his heroic strong man, Hercules. But this again was subtly modified by another and pervasive quality. The ear, small and shapely, the arch of the foot, the curve in mouth and nostril, even the indurated hand dyed to the orange-tawny of the toucan's bill, a hand telling alike of the halyards and tar bucket; but, above all, something in the mobile expression, and every chance attitude and movement, something suggestive of a mother eminently favored by Love and the Graces; all this strangely indicated a lineage in direct contradiction to his lot. The mysteriousness here became less mysterious through a matter of fact elicited when Billy at the capstan was being formally mustered into the service. Asked by the officer, a small, brisk little gentleman as it chanced, among other questions, his place of birth, he replied, "Please, sir, I don't know."

"Don't know where you were born? Who was your father?"

"God knows, sir."

Struck by the straightforward simplicity of these replies, the officer next asked, "Do you know anything about your beginning?"

"No, sir. But I have heard that I was found in a pretty silk-lined basket hanging one morning from the knocker of a good man's door in Bristol."

"Found, say you? Well," throwing back his head and looking up and down the new recruit; "well, it turns out to have been a pretty good find. Hope they'll find some more like you, my man; the fleet sadly needs them."

Yes, Billy Budd was a foundling, a presumable by-blow, and, evidently, no ignoble one. Noble descent was as evident in him as in a blood horse.

For the rest, with little or no sharpness of faculty or any trace of the wisdom of the serpent, nor yet quite a dove, he possessed that kind and degree of intelligence going along with the unconventional rectitude of a sound human creature, one to whom not yet has been proffered the questionable apple of knowledge. He was illiterate; he could not read, but he could sing, and like the illiterate nightingale was sometimes the composer of his own song.

Of self-consciousness he seemed to have little or none, or about as much as we may reasonably impute to a dog of Saint Bernard's breed.

Habitually living with the elements and knowing little more of the land than as a beach, or, rather, that portion of the terraqueous globe providentially set apart for dance-houses, doxies, and tapsters, in short what sailors call a "fiddler's green," his simple nature remained unsophisticated by those moral obliquities which are not in every case incompatible with that manufacturable thing known as respectability. But are sailors, frequenters of fiddlers' greens, without vices? No; but less often than with landsmen do their vices, so called, partake of crookedness of heart, seeming less to proceed from viciousness than exuberance of vitality after long constraint: frank manifestations in accordance with natural law. By his original constitution aided by the co-operating influences of his lot, Billy in many respects was little more than a sort of upright barbarian, much such perhaps as Adam presumably might have been ere the urbane Serpent wriggled himself into his company.

And here be it submitted that apparently going to corroborate the doctrine of man's Fall, a doctrine now popularly ignored, it is observable that where certain virtues pristine and unadulterate peculiarly characterize anybody in the external uniform of civilization, they will upon scrutiny seem not to be derived from custom or convention, but rather to be out of keeping with these, as if indeed exceptionally transmitted from a period prior to Cain's city and citified man. The character marked by such qualities has to an unvitiated taste an untampered-with flavor like that of berries, while the man thoroughly civilized, even in a fair specimen of the breed, has to the same moral palate a questionable smack as of a compounded wine. To any stray inheritor of these primitive qualities found, like Caspar Hauser,[11] wandering dazed in any Christian capital of our time, the good-natured poet's famous invocation, near two thousand years ago, of the good rustic out of his latitude in the Rome of the Caesars, still appropriately holds:

> Honest and poor, faithful in word and thought,
> What hath thee, Fabian, to the city brought?

Though our Handsome Sailor had as much of masculine beauty as one can expect anywhere to see; nevertheless, like the beautiful woman in one of Hawthorne's minor tales,[12] there was just one thing amiss in him. No visible blemish indeed, as with the lady; no, but an occasional liability to a vocal defect. Though in the hour of elemental uproar or peril he was everything that a sailor should be, yet under sudden provocation of strong heart-feeling his voice, otherwise singularly musical, as if expressive of the harmony within, was apt to develop an organic hesitancy, in fact more or less of a stutter or even worse. In this particular Billy was a striking instance that the arch interferer, the envious marplot of Eden, still has more or less to do with every human consignment to this planet of Earth. In every case, one way or another he is sure to slip in his little card, as much as to remind us—I too have a hand here.

The avowal of such an imperfection in the Handsome Sailor should be evidence not alone that he is not presented as a conventional hero, but also that the story in which he is the main figure is no romance.

3

At the time of Billy Budd's arbitrary enlistment into the *Bellipotent* that ship was on her way to join the Mediterranean fleet. No long time elapsed before the junction was effected. As one of that fleet the seventy-four participated in its movements, though at times on account of her superior sailing qualities, in the absence of

[11] A mysterious foundling who first appeared in 1828 wandering bewildered about the streets of Nuremberg.

[12] "The Birthmark."

frigates, dispatched on separate duty as a scout and at times on less temporary service. But with all this the story has little concernment, restricted as it is to the inner life of one particular ship and the career of an individual sailor.

It was the summer of 1797. In the April of that year had occurred the commotion at Spithead followed in May by a second and yet more serious outbreak in the fleet at the Nore.[13] The latter is known, and without exaggeration in the epithet, as "the Great Mutiny." It was indeed a demonstration more menacing to England than the contemporary manifestoes and conquering and proselyting armies of the French Directory.[14] To the British Empire the Nore Mutiny was what a strike in the fire brigade would be to London threatened by general arson. In a crisis when the kingdom might well have anticipated the famous signal that some years later published along the naval line of battle what it was that upon occasion England expected of Englishmen; *that* was the time when at the mastheads of the three-deckers and seventy-fours moored in her own roadstead—a fleet the right arm of a Power then all but the sole free conservative one of the Old World—the bluejackets, to be numbered by thousands, ran up with huzzas the British colors with the union and cross wiped out; by that cancellation transmuting the flag of founded law and freedom defined, into the enemy's red meteor of unbridled and unbounded revolt. Reasonable discontent growing out of practical grievances in the fleet had been ignited into irrational combustion as by live cinders blown across the Channel from France in flames.

The event converted into irony for a time those spirited strains of Dibdin[15]—as a song-writer no mean auxiliary to the English government at that European conjuncture—strains celebrating, among other things, the patriotic devotion of the British tar: "And as for my life, 'tis the King's!"

Such an episode in the Island's grand naval story her naval historians naturally abridge, one of them (William James)[16] candidly acknowledging that fain would he pass it over did not "impartiality

[13] These mutinies began on April 15, 1797, at Spithead, in the English Channel between Portsmouth and the Isle of Wight, and on May 20 at the Nore, near the mouth of the Thames.

[14] The body of five men which held the executive power from 1795 to 1799 in the First Republic.

[15] Charles Dibdin (1745-1814), English dramatist and songwriter, whose boast it was that his songs were "the solace of sailors in long voyages, in storms, in battle; and they have been quoted in mutinies to the restoration of order and discipline."

[16] Author of *The Naval History of Great Britain* (1860).

forbid fastidiousness." And yet his mention is less a narration than a reference, having to do hardly at all with details. Nor are these readily to be found in the libraries. Like some other events in every age befalling states everywhere, including America, the Great Mutiny was of such character that national pride along with views of policy would fain shade it off into the historical background. Such events cannot be ignored, but there is a considerate way of historically treating them. If a well-constituted individual refrains from blazoning aught amiss or calamitous in his family, a nation in the like circumstance may without reproach be equally discreet.

Though after parleyings between government and the ringleaders, and concessions by the former as to some glaring abuses, the first uprising—that at Spithead—with difficulty was put down, or matters for the time pacified; yet at the Nore the unforeseen renewal of insurrection on a yet larger scale, and emphasized in the conferences that ensued by demands deemed by the authorities not only inadmissible but aggressively insolent, indicated—if the Red Flag did not sufficiently do so—what was the spirit animating the men. Final suppression, however, there was; but only made possible perhaps by the unswerving loyalty of the marine corps and a voluntary resumption of loyalty among influential sections of the crews.

To some extent the Nore Mutiny may be regarded as analogous to the distempering irruption of contagious fever in a frame constitutionally sound, and which anon throws it off.

At all events, of these thousands of mutineers were some of the tars who not so very long afterwards—whether wholly prompted thereto by patriotism, or pugnacious instinct, or by both—helped to win a coronet for Nelson at the Nile, and the naval crown of crowns for him at Trafalgar. To the mutineers, those battles and especially Trafalgar were a plenary absolution and a grand one. For all that goes to make up scenic naval display and heroic magnificence in arms, those battles, especially Trafalgar, stand unmatched in human annals.

4

In this matter of writing, resolve as one may to keep to the main road, some bypaths have an enticement not readily to be withstood. I am going to err into such a bypath. If the reader will keep me company I shall be glad. At the least, we can promise ourselves that pleasure which is wickedly said to be in sinning, for a literary sin the divergence will be.

Very likely it is no new remark that the inventions of our time have at last brought about a change in sea warfare in degree corresponding to the revolution in all warfare effected by the original introduction from China into Europe of gunpowder. The first European firearm, a clumsy contrivance, was, as is well known, scouted by no few of the knights as a base implement, good enough peradventure for weavers too craven to stand up crossing steel with steel in frank fight. But as ashore knightly valor, though shorn of its blazonry, did not cease with the knights, neither on the seas—though nowadays in encounters there a certain kind of displayed gallantry be fallen out of date as hardly applicable under changed circumstances—did the nobler qualities of such naval magnates as Don John of Austria, Doria, Van Tromp, Jean Bart, the long line of British admirals, and the American Decaturs of 1812 become obsolete with their wooden walls.

Nevertheless, to anybody who can hold the Present at its worth without being inappreciative of the Past, it may be forgiven, if to such an one the solitary old hulk at Portsmouth, Nelson's *Victory*, seems to float there, not alone as the decaying monument of a fame incorruptible, but also as a poetic reproach, softened by its picturesqueness, to the *Monitors* and yet mightier hulls of the European ironclads. And this not altogether because such craft are unsightly, unavoidably lacking the symmetry and grand lines of the old battleships, but equally for other reasons.

There are some, perhaps, who while not altogether inaccessible to that poetic reproach just alluded to, may yet on behalf of the new order be disposed to parry it; and this to the extent of iconoclasm, if need be. For example, prompted by the sight of the star inserted in the *Victory*'s quarter-deck designating the spot where the Great Sailor fell, these martial utilitarians may suggest considerations implying that Nelson's ornate publication of his person in battle was not only unnecessary, but not military, nay, savored of foolhardiness and vanity. They may add, too, that at Trafalgar it was in effect nothing less than a challenge to death; and death came; and that but for his bravado the victorious admiral might possibly have survived the battle, and so, instead of having his sagacious dying injunctions overruled by his immediate successor in command, he himself when the contest was decided might have brought his shattered fleet to anchor, a proceeding which might have averted the deplorable loss of life by shipwreck in the elemental tempest that followed the martial one.

Well, should we set aside the more than disputable point whether for various reasons it was possible to anchor the fleet, then plausibly enough the Benthamites[17] of war may urge the above. But the *might-have-been* is but boggy ground to build on. And, certainly, in foresight as to the larger issue of an encounter, and anxious preparations for it—buoying the deadly way and mapping it out, as at Copenhagen—few commanders have been so painstakingly circumspect as this same reckless declarer of his person in fight.

Personal prudence, even when dictated by quite other than selfish considerations, surely is no special virtue in a military man; while an excessive love of glory, impassioning a less burning impulse, the honest sense of duty, is the first. If the name *Wellington* is not so much of a trumpet to the blood as the simpler name *Nelson,* the reason for this may perhaps be inferred from the above. Alfred in his funeral ode[18] on the victor of Waterloo ventures not to call him the greatest soldier of all time, though in the same ode he invokes Nelson as "the greatest sailor since our world began."

At Trafalgar Nelson on the brink of opening the fight sat down and wrote his last brief will and testament. If under the presentiment of the most magnificent of all victories to be crowned by his own glorious death, a sort of priestly motive led him to dress his person in the jewelled vouchers of his own shining deeds; if thus to have adorned himself for the altar and the sacrifice were indeed vainglory, then affectation and fustian is each more heroic line in the great epics and dramas, since in such lines the poet but embodies in verse those exaltations of sentiment that a nature like Nelson, the opportunity being given, vitalizes into acts.

5

Yes, the outbreak at the Nore was put down. But not every grievance was redressed. If the contractors, for example, were no longer permitted to ply some practices peculiar to their tribe everywhere, such as providing shoddy cloth, rations not sound, or false in the measure; not the less impressment, for one thing, went on. By custom sanctioned for centuries, and judicially maintained by a Lord Chancellor as late as Mansfield, that mode of manning the fleet, a mode now fallen into a sort of abeyance but never formally renounced, it was not practicable to give up in those years. Its abrogation would have crippled the indispensable fleet, one wholly under canvas, no steam power, its innumerable sails and thousands

[17] Followers of Jeremy Bentham (1748-1832), the philosopher who held the morality of actions to be determined by their utility.

[18] Lord Tennyson's "Ode on the Death of the Duke of Wellington."

of cannon, everything in short, worked by muscle alone; a fleet the more insatiate in demand for men, because then multiplying its ships of all grades against contingencies present and to come of the convulsed Continent.

Discontent foreran the Two Mutinies, and more or less it lurkingly survived them. Hence it was not unreasonable to apprehend some return of trouble sporadic or general. One instance of such apprehensions: In the same year with this story, Nelson, then Rear Admiral Sir Horatio, being with the fleet off the Spanish coast, was directed by the admiral in command to shift his pennant from the *Captain* to the *Theseus*; and for this reason: that the latter ship having newly arrived on the station from home, where it had taken part in the Great Mutiny, danger was apprehended from the temper of the men; and it was thought that an officer like Nelson was the one, not indeed to terrorize the crew into base subjection, but to win them, by force of his mere presence and heroic personality, back to an allegiance if not as enthusiastic as his own yet as true.

So it was that for a time, on more than one quarter-deck, anxiety did exist. At sea, precautionary vigilance was strained against relapse. At short notice an engagement might come on. When it did, the lieutenants assigned to batteries felt it incumbent on them, in some instances, to stand with drawn swords behind the men working the guns.

6

But on board the seventy-four in which Billy now swung his hammock, very little in the manner of the men and nothing obvious in the demeanor of the officers would have suggested to an ordinary observer that the Great Mutiny was a recent event. In their general bearing and conduct the commissioned officers of a warship naturally take their tone from the commander, that is if he have that ascendancy of character that ought to be his.

Captain the Honorable Edward Fairfax Vere, to give his full title, was a bachelor of forty or thereabouts, a sailor of distinction even in a time prolific of renowned seamen. Though allied to the higher nobility, his advancement had not been altogether owing to influences connected with that circumstance. He had seen much service, been in various engagements, always acquitting himself as an officer mindful of the welfare of his men, but never tolerating an infraction of discipline; thoroughly versed in the science of his profession, and intrepid to the verge of temerity, though never injudiciously so. For his gallantry in the West Indian waters as flag lieutenant under Rodney[19] in that admiral's crowning victory over De Grasse, he was made a post captain.

Ashore, in the garb of a civilian, scarce anyone would have taken him for a sailor, more especially that he never garnished unprofessional talk with nautical terms, and grave in his bearing, evinced little appreciation of mere humor. It was not out of keeping with these traits that on a passage when nothing demanded his paramount action, he was the most undemonstrative of men. Any landsman observing this gentleman not conspicuous by his stature and wearing no pronounced insignia, emerging from his cabin to the open deck, and noting the silent deference of the officers retiring to leeward, might have taken him for the King's guest, a civilian aboard the King's ship, some highly honorable discreet envoy on his way to an important post. But in fact this unobtrusiveness of demeanor may have proceeded from a certain unaffected modesty of manhood sometimes accompanying a resolute nature, a modesty evinced at all times not calling for pronounced action, which shown in any rank of life suggests a virtue aristocratic in kind. As with some others engaged in various departments of the world's more heroic activities, Captain Vere though practical enough upon occasion would at times betray a certain dreaminess of mood. Standing alone on the weather side of the quarter-deck, one hand holding by the rigging, he would absently gaze off at the blank sea. At the presentation to him then of some minor matter interrupting the current of his thoughts, he would show more or less irascibility; but instantly he would control it.

In the navy he was popularly known by the appellation "Starry Vere." How such a designation happened to fall upon one who whatever his sterling qualities was without any brilliant ones, was in this wise: A favorite kinsman, Lord Denton, a freehearted fellow, had been the first to meet and congratulate him upon his return to England from his West Indian cruise; and but the day previous turning over a copy of Andrew Marvell's poems had lighted, not for the first time, however, upon the lines entitled "Appleton House," the name of one of the seats of their common ancestor, a hero in the German wars of the seventeenth century, in which poem occur the lines:

> This 'tis to have been from the first
> In a domestic heaven nursed,
> Under the discipline severe
> Of Fairfax and the starry Vere.

---

[19] George Brydges, Baron Rodney (1719-1792), British admiral who defeated the French admiral de Grasse off Dominica in April 1782.

And so, upon embracing his cousin fresh from Rodney's great victory wherein he had played so gallant a part, brimming over with just family pride in the sailor of their house, he exuberantly exclaimed, "Give ye joy, Ed; give ye joy, my starry Vere!" This got currency, and the novel prefix serving in familiar parlance readily to distinguish the *Bellipotent*'s captain from another Vere his senior, a distant relative, an officer of like rank in the navy, it remained permanently attached to the surname.

7

In view of the part that the commander of the *Bellipotent* plays in scenes shortly to follow, it may be well to fill out that sketch of him outlined in the previous chapter.

Aside from his qualities as a sea officer Captain Vere was an exceptional character. Unlike no few of England's renowned sailors, long and arduous service with signal devotion to it had not resulted in absorbing and *salting* the entire man. He had a marked leaning toward everything intellectual. He loved books, never going to sea without a newly replenished library, compact but of the best. The isolated leisure, in some cases so wearisome, falling at intervals to commanders even during a war cruise, never was tedious to Captain Vere. With nothing of that literary taste which less heeds the thing conveyed than the vehicle, his bias was toward those books to which every serious mind of superior order occupying any active post of authority in the world naturally inclines: books treating of actual men and events no matter of what era—history, biography, and unconventional writers like Montaigne,[20] who, free from cant and convention, honestly and in the spirit of common sense philosophize upon realities. In this line of reading he found confirmation of his own more reserved thoughts—confirmation which he had vainly sought in social converse, so that as touching most fundamental topics, there had got to be established in him some positive convictions which he forefelt would abide in him essentially unmodified so long as his intelligent part remained unimpaired. In view of the troubled period in which his lot was cast, this was well for him. His settled convictions were as a dike against those invading waters of novel opinion social, political, and otherwise, which carried away as in a torrent no few minds in those days, minds by nature not inferior to his own. While other members of that aristocracy to which by birth he belonged were incensed at the innovators mainly

---

[20] Michel Eyquem de Montaigne (1533-1592), the French philosopher and essayist.

because their theories were inimical to the privileged classes, Captain Vere disinterestedly opposed them not alone because they seemed to him insusceptible of embodiment in lasting institutions, but at war with the peace of the world and the true welfare of mankind.

With minds less stored than his and less earnest, some officers of his rank, with whom at times he would necessarily consort, found him lacking in the companionable quality, a dry and bookish gentleman, as they deemed. Upon any chance withdrawal from their company one would be apt to say to another something like this: "Vere is a noble fellow, Starry Vere. 'Spite the gazettes, Sir Horatio" (meaning him who became Lord Nelson) "is at bottom scarce a better seaman or fighter. But between you and me now, don't you think there is a queer streak of the pedantic running through him? Yes, like the King's yarn in a coil of navy rope?"

Some apparent ground there was for this sort of confidential criticism; since not only did the captain's discourse never fall into the jocosely familiar, but in illustrating of any point touching the stirring personages and events of the time he would be as apt to cite some historic character or incident of antiquity as he would be to cite from the moderns. He seemed unmindful of the circumstance that to his bluff company such remote allusions, however pertinent they might really be, were altogether alien to men whose reading was mainly confined to the journals. But considerateness in such matters is not easy to natures constituted like Captain Vere's. Their honesty prescribes to them directness, sometimes far-reaching like that of a migratory fowl that in its flight never heeds when it crosses a frontier.

8

The lieutenants and other commissioned gentlemen forming Captain Vere's staff it is not necessary here to particularize, nor needs it to make any mention of any of the warrant officers. But among the petty officers was one who, having much to do with the story, may as well be forthwith introduced. His portrait I essay, but shall never hit it. This was John Claggart, the master-at-arms. But that sea title may to landsmen seem somewhat equivocal. Originally, doubtless, that petty officer's function was the instruction of the men in the use of arms, sword or cutlass. But very long ago, owing to the advance in gunnery making hand-to-hand encounters less frequent and giving to niter and sulphur the pre-eminence over steel, that function ceased; the master-at-arms of a great warship becoming a sort of chief of police charged among other matters with the duty of preserving order on the populous lower gun decks.

Claggart was a man about five-and-thirty, somewhat spare and tall, yet of no ill figure upon the whole. His hand was too small and shapely to have been accustomed to hard toil. The face was a notable one, the features all except the chin cleanly cut as those on a Greek medallion; yet the chin, beardless as Tecumseh's,[21] had something of strange protuberant broadness in its make that recalled the prints of the Reverend Dr. Titus Oates, the historic deponent with the clerical drawl in the time of Charles II and the fraud of the alleged Popish Plot.[22] It served Claggart in his office that his eye could cast a tutoring glance. His brow was of the sort phrenologically associated with more than average intellect; silken jet curls partly clustering over it, making a foil to the pallor below, a pallor tinged with a faint shade of amber akin to the hue of time-tinted marbles of old. This complexion, singularly contrasting with the red or deeply bronzed visages of the sailors, and in part the result of his official seclusion from the sunlight, though it was not exactly displeasing, nevertheless seemed to hint of something defective or abnormal in the constitution and blood. But his general aspect and manner were so suggestive of an education and career incongruous with his naval function that when not actively engaged in it he looked like a man of high quality, social and moral, who for reasons of his own was keeping incog. Nothing was known of his former life. It might be that he was an Englishman; and yet there lurked a bit of accent in his speech suggesting that possibly he was not such by birth, but through naturalization in early childhood. Among certain grizzled sea gossips of the gun decks and forecastle went a rumor perdue that the master-at-arms was a *chevalier*[23] who had volunteered into the King's navy by way of compounding for some mysterious swindle whereof he had been arraigned at the King's Bench. The fact that nobody could substantiate this report was, of course, nothing against its secret currency. Such a rumor once started on the gun decks in reference to almost anyone below the rank of a commissioned officer would, during the period assigned to this narrative, have seemed not altogether wanting in credibility to the tarry old wiseacres of a man-of-war crew. And indeed a man of Claggart's accomplishments, without prior nautical

[21] Tecumseh (1768?-1813), was a chief of the Shawnee Indians.

[22] The Reverend Titus Oates (1649-1705) alleged that there was a plot in 1678 to murder Charles II and establish the Roman Catholic religion by force in England.

[23] A "chevalier of fortune," one who lives by his wits.

experience entering the navy at mature life, as he did, and necessarily allotted at the start to the lowest grade in it; a man too who never made allusion to his previous life ashore; these were circumstances which in the dearth of exact knowledge as to his true antecedents opened to the invidious a vague field for unfavorable surmise.

But the sailors' dogwatch gossip concerning him derived a vague plausibility from the fact that now for some period the British navy could so little afford to be squeamish in the matter of keeping up the muster rolls, that not only were press gangs notoriously abroad both afloat and ashore, but there was little or no secret about another matter, namely, that the London police were at liberty to capture any able-bodied suspect, any questionable fellow at large, and summarily ship him to the dockyard or fleet. Furthermore, even among voluntary enlistments there were instances where the motive thereto partook neither of patriotic impulse nor yet of a random desire to experience a bit of sea life and martial adventure. Insolvent debtors of minor grade, together with the promiscuous lame ducks of morality, found in the navy a convenient and secure refuge, secure because, once enlisted aboard a King's ship, they were as much in sanctuary[24] as the transgressor of the Middle Ages harboring himself under the shadow of the altar. Such sanctioned irregularities, which for obvious reasons the government would hardly think to parade at the time and which consequently, and as affecting the least influential class of mankind, have all but dropped into oblivion, lend color to something for the truth whereof I do not vouch, and hence have some scruple in stating; something I remember having seen in print though the book I cannot recall; but the same thing was personally communicated to me now more than forty years ago by an old pensioner in a cocked hat with whom I had a most interesting talk on the terrace at Greenwich, a Baltimore Negro, a Trafalgar man. It was to this effect: In the case of a warship short of hands whose speedy sailing was imperative, the deficient quota, in lack of any other way of making it good, would be eked out by drafts culled direct from the jails. For reasons previously suggested it would not perhaps be easy at the present day directly to prove or disprove the allegation. But allowed as a verity, how significant would it be of England's straits at the time confronted by those wars which like a flight of harpies rose shrieking from the din and dust of the fallen Bastille. That era appears measurably clear to us who look back at it, and but read of it. But to the grandfathers of

[24] In England up until the Reformation certain churches were designated as places of asylum and afforded protection from arrest.

us graybeards, the more thoughtful of them, the genius of it presented an aspect like that of Camoëns' Spirit of the Cape,[25] an eclipsing menace mysterious and prodigious. Not America was exempt from apprehension. At the height of Napoleon's unexampled conquests, there were Americans who had fought at Bunker Hill who looked forward to the possibility that the Atlantic might prove no barrier against the ultimate schemes of this French portentous upstart from the revolutionary chaos who seemed in act of fulfilling judgment prefigured in the Apocalypse.[26]

But the less credence was to be given to the gun-deck talk touching Claggart, seeing that no man holding his office in a man-of-war can ever hope to be popular with the crew. Besides, in derogatory comments upon anyone against whom they have a grudge, or for any reason or no reason mislike, sailors are much like landsmen: they are apt to exaggerate or romance it.

About as much was really known to the *Bellipotent*'s tars of the master-at-arms' career before entering the service as an astronomer knows about a comet's travels prior to its first observable appearance in the sky. The verdict of the sea quidnuncs[27] has been cited only by way of showing what sort of moral impression the man made upon rude uncultivated natures whose conceptions of human wickedness were necessarily of the narrowest, limited to ideas of vulgar rascality—a thief among the swinging hammocks during a night watch, or the man-brokers and land-sharks of the seaports.

It was no gossip, however, but fact that though, as before hinted, Claggart upon his entrance into the navy was, as a novice, assigned to the least honorable section of a man-of-war's crew, embracing the drudgery, he did not long remain there. The superior capacity he immediately evinced, his constitutional sobriety, an ingratiating deference to superiors, together with a peculiar ferreting genius manifested on a singular occasion; all this, capped by a certain austere patriotism, abruptly advanced him to the position of master-at-arms.

Of this maritime chief of police the ship's corporals, so called, were the immediate subordinates, and compliant ones; and this, as is to be noted in some business departments ashore, almost to a degree inconsistent with entire moral volition. His place put various converging wires of underground influence under the chief's control, capable when astutely worked through his understrappers of operat-

---

[25] Adamastor is a monster who attempts to destroy Vasco da Gama and his crew in the *Lusiads* of the Portuguese epic poet Luis de Camoëns (1524-1580).

[26] The last book of the New Testament, *The Revelation of St. John the Divine*.

[27] Gossips.

ing to the mysterious discomfort, if nothing worse, of any of the sea commonalty.

9

Life in the foretop well agreed with Billy Budd. There, when not actually engaged on the yards yet higher aloft, the topmen, who as such had been picked out for youth and activity, constituted an aerial club lounging at ease against the smaller stun'sails rolled up into cushions, spinning yarns like the lazy gods, and frequently amused with what was going on in the busy world of the decks below. No wonder then that a young fellow of Billy's disposition was well content in such society. Giving no cause of offense to anybody, he was always alert at a call. So in the merchant service it had been with him. But now such a punctiliousness in duty was shown that his topmates would sometimes good-naturedly laugh at him for it. This heightened alacrity had its cause, namely, the impression made upon him by the first formal gangway-punishment he had ever witnessed, which befell the day following his impressment. It had been incurred by a little fellow, young, a novice afterguardsman absent from his assigned post when the ship was being put about; a dereliction resulting in a rather serious hitch to that maneuver, one demanding instantaneous promptitude in letting go and making fast. When Billy saw the culprit's naked back under the scourge, gridironed with red welts and worse, when he marked the dire expression in the liberated man's face as with his woolen shirt flung over him by the executioner he rushed forward from the spot to bury himself in the crowd, Billy was horrified. He resolved that never through remissness would he make himself liable to such a visitation or do or omit aught that might merit even verbal reproof. What then was his surprise and concern when ultimately he found himself getting into petty trouble occasionally about such matters as the stowage of his bag or something amiss in his hammock, matters under the police oversight of the ship's corporals of the lower decks, and which brought down on him a vague threat from one of them.

So heedful in all things as he was, how could this be? He could not understand it, and it more than vexed him. When he spoke to his young topmates about it they were either lightly incredulous or found something comical in his unconcealed anxiety. "Is it your bag, Billy?" said one. "Well, sew yourself up in it, bully boy, and then you'll be sure to know if anybody meddles with it."

Now there was a veteran aboard who because his years began to disqualify him for more active work had been recently assigned duty as mainmastman in his watch, looking to the gear belayed at the rail roundabout that great spar near the deck. At off-times the foretopman had picked up some acquaintance with him, and now in his trouble it occurred to him that he might be the sort of person to go to for wise counsel. He was an old Dansker[28] long anglicized in the service, of few words, many wrinkles, and some honorable scars. His wizened face, time-tinted and weather-stained to the complexion of an antique parchment, was here and there peppered blue by the chance explosion of a gun cartridge in action.

He was an *Agamemnon* man, some two years prior to the time of this story having served under Nelson when still captain in that ship immortal in naval memory, which dismantled and in part broken up to her bare ribs is seen a grand skeleton in Haden's etching.[29] As one of a boarding party from the *Agamemnon* he had received a cut slantwise along one temple and cheek leaving a long pale scar like a streak of dawn's light falling athwart the dark visage. It was on account of that scar and the affair in which it was known that he had received it, as well as from his blue-peppered complexion, that the Dansker went among the *Bellipotent*'s crew by the name of "Board-Her-in-the-Smoke."

Now the first time that his small weasel eyes happened to light on Billy Budd, a certain grim internal merriment set all his ancient wrinkles into antic play. Was it that his eccentric unsentimental old sapience, primitive in its kind, saw or thought it saw something which in contrast with the warship's environment looked oddly incongruous in the Handsome Sailor? But after slyly studying him at intervals, the old Merlin's[30] equivocal merriment was modified; for now when the twain would meet, it would start in his face a quizzing sort of look, but it would be but momentary and sometimes replaced by an expression of speculative query as to what might eventually befall a nature like that, dropped into a world not without some mantraps and against whose subtleties simple courage lacking experience and address, and without any touch of defensive ugliness, is of little avail; and where such innocence as man is capable of does yet in a moral emergency not always sharpen the faculties or enlighten the will.

However it was, the Dansker in his ascetic way rather took to Billy. Nor was this only because of a certain philosophic interest in

---

[28] Dane.

[29] "Breaking up of the 'Agamemnon,'" a well-known work by the English surgeon and etcher Sir Francis Seymour Haden (1818-1910).

[30] Merlin is the magician in the stories of King Arthur.

such a character. There was another cause. While the old man's eccentricities, sometimes bordering on the ursine, repelled the juniors, Billy, undeterred thereby, revering him as a salt hero, would make advances, never passing the old *Agamemnon* man without a salutation marked by that respect which is seldom lost on the aged, however crabbed at times or whatever their station in life.

There was a vein of dry humor, or what not, in the mastman; and, whether in freak of patriarchal irony touching Billy's youth and athletic frame, or for some other and more recondite reason, from the first in addressing him he always substituted *Baby* for Billy, the Dansker in fact being the originator of the name by which the foretopman eventually became known aboard ship.

Well then, in his mysterious little difficulty going in quest of the wrinkled one, Billy found him off duty in a dogwatch ruminating by himself, seated on a shot box of the upper gun deck, now and then surveying with a somewhat cynical regard certain of the more swaggering promenaders there. Billy recounted his trouble, again wondering how it all happened. The salt seer attentively listened, accompanying the foretopman's recital with queer twitchings of his wrinkles and problematical little sparkles of his small ferret eyes. Making an end of his story, the foretopman asked, "And now, Dansker, do tell me what you think of it."

The old man, shoving up the front of his tarpaulin and deliberately rubbing the long slant scar at the point where it entered the thin hair, laconically said, "Baby Budd, *Jemmy Legs*" (meaning the master-at-arms) "is down on you."

"*Jemmy Legs!*" ejaculated Billy, his welkin eyes expanding. "What for? Why, he calls me 'the sweet and pleasant young fellow,' they tell me."

"Does he so?" grinned the grizzled one; then said, "Ay, Baby lad, a sweet voice has Jemmy Legs."

"No, not always. But to me he has. I seldom pass him but there comes a pleasant word."

"And that's because he's down upon you, Baby Budd."

Such reiteration, along with the manner of it, incomprehensible to a novice, disturbed Billy almost as much as the mystery for which he had sought explanation. Something less unpleasingly oracular he tried to extract; but the old sea Chiron,[31] thinking perhaps that for the nonce he had sufficiently instructed his young Achilles, pursed his lips, gathered all his wrinkles together, and would commit himself to nothing further.

---

[31] Chiron: A learned Centaur, renowned for his kindness and wisdom, who was the tutor of Asclepius, Jason, and Achilles.

Years, and those experiences which befall certain shrewder men subordinated lifelong to the will of superiors, all this had developed in the Dansker the pithy guarded cynicism that was his leading characteristic.

10

The next day an incident served to confirm Billy Budd in his incredulity as to the Dansker's strange summing up of the case submitted. The ship at noon, going large before the wind, was rolling on her course, and he below at dinner and engaged in some sportful talk with the members of his mess, chanced in a sudden lurch to spill the entire contents of his soup pan upon the new-scrubbed deck. Claggart, the master-at-arms, official rattan in hand, happened to be passing along the battery in a bay of which the mess was lodged, and the greasy liquid streamed just across his path. Stepping over it, he was proceeding on his way without comment, since the matter was nothing to take notice of under the circumstances, when he happened to observe who it was that had done the spilling. His countenance changed. Pausing, he was about to ejaculate something hasty at the sailor, but checked himself, and pointing down to the streaming soup, playfully tapped him from behind with his rattan, saying in a low musical voice peculiar to him at times, "Handsomely done, my lad! And handsome is as handsome did it, too!" And with that passed on. Not noted by Billy as not coming within his view was the involuntary smile, or rather grimace, that accompanied Claggart's equivocal words. Aridly it drew down the thin corners of his shapely mouth. But everybody taking his remark as meant for humorous, and at which therefore as coming from a superior they were bound to laugh "with counterfeited glee," acted accordingly; and Billy, tickled, it may be, by the allusion to his being the Handsome Sailor, merrily joined in; then addressing his messmates exclaimed, "There now, who says that Jemmy Legs is down on me!"

"And who said he was, Beauty?" demanded one Donald with some surprise. Whereat the foretopman looked a little foolish, recalling that it was only one person, Board-Her-in-the-Smoke, who had suggested what to him was the smoky idea that this master-at-arms was in any peculiar way hostile to him. Meantime that functionary, resuming his path, must have momentarily worn some expression less guarded than that of the bitter smile, usurping the face from the heart—some distorting expression perhaps, for a drummer-boy heedlessly frolicking along from the opposite direction and chancing to come into light collision with his person was strangely disconcerted by his aspect. Nor was the impression lessened when the official, impetuously giving him a sharp cut with the rattan, vehemently exclaimed, "Look where you go!"

11

What was the matter with the master-at-arms? And, be the matter what it might, how could it have direct relation to Billy Budd, with whom prior to the affair of the spilled soup he had never come into any special contact official or otherwise? What indeed could the trouble have to do with one so little inclined to give offense as the merchant-ship's "peacemaker," even him who in Claggart's own phrase was "the sweet and pleasant young fellow"? Yes, why should Jemmy Legs, to borrow the Dansker's expression, be "down" on the Handsome Sailor? But, at heart and not for nothing, as the late chance encounter may indicate to the discerning, down on him, secretly down on him, he assuredly was.

Now to invent something touching the more private career of Claggart, something involving Billy Budd, of which something the latter should be wholly ignorant, some romantic incident implying that Claggart's knowledge of the young bluejacket began at some period anterior to catching sight of him on board the seventy-four —all this, not so difficult to do, might avail in a way more or less interesting to account for whatever of enigma may appear to lurk in the case. But in fact there was nothing of the sort. And yet the cause necessarily to be assumed as the sole one assignable is in its very realism as much charged with that prime element of Radcliffian romance,[32] the mysterious, as any that the ingenuity of the author of *The Mysteries of Udolpho* could devise. For what can more partake of the mysterious than an antipathy spontaneous and profound such as is evoked in certain exceptional mortals by the mere aspect of some other mortal, however harmless he may be, if not called forth by this very harmlessness itself?

Now there can exist no irritating juxtaposition of dissimilar personalities comparable to that which is possible aboard a great warship fully manned and at sea. There, every day among all ranks, almost every man comes into more or less of contact with almost every other man. Wholly there to avoid even the sight of an aggravating object one must needs give it Jonah's toss or jump overboard

---

[32] Such extravagant Gothic novels as *The Mysteries of Udolpho* by Mrs. Ann Radcliffe (1764-1823).

himself. Imagine how all this might eventually operate on some peculiar human creature the direct reverse of a saint!

But for the adequate comprehending of Claggart by a normal nature these hints are insufficient. To pass from a normal nature to him one must cross "the deadly space between." And this is best done by indirection.

Long ago an honest scholar, my senior, said to me in reference to one who like himself is now no more, a man so unimpeachably respectable that against him nothing was ever openly said though among the few something was whispered, "Yes, X—— is a nut not to be cracked by the tap of a lady's fan. You are aware that I am the adherent of no organized religion, much less of any philosophy built into a system. Well, for all that, I think that to try and get into X——, enter his labyrinth and get out again, without a clue derived from some source other that what is known as 'knowledge of the world'—that were hardly possible, at least for me."

"Why," said I, "X——, however singular a study to some, is yet human, and knowledge of the world assuredly implies the knowledge of human nature, and in most of its varieties."

"Yes, but a superficial knowledge of it, serving ordinary purposes. But for anything deeper, I am not certain whether to know the world and to know human nature be not two distinct branches of knowledge, which while they may coexist in the same heart, yet either may exist with little or nothing of the other. Nay, in an average man of the world, his constant rubbing with it blunts that finer spiritual insight indispensable to the understanding of the essential in certain exceptional characters, whether evil ones or good. In a matter of some importance I have seen a girl wind an old lawyer about her little finger. Nor was it the dotage of senile love. Nothing of the sort. But he knew law better than he knew the girl's heart. Coke and Blackstone[33] hardly shed so much light into obscure spiritual places as the Hebrew prophets. And who were they? Mostly recluses."

At the time, my inexperience was such that I did not quite see the drift of all this. It may be that I see it now. And, indeed, if that lexicon which is based on Holy Writ were any longer popular, one might with less difficulty define and denominate certain phenomenal men. As it is, one must turn to some authority not liable to the charge of being tinctured with the biblical element.

In a list of definitions included in the authentic translation of Plato, a list attributed to him, occurs this: "Natural Depravity:

[33] Sir Edward Coke (1552-1634) and Sir William Blackstone (1723-1780), famous British jurists and commentators on the law.

a depravity according to nature," a definition which, though savoring of Calvinism, by no means involves Calvin's dogma as to total mankind. Evidently its intent makes it applicable but to individuals. Not many are the examples of this depravity which the gallows and jail supply. At any rate, for notable instances, since these have no vulgar alloy of the brute in them, but invariably are dominated by intellectuality, one must go elsewhere. Civilization, especially if of the austerer sort, is auspicious to it. It folds itself in the mantle of respectability. It has its certain negative virtues serving as silent auxiliaries. It never allows wine to get within its guard. It is not going too far to say that it is without vices or small sins. There is a phenomenal pride in it that excludes them. It is never mercenary or avaricious. In short, the depravity here meant partakes nothing of the sordid or sensual. It is serious, but free from acerbity. Though no flatterer of mankind it never speaks ill of it.

But the thing which in eminent instances signalizes so exceptional a nature is this: Though the man's even temper and discreet bearing would seem to intimate a mind peculiarly subject to the law of reason, not the less in heart he would seem to riot in complete exemption from that law, having apparently little to do with reason further than to employ it as an ambidexter implement for effecting the irrational. That is to say: Toward the accomplishment of an aim which in wantonness of atrocity would seem to partake of the insane, he will direct a cool judgment sagacious and sound. These men are madmen, and of the most dangerous sort, for their lunacy is not continuous, but occasional, evoked by some special object; it is protectively secretive, which is as much as to say it is self-contained, so that when, moreover, most active it is to the average mind not distinguishable from sanity, and for the reason above suggested: that whatever its aims may be—and the aim is never declared—the method and the outward proceeding are always perfectly rational.

Now something such an one was Claggart, in whom was the mania of an evil nature, not engendered by vicious training or corrupting books or licentious living, but born with him and innate, in short "a depravity according to nature."

Dark sayings are these, some will say. But why? Is it because they somewhat savor of Holy Writ in its phrase "mystery of iniquity"? If they do, such savor was far enough from being intended, for little will it commend these pages to many a reader of today.

The point of the present story turning on the hidden nature of the master-at-arms has necessitated this chapter. With an added hint or two in connection with the incident at the mess, the resumed narrative must be left to vindicate, as it may, its own credibility.

12

That Claggart's figure was not amiss, and his face, save the chin, well molded, has already been said. Of these favorable points he seemed not insensible, for he was not only neat but careful in his dress. But the form of Billy Budd was heroic; and if his face was without the intellectual look of the pallid Claggart's, not the less was it lit, like his, from within, though from a different source. The bonfire in his heart made luminous the rose-tan in his cheek.

In view of the marked contrast between the persons of the twain, it is more than probable that when the master-at-arms in the scene last given applied to the sailor the proverb "Handsome is as handsome does," he there let escape an ironic inkling, not caught by the young sailors who heard it, as to what it was that had first moved him against Billy, namely, his significant personal beauty.

Now envy and antipathy, passions irreconcilable in reason, nevertheless in fact may spring conjoined like Chang and Eng[34] in one birth. Is Envy then such a monster? Well, though many an arraigned mortal has in hopes of mitigated penalty pleaded guilty to horrible actions, did ever anybody seriously confess to envy? Something there is in it universally felt to be more shameful than even felonious crime. And not only does everybody disown it, but the better sort are inclined to incredulity when it is in earnest imputed to an intelligent man. But since its lodgment is in the heart not the brain, no degree of intellect supplies a guarantee against it. But Claggart's was no vulgar form of the passion. Nor, as directed toward Billy Budd, did it partake of that streak of apprehensive jealousy that marred Saul's visage perturbedly brooding on the comely young David. Claggart's envy struck deeper. If askance he eyed the good looks, cheery health, and frank enjoyment of young life in Billy Budd, it was because these went along with a nature that, as Claggart magnetically felt, had in its simplicity never willed malice or experienced the reactionary bite of that serpent. To him, the spirit lodged within Billy, and looking out from his welkin eyes as from windows, that ineffability it was which made the dimple in his dyed cheek, suppled his joints, and dancing in his yellow curls

[34] The famous "Siamese Twins" (1811-1874).

made him pre-eminently the Handsome Sailor. One person excepted, the master-of-arms was perhaps the only man in the ship intellectually capable of adequately appreciating the moral phenomenon presented in Billy Budd. And the insight but intensified his passion, which assuming various secret forms within him, at times assumed that of cynic disdain, disdain of innocence—to be nothing more than innocent! Yet in an aesthetic way he saw the charm of it, the courageous free-and-easy temper of it, and fain would have shared it, but he despaired of it.

With no power to annul the elemental evil in him, though readily enough he could hide it; apprehending the good, but powerless to be it; a nature like Claggart's, surcharged with energy as such natures almost invariably are, what recourse is left to it but to recoil upon itself and, like the scorpion for which the Creator alone is responsible, act out to the end the part allotted it.

13

Passion, and passion in its profoundest, is not a thing demanding a palatial stage whereon to play its part. Down among the groundlings, among the beggars and rakers of the garbage, profound passion is enacted. And the circumstances that provoke it, however trivial or mean, are no measure of its power. In the present instance the stage is a scrubbed gun deck, and one of the external provocations a man-of-war's man's spilled soup.

Now when the master-at-arms noticed whence came that greasy fluid streaming before his feet, he must have taken it—to some extent wilfully, perhaps—not for the mere accident it assuredly was, but for the sly escape of a spontaneous feeling on Billy's part more or less answering to the antipathy on his own. In effect a foolish demonstration, he must have thought, and very harmless, like the futile kick of a heifer, which yet were the heifer a shod stallion would not be so harmless. Even so was it that into the gall of Claggart's envy he infused the vitriol of his contempt. But the incident confirmed to him certain telltale reports purveyed to his ear by "Squeak," one of his more cunning corporals, a grizzled little man, so nicknamed by the sailors on account of his squeaky voice and sharp visage ferreting about the dark corners of the lower decks after interlopers, satirically suggesting to them the idea of a rat in a cellar.

From his chief's employing him as an implicit tool in laying little traps for the worriment of the foretopman—for it was from the master-at-arms that the petty persecutions heretofore adverted to had proceeded—the corporal, having naturally enough concluded that his master could have no love for the sailor, made it his business, faithful understrapper that he was, to foment the ill blood by perverting to his chief certain innocent frolics of the good-natured foretopman, besides inventing for his mouth sundry contumelious epithets he claimed to have overheard him let fall. The master-at-arms never suspected the veracity of these reports, more especially as to the epithets, for he well knew how secretly unpopular may become a master-at-arms, at least a master-at-arms of those days, zealous in his function, and how the bluejackets shoot at him in private their raillery and wit; the nickname by which he goes among them (Jemmy Legs) implying under the form of merriment their cherished disrespect and dislike. But in view of the greediness of hate for pabulum it hardly needed a purveyor to feed Claggart's passion.

An uncommon prudence is habitual with the subtler depravity, for it has everything to hide. And in case of an injury but suspected, its secretiveness voluntarily cuts it off from enlightenment or disillusion; and, not unreluctantly, action is taken upon surmise as upon certainty. And the retaliation is apt to be in monstrous disproportion to the supposed offense; for when in anybody was revenge in its exactions aught else but an inordinate usurer? But how with Claggart's conscience? For though consciences are unlike as foreheads, every intelligence, not excluding the scriptural devils who "believe and tremble," has one. But Claggart's conscience being but the lawyer to his will, made ogres of trifles, probably arguing that the motive imputed to Billy in spilling the soup just when he did, together with the epithets alleged, these, if nothing more, made a strong case against him; nay, justified animosity into a sort of retributive righteousness. The Pharisee is the Guy Fawkes[35] prowling in the hid chambers underlying some natures like Claggart's. And they can really form no conception of an unreciprocated malice. Probably the master-at-arms' clandestine persecution of Billy was started to try the temper of the man; but it had not developed any quality in him that enmity could make official use of or even pervert into plausible self-justification; so that the occurrence at the mess, petty if it were, was a welcome one to that peculiar conscience assigned to be the private mentor of Claggart; and, for the rest, not improbably it put him upon new experiments.

---

[35] One of a group of Roman Catholics engaged in an aborted plot to blow up the Houses of Parliament on November 5, 1605.

14

Not many days after the last incident narrated, something befell Billy Budd that more graveled him than aught that had previously occurred.

It was a warm night for the latitude; and the foretopman, whose watch at the time was properly below, was dozing on the uppermost deck whither he had ascended from his hot hammock, one of hundreds suspended so closely wedged together over a lower gun deck that there was little or no swing to them. He lay as in the shadow of a hillside, stretched under the lee of the booms, a piled ridge of spare spars amidships between foremast and mainmast among which the ship's largest boat, the launch, was stowed. Alongside of three other slumberers from below, he lay near that end of the booms which approaches the foremast; his station aloft on duty as a foretopman being just over the deck-station of the forecastlemen, entitling him according to usage to make himself more or less at home in that neighborhood.

Presently he was stirred into semiconsciousness by somebody, who must have previously sounded the sleep of the others, touching his shoulder, and then, as the foretopman raised his head, breathing into his ear in a quick whisper, "Slip into the lee forechains, Billy; there is something in the wind. Don't speak. Quick, I will meet you there," and disappearing.

Now Billy, like sundry other essentially good-natured ones, had some of the weaknesses inseparable from essential good nature; and among these was a reluctance, almost an incapacity of plumply saying *no* to an abrupt proposition not obviously absurd on the face of it, nor obviously unfriendly, nor iniquitous. And being of warm blood, he had not the phlegm tacitly to negative any proposition by unresponsive inaction. Like his sense of fear, his apprehension as to aught outside of the honest and natural was seldom very quick. Besides, upon the present occasion, the drowse from his sleep still hung upon him.

However it was, he mechanically rose and, sleepily wondering what could be in the wind, betook himself to the designated place, a narrow platform, one of six, outside of the high bulwarks and screened by the great deadeyes[36] and multiple columned lanyards of the shrouds and backstays; and, in a great warship of that time, of dimensions commensurate to the hull's magnitude; a tarry bal-

[36] Wood blocks pierced with holes to receive the lanyard, used to set up shrouds and stays to support the mast.

cony in short, overhanging the sea, and so secluded that one mariner of the *Bellipotent,* a Nonconformist old tar of a serious turn, made it even in daytime his private oratory.

In this retired nook the stranger soon joined Billy Budd. There was no moon as yet; a haze obscured the starlight. He could not distinctly see the stranger's face. Yet from something in the outline and carriage, Billy took him, and correctly, for one of the afterguard.

"Hist! Billy," said the man, in the same quick cautionary whisper as before. "You were impressed, weren't you? Well, so was I"; and he paused, as to mark the effect. But Billy, not knowing exactly what to make of this, said nothing. Then the other: "We are not the only impressed ones, Billy. There's a gang of us.—Couldn't you —help—at a pinch?"

"What do you mean?" demanded Billy, here thoroughly shaking off his drowse.

"Hist, hist!" the hurried whisper now growing husky. "See here," and the man held up two small objects faintly twinkling in the night-light; "see, they are yours, Billy, if you'll only——"

But Billy broke in, and in his resentful eagerness to deliver himself his vocal infirmity somewhat intruded. "D—d—damme, I don't know what you are d—d—driving at, or what you mean, but you had better g—g—go where you belong!" For the moment the fellow, as confounded, did not stir; and Billy, springing to his feet, said, "If you d—don't start, I'll t—t—toss you back over the r—rail!" There was no mistaking this, and the mysterious emissary decamped, disappearing in the direction of the mainmast in the shadow of the booms.

"Hallo, what's the matter?" here came growling from a forecastleman awakened from his deck-doze by Billy's raised voice. And as the foretopman reappeared and was recognized by him: "Ah, Beauty, is it you? Well, something must have been the matter, for you st—st—stuttered."

"Oh," rejoined Billy, now mastering the impediment, "I found an afterguardsman in our part of the ship here, and I bid him be off where he belongs."

"And is that all you did about it, Foretopman?" gruffly demanded another, an irascible old fellow of brick-colored visage and hair who was known to his associate forecastlemen as "Red Pepper." "Such sneaks I should like to marry to the gunner's daughter!"—by that expression meaning that he would like to subject them to disciplinary castigation over a gun.

However, Billy's rendering of the matter satisfactorily accounted to these inquirers for the brief commotion, since of all the sections of a ship's company the forecastlemen, veterans for the most part and bigoted in their sea prejudices, are the most jealous in resenting territorial encroachments, especially on the part of any of the afterguard, of whom they have but a sorry opinion—chiefly landsmen, never going aloft except to reef or furl the mainsail, and in no wise competent to handle a marlinspike or turn in a deadeye, say.

15

This incident sorely puzzled Billy Budd. It was an entirely new experience, the first time in his life that he had ever been personally approached in underhand intriguing fashion. Prior to this encounter he had known nothing of the afterguardsman, the two men being stationed wide apart, one forward and aloft during his watch, the other on deck and aft.

What could it mean? And could they really be guineas, those two glittering objects the interloper had held up to his (Billy's) eyes? Where could the fellow get guineas? Why, even spare buttons are not so plentiful at sea. The more he turned the matter over, the more he was nonplussed, and made uneasy and discomfited. In his disgustful recoil from an overture which, though he but ill comprehended, he instinctively knew must involve evil of some sort, Billy Budd was like a young horse fresh from the pasture suddenly inhaling a vile whiff from some chemical factory, and by repeated snortings trying to get it out of his nostrils and lungs. This frame of mind barred all desire of holding further parley with the fellow, even were it but for the purpose of gaining some enlightenment as to his design in approaching him. And yet he was not without natural curiosity to see how such a visitor in the dark would look in broad day.

He espied him the following afternoon in his first dogwatch below, one of the smokers on that forward part of the upper gun deck allotted to the pipe. He recognized him by his general cut and build more than by his round freckled face and glassy eyes of pale blue, veiled with lashes all but white. And yet Billy was a bit uncertain whether indeed it were he—yonder chap about his own age chatting and laughing in freehearted way, leaning against a gun; a genial young fellow enough to look at, and something of a rattlebrain, to all appearance. Rather chubby too for a sailor, even an afterguardsman. In short, the last man in the world, one would think, to be overburdened with thoughts, especially those perilous thoughts that must needs belong to a conspirator in any serious project, or even to the underling of such a conspirator.

Although Billy was not aware of it, the fellow, with a sidelong watchful glance, had perceived Billy first, and then noting that Billy was looking at him, thereupon nodded a familiar sort of friendly recognition as to an old acquaintance, without interrupting the talk he was engaged in with the group of smokers. A day or two afterwards, chancing in the evening promenade on a gun deck to pass Billy, he offered a flying word of good-fellowship, as it were, which by its unexpectedness, and equivocalness under the circumstances, so embarrassed Billy that he knew not how to respond to it, and let it go unnoticed.

Billy was now left more at a loss than before. The ineffectual speculations into which he was led were so disturbingly alien to him that he did his best to smother them. It never entered his mind that here was a matter which, from its extreme questionableness, it was his duty as a loyal bluejacket to report in the proper quarter. And, probably, had such a step been suggested to him, he would have been deterred from taking it by the thought, one of novice magnanimity, that it would savor overmuch of the dirty work of a telltale. He kept the thing to himself. Yet upon one occasion he could not forbear a little disburdening himself to the old Dansker, tempted thereto perhaps by the influence of a balmy night when the ship lay becalmed; the twain, silent for the most part, sitting together on deck, their heads propped against the bulwarks. But it was only a partial and anonymous account that Billy gave, the unfounded scruples above referred to preventing full disclosure to anybody. Upon hearing Billy's version, the sage Dansker seemed to divine more than he was told; and after a little meditation, during which his wrinkles were pursed as into a point, quite effacing for the time that quizzing expression his face sometimes wore: "Didn't I say so, Baby Budd?"

"Say what?" demanded Billy.

"Why, *Jemmy Legs* is *down* on you."

"And what," rejoined Billy in amazement, "has *Jemmy Legs* to do with that cracked afterguardsman?"

"Ho, it was an afterguardsman, then. A cat's-paw, a cat's-paw!" And with that exclamation, whether it had reference to a light puff of air just then coming over the calm sea, or a subtler relation to the afterguardsman, there is no telling, the old Merlin gave a twisting wrench with his black teeth at his plug of tobacco, vouchsafing no reply to Billy's impetuous question, though now repeated, for it was his wont to relapse into grim silence when interrogated in skeptical sort as to any of his sententious oracles, not always very clear ones, rather partaking of that obscurity which invests most Delphic deliverances from any quarter.

Long experience had very likely brought this old man to that bitter prudence which never interferes in aught and never gives advice.

16

Yes, despite the Dansker's pithy insistence as to the master-at-arms being at the bottom of these strange experiences of Billy on board the *Bellipotent,* the young sailor was ready to ascribe them to almost anybody but the man who, to use Billy's own expression, "always had a pleasant word for him." This is to be wondered at. Yet not so much to be wondered at. In certain matters, some sailors even in mature life remain unsophisticated enough. But a young seafarer of the disposition of our athletic foretopman is much of a child-man. And yet a child's utter innocence is but its blank ignorance, and the innocence more or less wanes as intelligence waxes. But in Billy Budd intelligence, such as it was, had advanced while yet his simple-mindedness remained for the most part unaffected. Experience is a teacher indeed; yet did Billy's years make his experience small. Besides, he had none of that intuitive knowledge of the bad which in natures not good or incompletely so foreruns experience, and therefore may pertain, as in some instances it too clearly does pertain, even to youth.

And what could Billy know of man except of man as a mere sailor? And the old-fashioned sailor, the veritable man before the mast, the sailor from boyhood up, he, though indeed of the same species as a landsman, is in some respects singularly distinct from him. The sailor is frankness, the landsman is finesse. Life is not a game with the sailor, demanding the long head—no intricate game of chess where few moves are made in straightforwardness and ends are attained by indirection, an oblique, tedious, barren game hardly worth that poor candle burnt out in playing it.

Yes, as a class, sailors are in character a juvenile race. Even their deviations are marked by juvenility, this more especially holding true with the sailors of Billy's time. Then too, certain things which apply to all sailors do more pointedly operate here and there upon the junior one. Every sailor, too, is accustomed to obey orders without debating them; his life afloat is externally ruled for him; he is not brought into that promiscuous commerce with mankind where unobstructed free agency on equal terms—equal superficially, at least—soon teaches one that unless upon occasion he exercise a distrust keen in proportion to the fairness of the appearance, some foul turn may be served him. A ruled undemonstrative distrustfulness is so habitual, not with businessmen so much as with men who know their kind in less shallow relations than business, namely, certain men of the world, that they come at last to employ it all but unconsciously; and some of them would very likely feel real surprise at being charged with it as one of their general characteristics.

17

But after the little matter at the mess Billy Budd no more found himself in strange trouble at times about his hammock or his clothes bag or what not. As to that smile that occasionally sunned him, and the pleasant passing word, these were, if not more frequent, yet if anything more pronounced than before.

But for all that, there were certain other demonstrations now. When Claggart's unobserved glance happened to light on belted Billy rolling along the upper gun deck in the leisure of the second dogwatch, exchanging passing broadsides of fun with other young promenaders in the crowd, that glance would follow the cheerful sea Hyperion[37] with a settled meditative and melancholy expression, his eyes strangely suffused with incipient feverish tears. Then would Claggart look like the man of sorrows. Yes, and sometimes the melancholy expression would have in it a touch of soft yearning, as if Claggart could even have loved Billy but for fate and ban. But this was an evanescence, and quickly repented of, as it were, by an immitigable look, pinching and shriveling the visage into the momentary semblance of a wrinkled walnut. But sometimes catching sight in advance of the foretopman coming in his direction, he would, upon their nearing, step aside a little to let him pass, dwelling upon Billy for the moment with the glittering dental satire of a Guise.[38] But upon any abrupt unforeseen encounter a red light would flash forth from his eye like a spark from an anvil in a dusk smithy. That quick, fierce light was a strange one, darted from orbs which in repose were of a color nearest approaching a deeper violet, the softest of shades.

Though some of these caprices of the pit could not but be observed by their object, yet were they beyond the construing of such a nature. And the thews of Billy were hardly compatible with that

[37] A Titan, the father of Aurora, the Sun, and the Moon.

[38] A French ducal family associated in the sixteenth century with conspiracies and intrigues.

sort of sensitive spiritual organization which in some cases instinctively conveys to ignorant innocence an admonition of the proximity of the malign. He thought the master-at-arms acted in a manner rather queer at times. That was all. But the occasional frank air and pleasant word went for what they purported to be, the young sailor never having heard as yet of the "too fair-spoken man."

Had the foretopman been conscious of having done or said anything to provoke the ill will of the official, it would have been different with him, and his sight might have been purged if not sharpened. As it was, innocence was his blinder.

So was it with him in yet another matter. Two minor officers, the armorer and captain of the hold, with whom he had never exchanged a word, his position in the ship not bringing him into contact with them, these men now for the first began to cast upon Billy, when they chanced to encounter him, that peculiar glance which evidences that the man from whom it comes has been some way tampered with, and to the prejudice of him upon whom the glance lights. Never did it occur to Billy as a thing to be noted or a thing suspicious, though he well knew the fact, that the armorer and captain of the hold, with the ship's yeoman, apothecary, and others of that grade, were by naval usage messmates of the master-at-arms, men with ears convenient to his confidential tongue.

But the general popularity that came from our Handsome Sailor's manly forwardness upon occasion and irresistible good nature, indicating no mental superiority tending to excite an invidious feeling, this good will on the part of most of his shipmates made him the less to concern himself about such mute aspects toward him as those whereto allusion has just been made, aspects he could not so fathom as to infer their whole import.

As to the afterguardsman, though Billy for reasons already given necessarily saw little of him, yet when the two did happen to meet, invariably came the fellow's offhand cheerful recognition, sometimes accompanied by a passing pleasant word or two. Whatever that equivocal young person's original design may really have been, or the design of which he might have been the deputy, certain it was from his manner upon these occasions that he had wholly dropped it.

It was as if his precocity of crookedness (and every vulgar villain is precocious) had for once deceived him, and the man he had sought to entrap as a simpleton had through his very simplicity ignominiously baffled him.

But shrewd ones may opine that it was hardly possible for Billy to refrain from going up to the afterguardsman and bluntly demanding to know his purpose in the initial interview so abruptly closed in the forechains. Shrewd ones may also think it but natural in Billy to set about sounding some of the other impressed men of the ship in order to discover what basis, if any, there was for the emissary's obscure suggestions as to plotting disaffection aboard. Yes, shrewd ones may so think. But something more, or rather something else than mere shrewdness is perhaps needful for the due understanding of such a character as Billy Budd's.

As to Claggart, the monomania in the man—if that indeed it were—as involuntarily disclosed by starts in the manifestations detailed, yet in general covered over by his self-contained and rational demeanor; this, like a subterranean fire, was eating its way deeper and deeper in him. Something decisive must come of it.

18

After the mysterious interview in the forechains, the one so abruptly ended there by Billy, nothing especially germane to the story occurred until the events now about to be narrated.

Elsewhere it has been said that in the lack of frigates (of course better sailers than line-of-battle ships) in the English squadron up the Straits at that period, the *Bellipotent 74* was occasionally employed not only as an available substitute for a scout, but at times on detached service of more important kind. This was not alone because of her sailing qualities, not common in a ship of her rate, but quite as much, probably, that the character of her commander, it was thought, specially adapted him for any duty where under unforeseen difficulties a prompt initiative might have to be taken in some matter demanding knowledge and ability in addition to those qualities implied in good seamanship. It was on an expedition of the latter sort, a somewhat distant one, and when the *Bellipotent* was almost at her furthest remove from the fleet, that in the latter part of an afternoon watch she unexpectedly came in sight of a ship of the enemy. It proved to be a frigate. The latter, perceiving through the glass that the weight of men and metal would be heavily against her, invoking her light heels crowded sail to get away. After a chase urged almost against hope and lasting until about the middle of the first dogwatch, she signally succeeded in effecting her escape.

Not long after the pursuit had been given up, and ere the excitement incident thereto had altogether waned away, the master-at-arms, ascending from his cavernous sphere, made his appearance cap in hand by the mainmast respectfully waiting the notice of Captain Vere, then solitary walking the weather side of the quarter-deck, doubtless somewhat chafed at the failure of the pursuit. The spot where Claggart stood was the place allotted to men of lesser grades seeking some more particular interview either with the officer of the deck or the captain himself. But from the latter it was not often that a sailor or petty officer of those days would seek a hearing; only some exceptional cause would, according to established custom, have warranted that.

Presently, just as the commander, absorbed in his reflections, was on the point of turning aft in his promenade, he became sensible of Claggart's presence, and saw the doffed cap held in deferential expectancy. Here be it said that Captain Vere's personal knowledge of this petty officer had only begun at the time of the ship's last sailing from home, Claggart then for the first, in transfer from a ship detained for repairs, supplying on board the *Bellipotent* the place of a previous master-at-arms disabled and ashore.

No sooner did the commander observe who it was that now deferentially stood awaiting his notice than a peculiar expression came over him. It was not unlike that which uncontrollably will flit across the countenance of one at unawares encountering a person who, though known to him indeed, has hardly been long enough known for thorough knowledge, but something in whose aspect nevertheless now for the first provokes a vaguely repellent distaste. But coming to a stand and resuming much of his wonted official manner, save that a sort of impatience lurked in the intonation of the opening word, he said "Well? What is it, Master-at-arms?"

With the air of a subordinate grieved at the necessity of being a messenger of ill tidings, and while conscientiously determined to be frank yet equally resolved upon shunning overstatement, Claggart at this invitation, or rather summons to disburden, spoke up. What he said, conveyed in the language of no uneducated man, was to the effect following, if not altogether in these words, namely, that during the chase and preparations for the possible encounter he had seen enough to convince him that at least one sailor aboard was a dangerous character in a ship mustering some who not only had taken a guilty part in the late serious troubles, but others also who, like the man in question, had entered His Majesty's service under another form than enlistment.

At this point Captain Vere with some impatience interrupted him: "Be direct, man; say *impressed men.*"

Claggart made a gesture of subservience, and proceeded. Quite lately he (Claggart) had begun to suspect that on the gun decks some sort of movement prompted by the sailor in question was covertly going on, but he had not thought himself warranted in reporting the suspicion so long as it remained indistinct. But from what he had that afternoon observed in the man referred to, the suspicion of something clandestine going on had advanced to a point less removed from certainty. He deeply felt, he added, the serious responsibility assumed in making a report involving such possible consequences to the individual mainly concerned, besides tending to augment those natural anxieties which every naval commander must feel in view of extraordinary outbreaks so recent as those which, he sorrowfully said it, it needed not to name.

Now at the first broaching of the matter Captain Vere, taken by surprise, could not wholly dissemble his disquietude. But as Claggart went on, the former's aspect changed into restiveness under something in the testifier's manner in giving his testimony. However, he refrained from interrupting him. And Claggart, continuing, concluded with this: "God forbid, your honor, that the *Bellipotent*'s should be the experience of the——"

"Never mind that!" here peremptorily broke in the superior, his face altering with anger, instinctively divining the ship that the others was about to name, one in which the Nore Mutiny had assumed a singularly tragical character that for a time jeopardized the life of its commander. Under the circumstances he was indignant at the purposed allusion. When the commissioned officers themselves were on all occasions very heedful how they referred to the recent events in the fleet, for a petty officer unnecessarily to allude to them in the presence of his captain, this struck him as a most immodest presumption. Besides, to his quick sense of self-respect it even looked under the circumstances something like an attempt to alarm him. Nor at first was he without some surprise that one who so far as he had hitherto come under his notice had shown considerable tact in his function should in this particular evince such lack of it.

But these thoughts and kindred dubious ones flitting across his mind were suddenly replaced by an intuitional surmise which, though as yet obscure in form, served practically to affect his reception of the ill tidings. Certain it is that, long versed in everything pertaining to the complicated gun-deck life, which like every other form of life has its secret mines and dubious side, the side popularly disclaimed, Captain Vere did not permit himself to be unduly disturbed by the general tenor of his subordinate's report.

Furthermore, if in view of recent events prompt action should be taken at the first palpable sign of recurring insubordination, for all that, not judicious would it be, he thought, to keep the idea of lingering disaffection alive by undue forwardness in crediting an informer, even if his own subordinate and charged among other things with police surveillance of the crew. This feeling would not perhaps have so prevailed with him were it not that upon a prior occasion the patriotic zeal officially evinced by Claggart had somewhat irritated him as appearing rather supersensible and strained. Furthermore, something even in the official's self-possessed and somewhat ostentatious manner in making his specifications strangely reminded him of a bandsman, a perjurous witness in a capital case before a court-martial ashore of which when a lieutenant he (Captain Vere) had been a member.

Now the peremptory check given to Claggart in the matter of the arrested allusion was quickly followed up by this: "You say that there is at least one dangerous man aboard. Name him."

"William Budd, a foretopman, your honor."

"William Budd!" repeated Captain Vere with unfeigned astonishment. "And mean you the man that Lieutenant Ratcliffe took from the merchantman not very long ago, the young fellow who seems to be so popular with the men—Billy, the Handsome Sailor, as they call him?"

"The same, your honor; but for all his youth and good looks, a deep one. Not for nothing does he insinuate himself into the good will of his shipmates, since at the least they will at a pinch say—all hands will—a good word for him, and at all hazards. Did Lieutenant Ratcliffe happen to tell your honor of that adroit fling of Budd's, jumping up in the cutter's bow under the merchantman's stern when he was being taken off? It is even masked by that sort of good-humored air that at heart he resents his impressment. You have but noted his fair cheek. A mantrap may be under the ruddy-tipped daisies."

Now the Handsome Sailor as a signal figure among the crew had naturally enough attracted the captain's attention from the first. Though in general not very demonstrative to his officers, he had congratulated Lieutenant Ratcliffe upon his good fortune in lighting on such a fine specimen of the *genus homo,* who in the nude might have posed for a statue of young Adam before the Fall. As to Billy's adieu to the ship *Rights-of-Man,* which the boarding lieutenant had indeed reported to him, but, in a deferential way, more as a good story than aught else, Captain Vere, though mistakenly understanding it as a satiric sally, had but thought so much the better of the impressed man for it; as a military sailor, admiring the spirit that could take an arbitrary enlistment so merrily and sensibly. The foretopman's conduct, too, so far as it had fallen under the captain's notice, had confirmed the first happy augury, while the new recruit's qualities as a "sailor-man" seemed to be such that he had thought of recommending him to the executive officer for promotion to a place that would more frequently bring him under his own observation, namely, the captaincy of the mizzentop, replacing there in the starboard watch a man not so young whom partly for that reason he deemed less fitted for the post. Be it parenthesized here that since the mizzen-topmen have not to handle such breadths of heavy canvas as the lower sails on the mainmast and foremast, a young man if of the right stuff not only seems best adapted to duty there, but in fact is generally selected for the captaincy of that top, and the company under him are light hands and often but striplings. In sum, Captain Vere had from the beginning deemed Billy Budd to be what in the naval parlance of the time was called a "King's bargain": that is to say, for His Britannic Majesty's navy a capital investment at small outlay or none at all.

After a brief pause, during which the reminiscences above mentioned passed vividly through his mind and he weighed the import of Claggart's last suggestion conveyed in the phrase "mantrap under the daisies," and the more he weighed it the less reliance he felt in the informer's good faith, suddenly he turned upon him and in a low voice demanded: "Do you come to me, Master-at-arms, with so foggy a tale? As to Budd, cite me an act or spoken word of his confirmatory of what you in general charge against him. Stay," drawing nearer to him; "heed what you speak. Just now, and in a case like this, there is a yardarm-end for the false witness."

"Ah, your honor!" sighed Claggart, mildly shaking his shapely head as in sad deprecation of such unmerited severity of tone. Then, bridling—erecting himself as in virtuous self-assertion—he circumstantially alleged certain words and acts which collectively, if credited, led to presumptions mortally inculpating Budd. And for some of these averments, he added, substantiating proof was not far.

With gray eyes impatient and distrustful essaying to fathom to the bottom Claggart's calm violet ones, Captain Vere again heard him out; then for the moment stood ruminating. The mood he evinced, Claggart—himself for the time liberated from the other's scrutiny—steadily regarded with a look difficult to render: a look curious of the operation of his tactics, a look such as might have been that of the spokesman of the envious children of Jacob deceptively imposing upon the troubled patriarch the blood-dyed coat of young Joseph.

Though something exceptional in the moral quality of Captain Vere made him, in earnest encounter with a fellow man, a veritable touchstone of that man's essential nature, yet now as to Claggart and what was really going on in him his feeling partook less of intuitional conviction than of strong suspicion clogged by strange dubieties. The perplexity he evinced proceeded less from aught touching the man informed against—as Claggart doubtless opined—than from considerations how best to act in regard to the informer. At first, indeed, he was naturally for summoning that substantiation of his allegations which Claggart said was at hand. But such a proceeding would result in the matter at once getting abroad, which in the present stage of it, he thought, might undesirably affect the ship's company. If Claggart was a false witness—that closed the affair. And therefore, before trying the accusation, he would first practically test the accuser; and he thought this could be done in a quiet, undemonstrative way.

The measure he determined upon involved a shifting of the scene, a transfer to a place less exposed to observation than the broad quarter-deck. For although the few gun-room officers there at the time had, in due observance of naval etiquette, withdrawn to leeward the moment Captain Vere had begun his promenade on the deck's weather side; and though during the colloquy with Claggart they of course ventured not to diminish the distance; and though throughout the interview Captain Vere's voice was far from high, and Claggart's silvery and low; and the wind in the cordage and the wash of the sea helped the more to put them beyond earshot; nevertheless, the interview's continuance already had attracted observation from some topmen aloft and other sailors in the waist or further forward.

Having determined upon his measures, Captain Vere forthwith took action. Abruptly turning to Claggart, he asked, "Master-at-arms, is it now Budd's watch aloft?"

"No, your honor."

Whereupon, "Mr. Wilkes!" summoning the nearest midshipman. "Tell Albert to come to me." Albert was the captain's hammock-boy, a sort of sea valet in whose discretion and fidelity his master had much confidence. The lad appeared.

"You know Budd, the foretopman?"

"I do, sir."

"Go find him. It is his watch off. Manage to tell him out of earshot that he is wanted aft. Contrive it that he speaks to nobody. Keep him in talk yourself. And not till you get well aft here, not till then let him know that the place where he is wanted is my cabin. You understand. Go.—Master-at-arms, show yourself on the decks below, and when you think it time for Albert to be coming with his man, stand by quietly to follow the sailor in."

19

Now when the foretopman found himself in the cabin, closeted there, as it were, with the captain and Claggart, he was surprised enough. But it was a surprise unaccompanied by apprehension or distrust. To an immature nature essentially honest and humane, forewarning intimations of subtler danger from one's kind come tardily if at all. The only thing that took shape in the young sailor's mind was this: Yes, the captain, I have always thought, looks kindly upon me. Wonder if he's going to make me his coxswain. I should like that. And may be now he is going to ask the master-at-arms about me.

"Shut the door there, sentry," said the commander; "stand without, and let nobody come in.—Now, Master-at-arms, tell this man to his face what you told of him to me," and stood prepared to scrutinize the mutually confronting visages.

With the measured step and calm collected air of an asylum physician approaching in the public hall some patient beginning to show indications of a coming paroxysm, Claggart deliberately advanced within short range of Billy and, mesmerically looking him in the eye, briefly recapitulated the accusation.

Not at first did Billy take it in. When he did, the rose-tan of his cheek looked struck as by white leprosy. He stood like one impaled and gagged. Meanwhile the accuser's eyes, removing not as yet from the blue dilated ones, underwent a phenomenal change, their wonted rich violet color blurring into a muddy purple. Those lights of human intelligence, losing human expression, were gelidly protruding like the alien eyes of certain uncatalogued creatures of the deep. The first mesmeristic glance was one of serpent fascination; the last was as the paralyzing lurch of the torpedo fish.

"Speak, man!" said Captain Vere to the transfixed one, struck by his aspect even more than by Claggart's. "Speak! Defend yourself!" Which appeal caused but a strange dumb gesturing and gurgling in Billy; amazement at such an accusation so suddenly sprung on inexperienced nonage; this, and, it may be, horror of the accuser's eyes, serving to bring out his lurking defect and in this instance for the time intensifying it into a convulsed tongue-tie; while the intent head and entire form straining forward in an agony of ineffectual eagerness to obey the injunction to speak and defend himself, gave an expression to the face like that of a condemned vestal priestess in the moment of being buried alive, and in the first struggle against suffocation.

Though at the time Captain Vere was quite ignorant of Billy's liability to vocal impediment, he now immediately divined it, since vividly Billy's aspect recalled to him that of a bright young schoolmate of his whom he had once seen struck by much the same startling impotence in the act of eagerly rising in the class to be foremost in response to a testing question put to it by the master. Going close up to the young sailor, and laying a soothing hand on his shoulder, he said, "There is no hurry, my boy. Take your time, take your time." Contrary to the effect intended, these words so fatherly in tone, doubtless touching Billy's heart to the quick, prompted yet more violent efforts at utterance—efforts soon ending for the time in confirming the paralysis, and bringing to his face an expression which was as a crucifixion to behold. The next instant, quick as the flame from a discharged cannon at night, his right arm shot out, and Claggart dropped to the deck. Whether intentionally or but owing to the young athlete's superior height, the blow had taken effect full upon the forehead, so shapely and intellectual-looking a feature in the master-at-arms; so that the body fell over lengthwise, like a heavy plank tilted from erectness. A gasp or two, and he lay motionless.

"Fated boy," breathed Captain Vere in tone so low as to be almost a whisper, "what have you done! But here, help me."

The twain raised the felled one from the loins up into a sitting position. The spare form flexibly acquiesced, but inertly. It was like handling a dead snake. They lowered it back. Regaining erectness, Captain Vere with one hand covering his face stood to all appearance as impassive as the object at his feet. Was he absorbed in taking in all the bearings of the event and what was best not only now at once to be done, but also in the sequel? Slowly he uncovered his face; and the effect was as if the moon emerging from eclipse should reappear with quite another aspect than that which had gone into hiding. The father in him, manifested towards Billy thus far in the scene, was replaced by the military disciplinarian. In his official tone he bade the foretopman retire to a stateroom aft (pointing it out), and there remain till thence summoned. This order Billy in silence mechanically obeyed. Then going to the cabin door where it opened on the quarter-deck, Captain Vere said to the sentry without, "Tell somebody to send Albert here." When the lad appeared, his master so contrived it that he should not catch sight of the prone one. "Albert," he said to him, "tell the surgeon I wish to see him. You need not come back till called."

When the surgeon entered—a self-poised character of that grave sense and experience that hardly anything could take him aback—Captain Vere advanced to meet him, thus unconsciously intercepting his view of Claggart, and, interrupting the other's wonted ceremonious salutation, said, "Nay. Tell me how it is with yonder man," directing his attention to the prostrate one.

The surgeon looked, and for all his self-command somewhat started at the abrupt revelation. On Claggart's always pallid complexion, thick black blood was now oozing from nostril and ear. To the gazer's professional eye it was unmistakably no living man that he saw.

"Is it so, then?" said Captain Vere, intently watching him. "I thought it. But verify it." Whereupon the customary tests confirmed the surgeon's first glance, who now, looking up in unfeigned concern, cast a look of intense inquisitiveness upon his superior. But Captain Vere, with one hand to his brow, was standing motionless. Suddenly, catching the surgeon's arm convulsively, he exclaimed, pointing down to the body, "It is the divine judgment on Ananias! [39] Look!"

Disturbed by the excited manner he had never before observed in the *Bellipotent*'s captain, and as yet wholly ignorant of the affair, the prudent surgeon nevertheless held his peace, only again looking an earnest interrogatory as to what it was that had resulted in such a tragedy.

But Captain Vere was now again motionless, standing absorbed in thought. Again starting, he vehemently exclaimed, "Struck dead by an angel of God! Yet the angel must hang!"

At these passionate interjections, mere incoherences to the listener as yet unapprised of the antecedents, the surgeon was profoundly discomposed. But now, as recollecting himself, Captain Vere in less passionate tone briefly related the circumstances leading up to the event. "But come; we must dispatch," he added. "Help me to remove him" (meaning the body) "to yonder compartment," designating one opposite that where the foretopman remained immured. Anew disturbed by a request that, as implying a desire for secrecy, seemed unaccountably strange to him, there was nothing for the subordinate to do but comply.

"Go now," said Captain Vere with something of his wonted

[39] A follower of the apostles who, after being reproved by Peter for lying, fell dead.

manner. "Go now. I presently shall call a drumhead court. Tell the lieutenants what has happened, and tell Mr. Mordant" (meaning the captain of marines), "and charge them to keep the matter to themselves."

20

Full of disquietude and misgiving, the surgeon left the cabin. Was Captain Vere suddenly affected in his mind, or was it but a transient excitement, brought about by so strange and extraordinary a tragedy? As to the drumhead court, it struck the surgeon as impolitic, if nothing more. The thing to do, he thought, was to place Billy Budd in confinement, and in a way dictated by usage, and postpone further action in so extraordinary a case to such time as they should rejoin the squadron, and then refer it to the admiral. He recalled the unwonted agitation of Captain Vere and his excited exclamations, so at variance with his normal manner. Was he unhinged?

But assuming that he is, it is not so susceptible of proof. What then can the surgeon do? No more trying situation is conceivable than that of an officer subordinate under a captain whom he suspects to be not mad, indeed, but yet not quite unaffected in his intellects. To argue his order to him would be insolence. To resist him would be mutiny.

In obedience to Captain Vere, he communicated what had happened to the lieutenants and captain of marines, saying nothing as to the captain's state. They fully shared his own surprise and concern. Like him too, they seemed to think that such a matter should be referred to the admiral.

21

Who in the rainbow can draw the line where the violet tint ends and the orange tint begins? Distinctly we see the difference of the colors, but where exactly does the one first blendingly enter into the other? So with sanity and insanity. In pronounced cases there is no question about them. But in some supposed cases, in various degrees supposedly less pronounced, to draw the exact line of demarcation few will undertake, though for a fee becoming considerate some professional experts will. There is nothing namable but that some men will, or undertake to, do it for pay.

Whether Captain Vere, as the surgeon professionally and privately surmised, was really the sudden victim of any degree of aberration, every one must determine for himself by such light as this narrative may afford.

That the unhappy event which has been narrated could not have happened at a worse juncture was but too true. For it was close on the heel of the suppressed insurrections, an aftertime very critical to naval authority, demanding from every English sea commander two qualities not readily interfusable—prudence and rigor. Moreover, there was something crucial in the case.

In the jugglery of circumstances preceding and attending the event on board the *Bellipotent,* and in the light of that martial code whereby it was formally to be judged, innocence and guilt personified in Claggart and Budd in effect changed places. In a legal view the apparent victim of the tragedy was he who had sought to victimize a man blameless; and the indisputable deed of the latter, navally regarded, constituted the most heinous of military crimes. Yet more. The essential right and wrong involved in the matter, the clearer that might be, so much the worse for the responsibility of a loyal sea commander, inasmuch as he was not authorized to determine the matter on that primitive basis.

Small wonder then that the *Bellipotent*'s captain, though in general a man of rapid decision, felt that circumspectness not less than promptitude was necessary. Until he could decide upon his course, and in each detail; and not only so, but until the concluding measure was upon the point of being enacted, he deemed it advisable, in view of all the circumstances, to guard as much as possible against publicity. Here he may or may not have erred. Certain it is, however, that subsequently in the confidential talk of more than one or two gun rooms and cabins he was not a little criticized by some officers, a fact imputed by his friends and vehemently by his cousin Jack Denton to professional jealousy of Starry Vere. Some imaginative ground for invidious comment there was. The maintenance of secrecy in the matter, the confining all knowledge of it for a time to the place where the homicide occurred, the quarterdeck cabin; in these particulars lurked some resemblance to the policy adopted in those tragedies of the palace which have occurred more than once in the capital founded by Peter the Barbarian.[40]

The case indeed was such that fain would the *Bellipotent*'s captain have deferred taking any action whatever respecting it further than to keep the foretopman a close prisoner till the ship rejoined the squadron and then submitting the matter to the judgment of his admiral.

But a true military officer is in one particular like a true monk.

---

[40] Peter the Great of Russia (1672-1725), who founded St. Petersburg in 1703.

Not with more of self-abnegation will the latter keep his vows of monastic obedience than the former his vows of allegiance to martial duty.

Feeling that unless quick action was taken on it, the deed of the foretopman, so soon as it should be known on the gun decks, would tend to awaken any slumbering embers of the Nore among the crew, a sense of the urgency of the case overruled in Captain Vere every other consideration. But though a conscientious disciplinarian, he was no lover of authority for mere authority's sake. Very far was he from embracing opportunities for monopolizing to himself the perils of moral responsibility, none at least that could properly be referred to an official superior or shared with him by his official equals or even subordinates. So thinking, he was glad it would not be at variance with usage to turn the matter over to a summary court of his own officers, reserving to himself, as the one on whom the ultimate accountability would rest, the right of maintaining a supervision of it, or formally or informally interposing at need. Accordingly a drumhead court was summarily convened, he electing the individuals composing it: the first lieutenant, the captain of marines, and the sailing master.

In associating an officer of marines with the sea lieutenant and the sailing master in a case having to do with a sailor, the commander perhaps deviated from general custom. He was prompted thereto by the circumstance that he took that soldier to be a judicious person, thoughtful, and not altogether incapable of grappling with a difficult case unprecedented in his prior experience. Yet even as to him he was not without some latent misgiving, for withal he was an extremely good-natured man, an enjoyer of his dinner, a sound sleeper, and inclined to obesity—a man who though he would always maintain his manhood in battle might not prove altogether reliable in a moral dilemma involving aught of the tragic. As to the first lieutenant and the sailing master, Captain Vere could not but be aware that though honest natures, of approved gallantry upon occasion, their intelligence was mostly confined to the matter of active seamanship and the fighting demands of their profession.

The court was held in the same cabin where the unfortunate affair had taken place. This cabin, the commander's, embraced the entire area under the poop deck. Aft, and on either side, was a small stateroom, the one now temporarily a jail and the other a dead-house, and a yet smaller compartment, leaving a space between expanding forward into a goodly oblong of length coinciding with the ship's beam. A skylight of moderate dimension was overhead, and at each end of the oblong space were two sashed porthole windows easily convertible back into embrasures for short carronades.

All being quickly in readiness, Billy Budd was arraigned, Captain Vere necessarily appearing as the sole witness in the case, and as such temporarily sinking his rank, though singularly maintaining it in a matter apparently trivial, namely, that he testified from the ship's weather side, with that object having caused the court to sit on the lee side. Concisely he narrated all that had led up to the catastrophe, omitting nothing in Claggart's accusation and deposing as to the manner in which the prisoner had received it. At this testimony the three officers glanced with no little surprise at Billy Budd, the last man they would have suspected either of the mutinous design alleged by Claggart or the undeniable deed he himself had done. The first lieutenant, taking judicial primacy and turning toward the prisoner, said, "Captain Vere has spoken. Is it or is it not as Captain Vere says?"

In response came syllables not so much impeded in the utterance as might have been anticipated. They were these: "Captain Vere tells the truth. It is just as Captain Vere says, but it is not as the master-at-arms said. I have eaten the King's bread and I am true to the King."

"I believe you, my man," said the witness, his voice indicating a suppressed emotion not otherwise betrayed.

"God will bless you for that, your honor!" not without stammering said Billy, and all but broke down. But immediately he was recalled to self-control by another question, to which with the same emotional difficulty of utterance he said, "No, there was no malice between us. I never bore malice against the master-at-arms. I am sorry that he is dead. I did not mean to kill him. Could I have used my tongue I would not have struck him. But he foully lied to my face and in presence of my captain, and I had to say something, and I could only say it with a blow, God help me!"

In the impulsive aboveboard manner of the frank one the court saw confirmed all that was implied in words that just previously had perplexed them, coming as they did from the testifier to the tragedy and promptly following Billy's impassioned disclaimer of mutinous intent—Captain Vere's words, "I believe you, my man."

Next it was asked of him whether he knew of or suspected aught savoring of incipient trouble (meaning mutiny, though the explicit term was avoided) going on in any section of the ship's company.

The reply lingered. This was naturally imputed by the court to the same vocal embarrassment which had retarded or obstructed previous answers. But in main it was otherwise here, the question immediately recalling to Billy's mind the interview with the afterguardsman in the forechains. But an innate repugnance to playing a part at all approaching that of an informer against one's own shipmates—the same erring sense of uninstructed honor which had stood in the way of his reporting the matter at the time, though as a loyal man-of-war's man it was incumbent on him, and failure so to do, if charged against him and proven, would have subjected him to the heaviest of penalties; this, with the blind feeling now his that nothing really was being hatched, prevailed with him. When the answer came it was a negative.

"One question more," said the officer of marines, now first speaking and with a troubled earnestness. "You tell us that what the master-at-arms said against you was a lie. Now why should he have so lied, so maliciously lied, since you declare there was no malice between you?"

At that question, unintentionally touching on a spiritual sphere wholly obscure to Billy's thoughts, he was nonplussed, evincing a confusion indeed that some observers, such as can readily be imagined, would have construed into involuntary evidence of hidden guilt. Nevertheless, he strove some way to answer, but all at once relinquished the vain endeavor, at the same time turning an appealing glance towards Captain Vere as deeming him his best helper and friend. Captain Vere, who had been seated for a time, rose to his feet, addressing the interrogator. "The question you put to him comes naturally enough. But how can he rightly answer it?—or anybody else, unless indeed it be he who lies within there," designating the compartment where lay the corpse. "But the prone one there will not rise to our summons. In effect, though, as it seems to me, the point you make is hardly material. Quite aside from any conceivable motive actuating the master-at-arms, and irrespective of the provocation to the blow, a martial court must needs in the present case confine its attention to the blow's consequence, which consequence justly is to be deemed not otherwise than as the striker's deed."

This utterance, the full significance of which it was not at all likely that Billy took in, nevertheless caused him to turn a wistful interrogative look toward the speaker, a look in its dumb expressiveness not unlike that which a dog of generous breed might turn upon his master, seeking in his face some elucidation of a previous gesture ambiguous to the canine intelligence. Nor was the same utterance without marked effect upon the three officers, more especially the soldier. Couched in it seemed to them a meaning unanticipated, involving a prejudgment on the speaker's part. It served to augment a mental disturbance previously evident enough. The soldier once more spoke, in a tone of suggestive dubiety addressing at once his associates and Captain Vere: "Nobody is present—none of the ship's company, I mean—who might shed lateral light, if any is to be had, upon what remains mysterious in this matter."

"That is thoughtfully put," said Captain Vere; "I see your drift. Ay, there is a mystery; but, to use a scriptural phrase, it is a 'mystery of iniquity,' a matter for psychologic theologians to discuss. But what has a military court to do with it? Not to add that for us any possible investigation of it is cut off by the lasting tongue-tie of—him—in yonder," again designating the mortuary stateroom. "The prisoner's deed—with that alone we have to do."

To this, and particularly the closing reiteration, the marine soldier, knowing not how aptly to reply, sadly abstained from saying aught. The first lieutenant, who at the outset had not unnaturally assumed primacy in the court, now overrulingly instructed by a glance from Captain Vere, a glance more effective than words, resumed that primacy. Turning to the prisoner, "Budd," he said, and scarce in equable tones, "Budd, if you have aught further to say for yourself, say it now."

Upon this the young sailor turned another quick glance toward Captain Vere; then, as taking a hint from that aspect, a hint confirming his own instinct that silence was now best, replied to the lieutenant, "I have said all, sir."

The marine—the same who had been the sentinel without the cabin door at the time that the foretopman, followed by the master-at-arms, entered it—he, standing by the sailor throughout these judicial proceedings, was now directed to take him back to the after compartment originally assigned to the prisoner and his custodian. As the twain disappeared from view, the three officers, as partially liberated from some inward constraint associated with Billy's mere presence, simultaneously stirred in their seats. They exchanged looks of troubled indecision, yet feeling that decide they must and without long delay. For Captain Vere, he for the time stood—unconsciously with his back toward them, apparently in one of his absent fits—gazing out from a sashed porthole to windward upon the monotonous blank of the twilight sea. But the court's silence continuing, broken only at moments by brief consultations, in low earnest tones, this served to arouse him and energize him. Turning, he to-and-fro paced the cabin athwart; in the returning ascent to windward climbing the slant deck in the ship's lee roll, without knowing it symbolizing thus in his action a mind resolute to surmount difficulties even if against primitive instincts strong as the wind and the sea. Presently he came to a stand before the three. After scanning their faces he stood less as mustering his thoughts for expression than as one inly deliberating how best to put them to well-meaning men not intellectually mature, men with whom it was necessary to demonstrate certain principles that were axioms to himself. Similar impatience as to talking is perhaps one reason that deters some minds from addressing any popular assemblies.

When speak he did, something, both in the substance of what he said and his manner of saying it, showed the influence of unshared studies modifying and tempering the practical training of an active career. This, along with his phraseology, now and then was suggestive of the grounds whereon rested that imputation of a certain pedantry socially alleged against him by certain naval men of wholly practical cast, captains who nevertheless would frankly concede that His Majesty's navy mustered no more efficient officer of their grade than Starry Vere.

What he said was to this effect: "Hitherto I have been but the witness, little more; and I should hardly think now to take another tone, that of your coadjutor for the time, did I not perceive in you—at the crisis too—a troubled hesitancy, proceeding, I doubt not, from the clash of military duty with moral scruple—scruple vitalized by compassion. For the compassion, how can I otherwise than share it? But, mindful of paramount obligations, I strive against scruples that may tend to enervate decision. Not, gentlemen, that I hide from myself that the case is an exceptional one. Speculatively regarded, it well might be referred to a jury of casuists. But for us here, acting not as casuists or moralists, it is a case practical, and under martial law practically to be dealt with.

"But your scruples: do they move as in a dusk? Challenge them. Make them advance and declare themselves. Come now; do they import something like this: If, mindless of palliating circumstances, we are bound to regard the death of the master-at-arms as the prisoner's deed, then does that deed constitute a capital crime whereof the penalty is a mortal one. But in natural justice is nothing but the prisoner's overt act to be considered? How can we adjudge to summary and shameful death a fellow creature innocent before God, and whom we feel to be so?—Does that state it aright? You sign sad assent. Well, I too feel that, the full force of that. It is Nature. But do these buttons that we wear attest that our allegiance is to Nature? No, to the King. Though the ocean, which is inviolate Nature primeval, though this be the element where we move and have our being as sailors, yet as the King's officers lies our duty in a sphere correspondingly natural? So little is that true, that in receiving our commissions we in the most important regards ceased to be natural free agents. When war is declared are we the commissioned fighters previously consulted? We fight at command. If our judgments approve the war, that is but coincidence. So in other particulars. So now. For suppose condemnation to follow these present proceedings. Would it be so much we ourselves that would condemn as it would be martial law operating through us? For that law and the rigor of it, we are not responsible. Our vowed responsibility is in this: That however pitilessly that law may operate in any instances, we nevertheless adhere to it and administer it.

"But the exceptional in the matter moves the hearts within you. Even so too is mine moved. But let not warm hearts betray heads that should be cool. Ashore in a criminal case, will an upright judge allow himself off the bench to be waylaid by some tender kinswoman of the accused seeking to touch him with her tearful plea? Well, the heart here, sometimes the feminine in man, is as that piteous woman, and hard though it be, she must here be ruled out."

He paused, earnestly studying them for a moment; then resumed.

"But something in your aspect seems to urge that it is not solely the heart that moves in you, but also the conscience, the private conscience. But tell me whether or not, occupying the position we do, private conscience should not yield to that imperial one formulated in the code under which alone we officially proceed?"

Here the three men moved in their seats, less convinced than agitated by the course of an argument troubling but the more the spontaneous conflict within.

Perceiving which, the speaker paused for a moment; then abruptly changing his tone, went on.

"To steady us a bit, let us recur to the facts.—In wartime at sea a man-of-war's man strikes his superior in grade, and the blow kills. Apart from its effect the blow itself is, according to the Articles of War, a capital crime. Furthermore ——"

"Ay, sir," emotionally broke in the officer of marines, "in one sense it was. But surely Budd purposed neither mutiny nor homicide."

"Surely not, my good man. And before a court less arbitrary and more merciful than a martial one, that plea would largely extenuate. At the Last Assizes it shall acquit. But how here? We proceed under the law of the Mutiny Act. In feature no child can resemble his father more than that Act resembles in spirit the thing from which it derives—War. In His Majesty's service—in this ship, indeed—there are Englishmen forced to fight for the King against their will. Against their conscience, for aught we know. Though as their fellow creatures some of us may appreciate their position, yet as navy officers what reck we of it? Still less recks the enemy. Our impressed men he would fain cut down in the same swath with our volunteers. As regards the enemy's naval conscripts, some of whom may even share our own abhorrence of the regicidal French Directory, it is the same on our side. War looks but to the frontage, the appearance. And the Mutiny Act, War's child, takes after the father. Budd's intent or non-intent is nothing to the purpose.

"But while, put to it by those anxieties in you which I cannot but respect, I only repeat myself—while thus strangely we prolong proceedings that should be summary—the enemy may be sighted and an engagement result. We must do; and one of two things must we do—condemn or let go."

"Can we not convict and yet mitigate the penalty?" asked the sailing master, here speaking, and falteringly, for the first.

"Gentlemen, were that clearly lawful for us under the circumstances, consider the consequences of such clemency. The people" (meaning the ship's company) "have native sense; most of them are familiar with our naval usage and tradition; and how would they take it? Even could you explain to them—which our official position forbids—they, long molded by arbitrary discipline, have not that kind of intelligent responsiveness that might qualify them to comprehend and discriminate. No, to the people the foretopman's deed, however it be worded in the announcement, will be plain homicide committed in a flagrant act of mutiny. What penalty for that should follow, they know. But it does not follow. *Why?* they will ruminate. You know what sailors are. Will they not revert to the recent outbreak at the Nore? Ay. They know the well-founded alarm—the panic it struck throughout England. Your clement sentence they would account pusillanimous. They would think that we flinch, that we are afraid of them—afraid of practicing a lawful rigor singularly demanded at this juncture, lest it should provoke new troubles. What shame to us such a conjecture on their part, and how deadly to discipline. You see then, whither, prompted by duty and the law, I steadfastly drive. But I beseech you, my friends, do not take me amiss. I feel as you do for this unfortunate boy. But did he know our hearts, I take him to be of that generous nature that he would feel even for us on whom in this military necessity so heavy a compulsion is laid."

With that, crossing the deck he resumed his place by the sashed porthole, tacitly leaving the three to come to a decision. On the cabin's opposite side the troubled court sat silent. Loyal lieges, plain and practical, though at bottom they dissented from some points Captain Vere had put to them, they were without the faculty, hardly had the inclination, to gainsay one whom they felt to be an earnest man, one too not less their superior in mind than in naval rank. But it is not improbable that even such of his words as were not without influence over them, less came home to them than his closing appeal to their instinct as sea officers: in the forethought he threw out as to the practical consequences to discipline, considering the unconfirmed tone of the fleet at the time, should a man-of-war's man's violent killing at sea of a superior in grade be allowed to pass for aught else than a capital crime demanding prompt infliction of the penalty.

Not unlikely they were brought to something more or less akin to that harassed frame of mind which in the year 1842 actuated the commander[41] of the U.S. brig-of-war *Somers* to resolve, under the so-called Articles of War, Articles modeled upon the English Mutiny Act, to resolve upon the execution at sea of a midshipman and two sailors as mutineers designing the seizure of the brig. Which resolution was carried out though in a time of peace and within not many days' sail of home. An act vindicated by a naval court of inquiry subsequently convened ashore. History, and here cited without comment. True, the circumstances on board the *Somers* were different from those on board the *Bellipotent*. But the urgency felt, well-warranted or otherwise, was much the same.

Says a writer whom few know, "Forty years after a battle it is easy for a noncombatant to reason about how it ought to have been fought. It is another thing personally and under fire to have to direct the fighting while involved in the obscuring smoke of it. Much so with respect to other emergencies involving considerations both practical and moral, and when it is imperative promptly to act. The greater the fog the more it imperils the steamer, and speed is put on though at the hazard of running somebody down. Little ween the snug card players in the cabin of the responsibilities of the sleepless man on the bridge."

In brief, Billy Budd was formally convicted and sentenced to be

---

[41] Alexander Slidell Mackenzie; Melville's cousin, Guert Gansevoort, was first lieutenant of the *Somers* at the time of the hangings.

hung at the yardarm in the early morning watch, it being now night. Otherwise, as is customary in such cases, the sentence would forthwith have been carried out. In wartime on the field or in the fleet, a mortal punishment decreed by a drumhead court—on the field sometimes decreed by but a nod from the general—follows without delay on the heel of conviction, without appeal.

22

It was Captain Vere himself who of his own motion communicated the finding of the court to the prisoner, for that purpose going to the compartment where he was in custody and bidding the marine there to withdraw for the time.

Beyond the communication of the sentence, what took place at this interview was never known. But in view of the character of the twain briefly closeted in that stateroom, each radically sharing in the rarer qualities of our nature—so rare indeed as to be all but incredible to average minds however much cultivated—some conjectures may be ventured.

It would have been in consonance with the spirit of Captain Vere should he on this occasion have concealed nothing from the condemned one—should he indeed have frankly disclosed to him the part he himself had played in bringing about the decision, at the same time revealing his actuating motives. On Billy's side it is not improbable that such a confession would have been received in much the same spirit that prompted it. Not without a sort of joy, indeed, he might have appreciated the brave opinion of him implied in his captain's making such a confidant of him. Nor, as to the sentence itself, could he have been insensible that it was imparted to him as to one not afraid to die. Even more may have been. Captain Vere in end may have developed the passion sometimes latent under an exterior stoical or indifferent. He was old enough to have been Billy's father. The austere devotee of military duty, letting himself melt back into what remains primeval in our formalized humanity, may in end have caught Billy to his heart, even as Abraham may have caught young Isaac on the brink of resolutely offering him up in obedience to the exacting behest. But there is no telling the sacrament, seldom if in any case revealed to the gadding world, wherever under circumstances at all akin to those here attempted to be set forth two of great Nature's nobler order embrace. There is privacy at the time, inviolable to the survivor; and holy oblivion, the sequel to each diviner magnanimity, providentially covers all at last.

The first to encounter Captain Vere in act of leaving the compartment was the senior lieutenant. The face he beheld, for the moment one expressive of the agony of the strong, was to that officer, though a man of fifty, a startling revelation. That the condemned one suffered less than he who mainly had effected the condemnation was apparently indicated by the former's exclamation in the scene soon perforce to be touched upon.

23

Of a series of incidents within a brief term rapidly following each other, the adequate narration may take up a term less brief, especially if explanation or comment here and there seem requisite to the better understanding of such incidents. Between the entrance into the cabin of him who never left it alive, and him who when he did leave it left it as one condemned to die; between this and the closeted interview just given, less than an hour and a half had elapsed. It was an interval long enough, however, to awaken speculations among no few of the ship's company as to what it was that could be detaining in the cabin the master-at-arms and the sailor; for a rumor that both of them had been seen to enter it and neither of them had been seen to emerge, this rumor had got abroad upon the gun decks and in the tops, the people of a great warship being in one respect like villagers, taking microscopic note of every outward movement or non-movement going on. When therefore, in weather not at all tempestuous, all hands were called in the second dogwatch, a summons under such circumstances not usual in those hours, the crew were not wholly unprepared for some announcement extraordinary, one having connection too with the continued absence of the two men from their wonted haunts.

There was a moderate sea at the time; and the moon, newly risen and near to being at its full, silvered the white spar deck wherever not blotted by the clear-cut shadows horizontally thrown of fixtures and moving men. On either side the quarterdeck the marine guard under arms was drawn up; and Captain Vere, standing in his place surrounded by all the wardroom officers, addressed his men. In so doing, his manner showed neither more nor less than that properly pertaining to his supreme position aboard his own ship. In clear terms and concise he told them what had taken place in the cabin: that the master-at-arms was dead, that he who had killed him had been already tried by a summary court and condemned to death, and that the execution would take place in the early morning watch. The word *mutiny* was not named in what he said. He refrained too from making the occasion an opportunity for any preachment as to the maintenance of discipline, thinking perhaps that under existing circumstances in the navy the consequence of violating discipline should be made to speak for itself.

Their captain's announcement was listened to by the throng of standing sailors in a dumbness like that of a seated congregation of believers in hell listening to the clergyman's announcement of his Calvinistic text.

At the close, however, a confused murmur went up. It began to wax. All but instantly, then, at a sign, it was pierced and suppressed by shrill whistles of the boatswain and his mates. The word was given to about ship.

To be prepared for burial Claggart's body was delivered to certain petty officers of his mess. And here, not to clog the sequel with lateral matters, it may be added that at a suitable hour, the master-at-arms was committed to the sea with every funeral honor properly belonging to his naval grade.

In this proceeding as in every public one growing out of the tragedy strict adherence to usage was observed. Nor in any point could it have been at all deviated from, either with respect to Claggart or Billy Budd, without begetting undesirable speculations in the ship's company, sailors, and more particularly men-of-war's men, being of all men the greatest sticklers for usage. For similar cause, all communication between Captain Vere and the condemned one ended with the closeted interview already given, the latter being now surrendered to the ordinary routine preliminary to the end. His transfer under guard from the captain's quarters was effected without unusual precautions—at least no visible ones. If possible, not to let the men so much as surmise that their officers anticipate aught amiss from them is the tacit rule in a military ship. And the more that some sort of trouble should really be apprehended, the more do the officers keep that apprehension to themselves, though not the less unostentatious vigilance may be augmented. In the present instance, the sentry placed over the prisoner had strict orders to let no one have communication with him but the chaplain. And certain unobtrusive measures were taken absolutely to insure this point.

24

In a seventy-four of the old order the deck known as the upper gun deck was the one covered over by the spar deck, which last, though not without its armament, was for the most part exposed to the weather. In general it was at all hours free from hammocks; those of the crew swinging on the lower gun deck and berth deck, the latter being not only a dormitory but also the place for the stowing of the sailors' bags, and on both sides lined with the large chests or movable pantries of the many messes of the men.

On the starboard side of the *Bellipotent*'s upper gun deck, behold Billy Budd under sentry lying prone in irons in one of the bays formed by the regular spacing of the guns comprising the batteries on either side. All these pieces were of the heavier caliber of that period. Mounted on lumbering wooden carriages, they were hampered with cumbersome harness of breeching and strong side-tackles for running them out. Guns and carriages, together with the long rammers and shorter linstocks lodged in loops overhead—all these, as customary, were painted black; and the heavy hempen breechings, tarred to the same tint, wore the like livery of the undertakers. In contrast with the funereal hue of these surroundings, the prone sailor's exterior apparel, white jumper and white duck trousers, each more or less soiled, dimly glimmered in the obscure light of the bay like a patch of discolored snow in early April lingering at some upland cave's black mouth. In effect he is already in his shroud, or the garments that shall serve him in lieu of one. Over him but scarce illuminating him, two battle lanterns swing from two massive beams of the deck above. Fed with the oil supplied by the war contractors (whose gains, honest or otherwise, are in every land an anticipated portion of the harvest of death), with flickering splashes of dirty yellow light they pollute the pale moonshine all but ineffectually struggling in obstructed flecks through the open ports from which the tampioned cannon protrude. Other lanterns at intervals serve but to bring out somewhat the obscurer bays which, like small confessionals or side-chapels in a cathedral, branch from the long dim-vistaed broad aisle between the two batteries of that covered tier.

Such was the deck where now lay the Handsome Sailor. Through the rose-tan of his complexion no pallor could have shown. It would have taken days of sequestration from the winds and the sun to have brought about the effacement of that. But the skeleton in the cheekbone at the point of its angle was just beginning delicately to be defined under the warm-tinted skin. In fervid hearts self-contained, some brief experiences devour our human tissue as secret fire in a ship's hold consumes cotton in the bale.

But now lying between the two guns, as nipped in the vice of fate, Billy's agony, mainly proceeding from a generous young heart's virgin experience of the diabolical incarnate and effective in some men—the tension of that agony was over now. It survived not the something healing in the closeted interview with Captain Vere. Without movement, he lay as in a trance, that adolescent expression previously noted as his taking on something akin to the look of a slumbering child in the cradle when the warm hearth-glow of the still chamber at night plays on the dimples that at whiles mysteriously form in the cheek, silently coming and going there. For now and then in the gyved [42] one's trance a serene happy light born of some wandering reminiscence or dream would diffuse itself over his face, and then wane away only anew to return.

The chaplain, coming to see him and finding him thus, and perceiving no sign that he was conscious of his presence, attentively regarded him for a space, then slipping aside, withdrew for the time, peradventure feeling that even he, the minister of Christ though receiving his stipend from Mars, had no consolation to proffer which could result in a peace transcending that which he beheld. But in the small hours he came again. And the prisoner, now awake to his surroundings, noticed his approach, and civilly, all but cheerfully, welcomed him. But it was to little purpose that in the interview following, the good man sought to bring Billy Budd to some godly understanding that he must die, and at dawn. True, Billy himself freely referred to his death as a thing close at hand; but it was something in the way that children will refer to death in general, who yet among their other sports will play a funeral with hearse and mourners.

Not that like children Billy was incapable of conceiving what death really is. No, but he was wholly without irrational fear of it, a fear more prevalent in highly civilized communities than those so-called barbarous ones which in all respects stand nearer to unadulterate Nature. And, as elsewhere said, a barbarian Billy radically was—as much so, for all the costume, as his countrymen the British captives, living trophies, made to march in the Roman triumph of Germanicus.[43] Quite as much so as those later barbarians, young men probably, and picked specimens among the earlier British converts to Christianity, at least nominally such, taken to Rome (as today converts from lesser isles of the sea may be taken to London), of whom the Pope of that time, admiring the strangeness of their personal beauty so unlike the Italian stamp, their clear ruddy complexion and curled flaxen locks, exclaimed, "Angles" (meaning *English*, the modern derivative), "Angles, do

---

[42] Fettered.

[43] Germanicus Julius Caesar (15 B.C.-A.D. 19), a Roman general who received a triumph at Rome in A.D. 17.

you call them? And is it because they look so like angels?" Had it been later in time, one would think that the Pope had in mind Fra Angelico's[44] seraphs, some of whom, plucking apples in gardens of the Hesperides, have the faint rosebud complexion of the more beautiful English girls.

If in vain the good chaplain sought to impress the young barbarian with ideas of death akin to those conveyed in the skull, dial, and crossbones on old tombstones, equally futile to all appearance were his efforts to bring home to him the thought of salvation and a Savior. Billy listened, but less out of awe or reverence, perhaps, than from a certain natural politeness, doubtless at bottom regarding all that in much the same way that most mariners of his class take any discourse abstract or out of the common tone of the workaday world. And this sailor way of taking clerical discourse is not wholly unlike the way in which the primer of Christianity, full of transcendent miracles, was received long ago on tropic isles by any superior *savage*, so called—a Tahitian, say, of Captain Cook's time or shortly after that time. Out of natural courtesy he received, but did not appropriate. It was like a gift placed in the palm of an outreached hand upon which the fingers do not close.

But the *Bellipotent*'s chaplain was a discreet man possessing the good sense of a good heart. So he insisted not in his vocation here. At the instance of Captain Vere, a lieutenant had apprised him of pretty much everything as to Billy; and since he felt that innocence was even a better thing than religion wherewith to go to Judgment, he reluctantly withdrew; but in his emotion not without first performing an act strange enough in an Englishman, and under the circumstances yet more so in any regular priest. Stooping over, he kissed on the fair cheek his fellow man, a felon in martial law, one whom though on the confines of death he felt he could never convert to a dogma; nor for all that did he fear for his future.

Marvel not that having been made acquainted with the young sailor's essential innocence the worthy man lifted not a finger to avert the doom of such a martyr to martial discipline. So to do would not only have been as idle as invoking the desert, but would also have been an audacious transgression of the bounds of his function, one as exactly prescribed to him by military law as that of the boatswain or any other naval officer. Bluntly put, a chaplain is the minister of the Prince of Peace serving in the host of the God of War—Mars. As such, he is as incongruous as a musket would be on the altar at Christmas. Why, then, is he there? Because he indirectly

---

[44] The name by which Guido di Pietro of Fiesole (1387-1455), is usually known; he was a celebrated Italian painter of religious subjects.

subserves the purpose attested by the cannon; because too he lends the sanction of the religion of the meek to that which practically is the abrogation of everything but brute Force.

25

The night so luminous on the spar deck, but otherwise on the cavernous ones below, levels so like the tiered galleries in a coal mine—the luminous night passed away. But like the prophet[45] in the chariot disappearing in heaven and dropping his mantle to Elisha, the withdrawing night transferred its pale robe to the breaking day. A meek, shy light appeared in the East, where stretched a diaphanous fleece of white furrowed vapor. That light slowly waxed. Suddenly *eight bells* was struck aft, responded to by one louder metallic stroke from forward. It was four o'clock in the morning. Instantly the silver whistles were heard summoning all hands to witness punishment. Up through the great hatchways rimmed with racks of heavy shot the watch below came pouring, overspreading with the watch already on deck the space between the mainmast and foremast including that occupied by the capacious launch and the black booms tiered on either side of it, boat and booms making a summit of observation for the powder-boys and younger tars. A different group comprising one watch of topmen leaned over the rail of that sea balcony, no small one in a seventy-four, looking down on the crowd below. Man or boy, none spake but in whisper, and few spake at all. Captain Vere—as before, the central figure among the assembled commissioned officers—stood nigh the break of the poop deck facing forward. Just below him on the quarter-deck the marines in full equipment were drawn up much as at the scene of the promulgated sentence.

At sea in the old time, the execution by halter of a military sailor was generally from the foreyard. In the present instance, for special reasons the mainyard was assigned. Under an arm of that yard the prisoner was presently brought up, the chaplain attending him. It was noted at the time, and remarked upon afterwards, that in this final scene the good man evinced little or nothing of the perfunctory. Brief speech indeed he had with the condemned one, but the genuine Gospel was less on his tongue than in his aspect and manner towards him. The final preparations personal to the latter being speedily brought to an end by two boatswain's mates, the consummation impended. Billy stood facing aft. At the penultimate moment, his words, his only ones, words wholly unobstructed in the utterance,

[45] Elijah.

were these: "God bless Captain Vere!" Syllables so unanticipated coming from one with the ignominious hemp about his neck—a conventional felon's benediction directed aft towards the quarters of honor; syllables too delivered in the clear melody of a singing bird on the point of launching from the twig—had a phenomenal effect, not unenhanced by the rare personal beauty of the young sailor, spiritualized now through late experiences so poignantly profound.

Without volition, as it were, as if indeed the ship's populace were but the vehicles of some vocal current electric, with one voice from alow and aloft came a resonant sympathetic echo: "God bless Captain Vere!" And yet at that instant Billy alone must have been in their hearts, even as in their eyes.

At the pronounced words and the spontaneous echo that voluminously rebounded them, Captain Vere, either through stoic self-control or a sort of momentary paralysis induced by emotional shock, stood erectly rigid as a musket in the ship-armorer's rack.

The hull, deliberately recovering from the periodic roll to leeward, was just regaining an even keel when the last signal, a preconcerted dumb one, was given. At the same moment it chanced that the vapory fleece hanging low in the East was shot through with a soft glory as of the fleece of the Lamb of God seen in mystical vision, and simultaneously therewith, watched by the wedged mass of upturned faces, Billy ascended; and, ascending, took the full rose of the dawn.

In the pinioned figure arrived at the yard-end, to the wonder of all no motion was apparent, none save that created by the slow roll of the hull in moderate weather, so majestic in a great ship ponderously cannoned.

26

When some days afterwards, in reference to the singularity just mentioned, the purser, a rather ruddy, rotund person more accurate as an accountant than profound as a philosopher, said at mess to the surgeon, "What testimony to the force lodged in will power," the latter, saturnine, spare, and tall, one in whom a discreet causticity went along with a manner less genial than polite, replied, "Your pardon, Mr. Purser. In a hanging scientifically conducted—and under special orders I myself directed how Budd's was to be effected—any movement following the completed suspension and originating in the body suspended, such movement indicates mechanical spasm in the muscular system. Hence the absence of that is no more attributable to will power, as you call it, than to horsepower—begging your pardon."

"But this muscular spasm you speak of, is not that in a degree more or less invariable in these cases?"

"Assuredly so, Mr. Purser."

"How then, my good sir, do you account for its absence in this instance?"

"Mr. Purser, it is clear that your sense of the singularity in this matter equals not mine. You account for it by what you call will power—a term not yet included in the lexicon of science. For me, I do not, with my present knowledge, pretend to account for it at all. Even should we assume the hypothesis that at the first touch of the halyards the action of Budd's heart, intensified by extraordinary emotion at its climax, abruptly stopped—much like a watch when in carelessly winding it up you strain at the finish, thus snapping the chain—even under that hypothesis how account for the phenomenon that followed?"

"You admit, then, that the absence of spasmodic movement was phenomenal."

"It was phenomenal, Mr. Purser, in the sense that it was an appearance the cause of which is not immediately to be assigned."

"But tell me, my dear sir," pertinaciously continued the other, "was the man's death effected by the halter, or was it a species of euthanasia?"

"*Euthanasia,* Mr. Purser, is something like your *will power:* I doubt its authenticity as a scientific term—begging your pardon again. It is at once imaginative and metaphysical—in short, Greek. —But," abruptly changing his tone, "there is a case in the sick bay that I do not care to leave to my assistants. Beg your pardon, but excuse me." And rising from the mess he formally withdrew.

27

The silence at the moment of execution and for a moment or two continuing thereafter, a silence but emphasized by the regular wash of the sea against the hull or the flutter of a sail caused by the helmsman's eyes being tempted astray, this emphasized silence was gradually disturbed by a sound not easily to be verbally rendered. Whoever has heard the freshet-wave of a torrent suddenly swelled by pouring showers in tropical mountains, showers not shared by the plain; whoever has heard the first muffled murmur of its sloping advance through precipitous woods may form some conception of the sound now heard. The seeming remoteness of its source was because of its murmurous indistinctness, since it came from close by, even from the men massed on the ship's open deck. Being inarticulate, it was dubious in significance further than it seemed to indicate some capricious revulsion of thought or feeling such as mobs ashore are liable to, in the present instance possibly implying a sullen revocation on the men's part of their involuntary echoing of Billy's benediction. But ere the murmur had time to wax into clamor it was met by a strategic command, the more telling that it came with abrupt unexpectedness: "Pipe down the starboard watch, Boatswain, and see that they go."

Shrill as the shriek of the sea hawk, the silver whistles of the boatswain and his mates pierced that ominous low sound, dissipating it; and yielding to the mechanism of discipline the throng was thinned by one-half. For the remainder, most of them were set to temporary employments connected with trimming the yards and so forth, business readily to be got up to serve occasion by any officer of the deck.

Now each proceeding that follows a mortal sentence pronounced at sea by a drumhead court is characterized by promptitude not perceptibly merging into hurry, though bordering that. The hammock, the one which had been Billy's bed when alive, having already been ballasted with shot and otherwise prepared to serve for his canvas coffin, the last offices of the sea undertakers, the sailmaker's mates, were now speedily completed. When everything was in readiness a second call for all hands, made necessary by the strategic movement before mentioned, was sounded, now to witness burial.

The details of this closing formality it needs not to give. But when the tilted plank let slide its freight into the sea, a second strange human murmur was heard, blended now with another inarticulate sound proceeding from certain larger seafowl who, their attention having been attracted by the peculiar commotion in the water resulting from the heavy sloped dive of the shotted hammock into the sea, flew screaming to the spot. So near the hull did they come, that the stridor or bony creak of their gaunt double-jointed pinions was audible. As the ship under light airs passed on, leaving the burial spot astern, they still kept circling it low down with the moving shadow of their outstretched wings and the croaked requiem of their cries.

Upon sailors as superstitious as those of the age preceding ours, men-of-war's men too who had just beheld the prodigy of repose in the form suspended in air, and now foundering in the deeps; to such mariners the action of the seafowl, though dictated by mere animal greed for prey, was big with no prosaic significance. An uncertain movement began among them, in which some encroachment was made. It was tolerated but for a moment. For suddenly the drum beat to quarters, which familiar sound happening at least twice every day, had upon the present occasion a signal peremptoriness in it. True martial discipline long continued superinduces in average man a sort of impulse whose operation at the official word of command much resembles in its promptitude the effect of an instinct.

The drumbeat dissolved the multitude, distributing most of them along the batteries of the two covered gun decks. There, as wonted, the guns' crews stood by their respective cannon erect and silent. In due course the first officer, sword under arm and standing in his place on the quarter-deck, formally received the successive reports of the sworded lieutenants commanding the sections of batteries below; the last of which reports being made, the summed report he delivered with the customary salute to the commander. All this occupied time, which in the present case was the object in beating to quarters at an hour prior to the customary one. That such variance from usage was authorized by an officer like Captain Vere, a martinet as some deemed him, was evidence of the necessity for unusual action implied in what he deemed to be temporarily the mood of his men. "With mankind," he would say, "forms, measured forms, are everything; and that is the import couched in the story of Orpheus[46] with his lyre spellbinding the wild denizens of the wood." And this he once applied to the disruption of forms going on across the Channel and the consequences thereof.

At this unwonted muster at quarters, all proceeded as at the regular hour. The band on the quarter-deck played a sacred air, after which the chaplain went through the customary morning service. That done, the drum beat the retreat; and toned by music and religious rites subserving the discipline and purposes of war, the men in their wonted orderly manner dispersed to the places allotted them when not at the guns.

And now it was full day. The fleece of low-hanging vapor had vanished, licked up by the sun that late had so glorified it. And the circumambient air in the clearness of its serenity was like smooth white marble in the polished block not yet removed from the marble-dealer's yard.

28

The symmetry of form attainable in pure fiction cannot so readily be achieved in a narration essentially having less to do with fable than with fact. Truth uncompromisingly told will always have its ragged edges; hence the conclusion of such a narration is apt to be less finished than an architectural finial.

How it fared with the Handsome Sailor during the year of the

---

[46] Son of the muse Calliope and Apollo, he was the greatest musician and singer of classical myth and could influence men and beasts to do his bidding.

Great Mutiny has been faithfully given. But though properly the story ends with his life, something in way of sequel will not be amiss. Three brief chapters will suffice.

In the general rechristening under the Directory of the craft originally forming the navy of the French monarchy, the *St. Louis* line-of-battle ship was named the *Athée* (the *Atheist*). Such a name, like some other substituted ones in the Revolutionary fleet, while proclaiming the infidel audacity of the ruling power, was yet, though not so intended to be, the aptest name, if one consider it, ever given to a warship; far more so indeed than the *Devastation*, the *Erebus* (the *Hell*), and similar names bestowed upon fighting ships.

On the return passage to the English fleet from the detached cruise during which occurred the events already recorded, the *Bellipotent* fell in with the *Athée*. An engagement ensued, during which Captain Vere, in the act of putting his ship alongside the enemy with a view of throwing his boarders across her bulwarks, was hit by a musket ball from a porthole of the enemy's main cabin. More than disabled, he dropped to the deck and was carried below to the same cockpit where some of his men already lay. The senior lieutenant took command. Under him the enemy was finally captured, and though much crippled was by rare good fortune successfully taken into Gibraltar, an English port not very distant from the scene of the fight. There, Captain Vere with the rest of the wounded was put ashore. He lingered for some days, but the end came. Unhappily he was cut off too early for the Nile and Trafalgar. The spirit that 'spite its philosophic austerity may yet have indulged in the most secret of all passions, ambition, never attained to the fulness of fame.

Not long before death, while lying under the influence of that magical drug which, soothing the physical frame, mysteriously operates on the subtler element in man, he was heard to murmur words inexplicable to his attendant: "Billy Budd, Billy Budd." That these were not the accents of remorse would seem clear from what the attendant said to the *Bellipotent*'s senior officer of marines, who, as the most reluctant to condemn of the members of the drumhead court, too well knew, though here he kept the knowledge to himself, who Billy Budd was.

29

Some few weeks after the execution, among other matters under the head of "News from the Mediterranean," there appeared in a naval chronicle of the time, an authorized weekly publication, an account of the affair. It was doubtless for the most part written in good faith, though the medium, partly rumor, through which the facts must have reached the writer served to deflect and in part falsify them. The account was as follows:

"On the tenth of the last month a deplorable occurrence took place on board H.M.S. *Bellipotent*. John Claggart, the ship's master-at-arms, discovering that some sort of plot was incipient among an inferior section of the ship's company, and that the ringleader was one William Budd; he, Claggart, in the act of arraigning the man before the captain, was vindictively stabbed to the heart by the suddenly drawn sheath knife of Budd.

"The deed and the implement employed sufficiently suggest that though mustered into the service under an English name the assassin was no Englishman, but one of those aliens adopting English cognomens whom the present extraordinary necessities of the service have caused to be admitted into it in considerable numbers.

"The enormity of the crime and the extreme depravity of the criminal appear the greater in view of the character of the victim, a middle-aged man respectable and discreet, belonging to that minor official grade, the petty officers, upon whom, as none know better than the commissioned gentlemen, the efficiency of His Majesty's navy so largely depends. His function was a responsible one, at once onerous and thankless; and his fidelity in it the greater because of his strong patriotic impulse. In this instance as in so many other instances in these days, the character of this unfortunate man signally refutes, if refutation were needed, that peevish saying attributed to the late Dr. Johnson, that patriotism is the last refuge of a scoundrel.

"The criminal paid the penalty of his crime. The promptitude of the punishment has proved salutary. Nothing amiss is now apprehended aboard H.M.S. *Bellipotent*."

The above, appearing in a publication now long ago superannuated and forgotten, is all that hitherto has stood in human record to attest what manner of men respectively were John Claggart and Billy Budd.

30

Everything is for a term venerated in navies. Any tangible object associated with some striking incident of the service is converted into a monument. The spar from which the foretopman was suspended was for some few years kept trace of by the bluejackets. Their knowledges followed it from ship to dockyard and again from dockyard to ship, still pursuing it even when at last reduced to a mere dockyard boom. To them a chip of it was as a piece of the Cross. Ignorant though they were of the secret facts of the tragedy, and not thinking but that the penalty was somehow unavoidably inflicted from the naval point of view, for all that, they instinctively felt that Billy was a sort of man as incapable of mutiny as of wilful murder. They recalled the fresh young image of the Handsome Sailor, that face never deformed by a sneer or subtler vile freak of the heart within. This impression of him was doubtless deepened by the fact that he was gone, and in a measure mysteriously gone. On the gun decks of the *Bellipotent* the general estimate of his nature and its unconscious simplicity eventually found rude utterance from another foretopman, one of his own watch, gifted, as some sailors are, with an artless *poetic* temperament. The tarry hand made some lines which, after circulating among the shipboard crews for a while, finally got rudely printed at Portsmouth as a ballad. The title given to it was the sailor's.

Billy in the Darbies[47]

Good of the chaplain to enter Lone Bay
And down on his marrowbones here and pray
For the likes just o' me, Billy Budd.—But, look:
Through the port comes the moonshine astray!
It tips the guard's cutlass and silvers this nook;
But 'twill die in the dawning of Billy's last day.
A jewel-block they'll make of me tomorrow,
Pendant pearl from the yardarm-end
Like the eardrop I gave to Bristol Molly—
O, 'tis me, not the sentence they'll suspend.
Ay, ay, all is up; and I must up too,
Early in the morning, aloft from alow.
On an empty stomach now never it would do.
They'll give me a nibble—bit o' biscuit ere I go.
Sure, a messmate will reach me the last parting cup;
But, turning heads away from the hoist and the belay,
Heaven knows who will have the running of me up!
No pipe to those halyards.—But aren't it all sham?
A blur's in my eyes; it is dreaming that I am.
A hatchet to my hawser? All adrift to go?
The drum roll to grog, and Billy never know?

---

[47] Handcuffs.

But Donald he has promised to stand by the plank;
So I'll shake a friendly hand ere I sink.
But—no! It is dead then I'll be, come to think.
I remember Taff the Welshman when he sank.
And his cheek it was like the budding pink.
But me they'll lash in hammock, drop me deep.
Fathoms down, fathoms down, how I'll dream fast asleep.
I feel it stealing now. Sentry, are you there?
Just ease these darbies at the wrist,
And roll me over fair!
I am sleepy, and the oozy weeds about me twist.

Appendix

Some Supplementary Works

Cooper, James Fenimore. *The Deerslayer.*
Dreiser, Theodore. *An American Tragedy.*
Faulkner, William. *The Bear.*
Fielding, Henry. *Joseph Andrews.*
Golding, William. *Lord of the Flies.*
Hawthorne, Nathaniel. *The Marble Faun;* "The Maypole of Merry Mount."
James, Henry. *The American; The Golden Bowl.*
Twain, Mark. *The Adventures of Huckleberry Finn.*
West, Nathanael. *A Cool Million.*

Hopkins, Gerard Manley. "Spring and Fall: To a Young Child."
Marvell, Andrew. "The Garden."
Milton, John. *Paradise Lost.*
Spenser, Edmund. *Shepheards Calendar.*
Tennyson, Alfred. "Sir Galahad."
Thomas, Dylan. "Fern Hill."
Traherne, Thomas. "Innocence"; "Wonder."
Vaughan, Henry. "The Retreat."
Whitman, Walt. *Leaves of Grass.*
Wordsworth, William. "Ode: Intimations of Immortality."
Yeats, William Butler. "A Prayer for My Daughter."

Coxe, Louis O., and Robert Chapman. *Billy Budd: A Play in Three Acts.*
James, Henry. *Daisy Miller: A Comedy in Three Acts.*
Miller, Arthur. *The Crucible.*
O'Neill, Eugene. *Anna Christie.*
Shakespeare, William. *The Winter's Tale.*
Shaw, George Bernard. *Saint Joan.*

Suggested Seminar Paper Topics

1. What is the nature and fate of innocence as described by Shakespeare in *The Tempest*? How does this conception of innocence compare with that found in the Genesis story of the Fall?

2. E. M. W. Tillyard has described Shakespeare's last plays as "romances" (see *Shakespeare's Last Plays*). What are some of the similarities of form and content between *The Winter's Tale* and *The Tempest* that might support Tillyard's contention? (It would be helpful, by way of illustration, to contrast these two late plays with an earlier Shakespearean comedy with which you are familiar.) Discuss the ways in which the "romance" is especially suitable for a presentation of the theme of innocence.

3. Investigate what you consider to be the important image patterns in *The Tempest* and try to relate them to the dominant themes of the play, in particular the theme of innocence.

4. Compare and contrast Shakespeare's use of songs in *The Tempest* and *As You Like It*.

5. In the recent past, a lively critical controversy has developed concerning the meaning of *Comus*. Discuss the interpretive views of such critics as A. S. P. Woodhouse, E. M. W. Tillyard, J. C. Maxwell, and Rosemond Tuve and set forth your own critical position.

6. What is the pastoral tradition in poetry and how does Milton exploit it in his treatment of the fate of innocence in *Comus*?

7. *Comus* is an essentially Christian poem that abounds in pagan references. Discuss the relevance of these references to the theme of the work.

8. Report on the history of the masque in Italy and England. In what ways is *Comus* different from the traditional masque? Why do you think Shakespeare includes a masque in *The Tempest*?

9. Discuss the imagery of innocence in Blake's *Songs of Innocence* and its relationship to childhood. Does this imagery differ from that found in the world of *Experience*?

10. Blake has been called an idealistic revolutionary. Comment on the *Songs of Experience* as late eighteenth-century social criticism.

11. Give a detailed analysis of "The Chimney Sweeper" poems in *Songs of Innocence and of Experience* and explain how each is representative of the context in which it appears.

12. Everything that "submits, mortifies, constricts, and denies" was anathema to William Blake. How is this attitude related to the poet's conception of innocence in his *Songs* and of the "higher innocence" represented in his belief in the New Jerusalem (see Blake's Preface to *Milton*)?

13. How does James characterize and contrast his Americans and his Europeans (or Europeanized Americans) in *Daisy Miller* and *An International Episode*?

14. How is the point of view from which the events of James's *novella* are seen related to the meaning of the work?

15. Henry James has written that, "Poor little Daisy Miller was, as I understand her, above all things *innocent*. . . . She never took the measure really of the scandal she produced, and had no means of doing so: she was too ignorant, too irreflective, too little versed in the proportions of things." What is the nature of Daisy's innocence? Has James described it accurately or must his remarks be qualified?

16. Explore the similarities and differences between the female innocents in *The Tempest, Comus,* and *Daisy Miller.*

17. Analyze James's prose style (for example, diction, imagery, syntax, choice of detail) in *Daisy Miller* and compare it with that of Melville in *Billy Budd.* Consider the relationship between style and principal themes in both instances.

18. *Billy Budd* has been called Melville's "Testament of Acceptance." What is the meaning of this expression and is it critically sound?

19. Some critics have termed the innocent Billy a figure symbolic of Christ. Comment on their argument, and in determining its worth, present criteria for evaluating the validity of a symbolic interpretation of literature.

20. Discuss the alleged mutiny that occurred aboard the U.S. Brig *Somers* and its connection with Melville and *Billy Budd.* Particular emphasis should be placed on how Melville altered historical fact and why he might have done so.

21. Although initially it may seem that Melville's characters in *Billy Budd* lack depth, one soon discovers their complex nature through the human ambiguities that characterize them. Discuss.

Suggested Term Paper Topics

1. Milton's representation of innocence before the Fall in *Paradise Lost.*

2. Childhood innocence in William Golding's *Lord of the Flies* and Dylan Thomas's *Portrait of the Artist as a Young Dog.*

3. Joyce Cary's use of the poetry and ideas of William Blake in *The Horse's Mouth.*

4. The effect of Europe on Americans in *Daisy Miller, The Portrait of a Lady,* and *The Ambassadors.*

5. Shakespeare's tragic innocents: Juliet, Desdemona, Ophelia, and Cordelia.

6. Complex innocence in the poems of Theodore Roethke.

7. The operation of guilt in Joseph Conrad's *Lord Jim* and Malcolm Lowry's *Under the Volcano.*

8. Innocence and deception in Henry Fielding's *Jonathan Wild* and *Joseph Andrews.*

9. The fool in *As You Like It, Twelfth Night,* and *King Lear.*

10. The relationship of Blake's engravings to his *Songs of Innocence and of Experience.*

11. Innocence in the *Bildungsroman:* Samuel Butler's *The Way of All Flesh* and Somerset Maugham's *Of Human Bondage.*

12. The evolution of Melville's thought from the innocence of *Typee* to the experience of *The Confidence Man.*

13. In quest of the earthly paradise: Utopias and innocence.

14. Milton's concept of the topography of innocence in *Arcades, Comus,* and *Paradise Lost.*

15. Society and the courts: the trial of innocence in Theodore Dreiser's *An American Tragedy* and Arthur Miller's *The Crucible.*

Some Useful Reference Works for Literary Research

"Articles on American Literature in Current Periodicals," *American Literature* (1929-).

Baugh, Albert C., et al., *A Literary History of England.* New York, 1948.

Besterman, Theodore, *A World Bibliography of Bibliographies,* 4 vols. Geneva, 1955-1956.

Bibliographic Index: A Cumulative Bibliography of Bibliographies (1937-).

The Cambridge Bibliography of English Literature, 4 vols., ed. F. W. Bateson. Cambridge, Eng., 1941. Volume V (Supplement), ed. George Watson. Cambridge, Eng., 1957.

International Index to Periodicals (1907-).

Leary, Lewis, *Articles on American Literature, 1900-1950.* Durham, N.C., 1954.

The Oxford Companion to American Literature, ed. James D. Hart. New York, 1956.

The Oxford Companion to English Literature, ed. Paul Harvey. Oxford, 1946.

PMLA: Publications of the Modern Language Association of America, "Annual Bibliography" (1921-).

Reader's Guide to Periodical Literature (1900-).

"Shakespeare: An Annotated Bibliography," *Shakespeare Quarterly* (1949-).

Spiller, Robert E., et al., *Literary History of the United States,* 3 vols. New York, 1948.

The Year's Work in English Studies (1919-).

General Bibliography

Bloomfield, Reginald, *The Formal Garden*. London, 1936.

Brumm, Ursula, "The Figure of Christ in American Literature," *Partisan Review*, XXIV, No. 3 (Summer 1957), 403-13.

Busby, Olive Mary, *Studies in the Development of the Fool in the Elizabethan Drama*. Oxford, 1923.

Fiedler, Leslie A., *An End to Innocence*. Boston, 1955.

Frye, Northrop, *Anatomy of Criticism*. Princeton, N.J., 1957.

———, *Fables of Identity: Studies in Poetic Mythology*. New York, 1963.

Greg, W. W., *Pastoral Poetry and Pastoral Drama*. London, 1906.

Hartt, Julian N., *The Lost Image of Man*. Baton Rouge, La., 1963.

Hassan, Ihab, *Radical Innocence: Studies in the Contemporary American Novel*. Princeton, N.J., 1961.

Hofmann, Werner, *The Earthly Paradise: Art in the Nineteenth Century*. New York, 1961.

Howe, Susanne, *Wilhelm Meister and His English Kinsmen*. New York, 1930.

Kermode, Frank, *English Pastoral Poetry from the Beginnings to Marvell*. London, 1952.

LeRoy, Gaylord C., "American Innocence Reconsidered," *The Massachusetts Review* (Summer 1963), 623-46.

Lewis, R. W. B., *The American Adam: Innocence, Tragedy and Tradition in the Nineteenth Century*. Chicago, 1955.

Lovejoy, Arthur O., "Milton and the Paradox of the Fortunate Fall," *Essays in the History of Ideas* (Baltimore, Md., 1948), pp. 277-95.

MacCaffrey, Isabel G., *Paradise Lost as "Myth."* Cambridge, Mass., 1959.

Marx, Leo, "Two Kingdoms of Force," *The Massachusetts Review* (Fall 1959), 62-95.

Matthiessen, F. O., *American Renaissance*. New York, 1941.

Negley, Glenn, and J. Max Patrick, *The Quest for Utopia*. New York, 1952.

Parkes, Henry Bamford, *The American Experience: an Interpretation of the History and Civilization of the American People*. New York, 1947.

Price, Martin, *To the Palace of Wisdom: Studies in Order and Energy from Dryden to Blake*. New York, 1964.

Rahv, Philip, ed., *Discovery of Europe: The Story of American Experience in the Old World*. New York, 1960.

Reik, Theodor, *Myth and Guilt: The Crime and Punishment of Mankind*. New York, 1957.

Tillyard, E. M. W., *The Elizabethan World Picture*. New York, 1944.

Welsford, Enid, *The Court Masque*. New York, 1938.

William Shakespeare

Bushnell, N. S., "Natural Supernaturalism in 'The Tempest,'" *PMLA*, XLVII (September 1932), 684-98.

Camden, C., "Songs and Choruses in 'The Tempest,'" *Philological Quarterly,* XLI (January 1962), 114-22.

Craig, Hardin, "Prospero's Renunciation," *Shakespeare Newsletter,* III (1953), 13.

Cutts, J. P., "Music and the Supernatural in *The Tempest:* A Study in Interpretation," *Music and Letters,* XXXIX (October 1958), 347-58.

Ebisch, Walther, *A Shakespeare Bibliography.* Oxford, 1931.

———, Supplement for 1930-1935. Oxford, 1937.

Gesner, Carol, "*The Tempest* as Pastoral Romance," *Shakespeare Quarterly,* X (Fall 1959), 531-39.

Hankins, J. E., "Caliban the Bestial Man," *PMLA,* LXII (September 1947), 793-801.

Hoeniger, F. D., "Prospero's Storm and Miracle," *Shakespeare Quarterly,* VII (Winter 1956), 33-38.

Kermode, Frank, "Introduction to *The Tempest*" (The Arden Edition). London, 1958, pp. xi-xciii.

Knight, George Wilson, *The Shakespearean Tempest.* London, 1932.

———, *The Crown of Life.* London, 1947.

Knox, B., "*The Tempest* and the Ancient Comic Tradition," *Virginia Quarterly Review,* XXXI (Winter 1955), 73-89.

Leech, Clifford, "The Structure of the Last Plays," *The Shakespeare Survey,* XI (1958), 19-30.

McManaway, J. G., "Songs and Masques in *The Tempest,*" *Theatre Miscellany: Six Pieces Connected with the Seventeenth-century Stage,* Luttrell Society, No. 14 (1953), pp. 69-96.

Marx, Leo, "Shakespeare's American Fable," *The Massachusetts Review* (Autumn 1960), 40-71.

Muir, Kenneth, *Last Periods of Shakespeare, Racine, Ibsen.* Detroit, Mich., 1961.

Nosworthy, J. M., "Narrative Sources of *The Tempest,*" *Review of English Studies,* XXIV (October 1948), 281-94.

Ralli, Augustus, *A History of Shakespearean Criticism,* 2 vols. Oxford, 1932.

Rose, Brian W., "*The Tempest:* A Reconsideration of Its Meaning," *English Studies in Africa,* I (1958), 205-16.

Simpson, P., "Supposed Crux in *The Tempest,*" *Review of English Studies,* XXII (July 1946), 224-25.

Spencer, Theodore, "Shakespeare and the Nature of Man: *The Tempest*," *Shakespeare: Modern Essays in Criticism*, ed. Leonard F. Dean, pp. 411-16. New York, 1957.

Still, Colin, *Shakespeare's Mystery Play: A Study of "The Tempest."* London, 1921.

Stoll, Elmer Edgar, *"The Tempest," PMLA*, XLVII (September 1932), 699-726.

Tillyard, E. M. W., *Shakespeare's Last Plays*. London, 1938.

Traversi, Derek A., *Shakespeare: the Last Phase*. New York, 1955.

Wagner, Emma Brockway, *Shakespeare's "The Tempest," An Allegorical Interpretation*. Yellow Springs, Ohio, 1933.

Wilson, Harold S., "Action and Symbol in *Measure for Measure* and *The Tempest*," *Shakespeare Quarterly*, IV (1953), 377-84.

Wilson, John Dover, *The Meaning of "The Tempest,"* Newcastle upon Tyne, Eng., 1936.

Zimbardo, Rose A., "Form and Disorder in *The Tempest*," *Shakespeare Quarterly* (Winter 1963), 49-56.

John Milton

Adams, Robert M., "Reading *Comus*," *Modern Philology*, LI (August 1953), 18-32.

Allen, D. C., "Milton's *Comus* as a Failure in Artistic Compromise," *ELH*, XVI (June 1949), 104-19.

Arthos, John, *On a Mask Presented at Ludlow-Castle, by John Milton*. Ann Arbor, Mich., 1954.

———, "Realms of Being in the Epilogue of *Comus*," *Modern Language Notes*, LXXVI (April 1961), 321-24.

Bowers, Robert H., "The Accent on Youth in *Comus*," *South Atlantic Modern Language Association*, ed. J. Max Patrick, pp. 72-79. Gainesville, Fla., 1953.

Bruser, F., "*Comus* and the Rose Song," *Studies in Philology*, XLIV (October 1947), 625-44.

Diekhoff, John S., "The Punctuation of *Comus*," *PMLA*, LI (September 1936), 757-68.

Dyson, A. E., "The Interpretation of *Comus*," *Essays and Studies* (1955), 90-91.

Finney, G. L., "*Comus*, Dramma Per Musica," *Studies in Philology*, XXXVII (July 1940), 482-500.

Fletcher, Harris Francis, *Contributions to a Milton Bibliography, 1800-1930*. Urbana, Ill., 1931.

Gossman, A., and G. W. Whiting, "*Comus*, Once More, 1761," *Review of English Studies*, n.s., XI (February 1960), 56-60.

Hanford, James Holly, *A Milton Handbook.* New York, 1954.

Haun, Eugene, "An Inquiry into the Genre of *Comus,*" *Essays in Honor of W. C. Curry,* pp. 221-39. Nashville, Tenn., 1955.

Huckabay, Calvin, *John Milton; A Bibliographical Supplement, 1929-1957.* Pittsburgh, Pa., 1960.

Jayne, S., "The Subject of Milton's Ludlow Mask," *PMLA,* LXXIV (December 1959), 533-43.

Leahy, William, "Pollution and *Comus,*" *Essays in Criticism,* XI (1961), 111.

Major, John M., "*Comus* and *The Tempest,*" *Shakespeare Quarterly,* X (Spring 1959), 177-83.

Maxwell, J. C., "The Pseudo-Problem of *Comus,*" *Cambridge Journal,* I (1947-1948), 376-80.

Rideout, G. H., "Informal Ethics and the Study of *Comus,*" *English Journal,* XVII (May 1928), 417-20.

Seaton, Ethel, "*Comus* and Shakespeare," *Essays and Studies by Members of the English Association,* XXXI (1945), 68-80.

Sensabaugh, G. F., "The Milieu of *Comus,*" *Studies in Philology,* XLI (April 1944), 238-49.

Stevens, C., "Milton's Nymph: Sabrina," *English Journal,* XVII (September 1928), 571-75.

Stevens, David Harrison, *Reference Guide to Milton: From 1800 to the Present Day.* Chicago, 1930.

Tillyard, E. M. W., *The Miltonic Setting, Past and Present.* Cambridge, Eng., 1938.

———, *Studies in Milton.* New York, 1951.

———, *Milton.* London, 1956.

Tuve, Rosemond, *Images and Themes in Five Poems by Milton.* Cambridge, Mass., 1957.

Woodhouse, A. S. P., "The Argument of Milton's *Comus,*" *University of Toronto Quarterly,* XI (1941), 46-71.

———, "*Comus* Once More," *University of Toronto Quarterly,* XIX (1950), 218-23.

William Blake

Adams, Hazard, "Blake and Gulley Jimson: English Symbolists," *Critique: Studies in Modern Fiction* (Spring-Fall 1959), 3-14.

Adler, J. H., "Symbol and Meaning in 'The Little Black Boy,' " *Modern Language Notes,* LXXII (June 1957), 412-15.

Bloom, Harold, *Blake's Apocalypse—A Study in Poetic Argument.* New York, 1963.

Brennan, Joseph X., "The Symbolic Framework of Blake's 'The Tyger,'" *College English,* XXII (1961), 406-7.

Dike, D. A., "Difficult Innocence: Blake's Songs and Pastoral," *ELH,* XXVIII (December 1961), 353-75.

Eberly, Ralph D., "Blake's 'The Little Black Boy,'" *Explicator,* XV (1957), item 42.

Freeman, J., "Blake's Innocence and Experience Rationalised," *Bookman* (London), LXXV (October 1928), 17-19.

Frye, Northrop, *Fearful Symmetry, A Study of William Blake.* Princeton, N.J., 1947.

———, "Blake's Introduction to Experience," *Huntington Library Quarterly,* XXI (1957), 57-67.

Gleckner, Robert F., "Irony in Blake's 'Holy Thursday,'" *Modern Language Notes,* LXXI (June 1956), 412-15.

———, "Blake's *Tiriel* and the State of Experience," *Philological Quarterly,* XXXVI (April 1957), 195-210.

———, "Point of View and Context in Blake's Songs," *Bulletin of New York Public Library,* LXI (1957), 531-38.

———, *The Piper and the Bard.* Detroit, Mich., 1959.

———, "William Blake and the Human Abstract," *PMLA,* LXXVI (1961), 373-79.

Harper, George M., "The Source of Blake's 'Ah! Sun-Flower,'" *Modern Language Review,* XLVIII (April 1953), 139-42.

Hendry, J. F., "The Social Philosophy of William Blake," *Life and Letters To-day,* XXXIX (December 1943), 156-63.

Justin, Howard, "Blake's 'Introduction' to *Songs of Innocence,*" *Explicator,* XI (1952), item 1.

Larrabee, S. A., "Interpretation of Blake's 'A Divine Image,'" *Modern Language Notes,* XLVII (May 1932), 305-8.

McElderry, R. B., Jr., "Coleridge on Blake's Songs," *Modern Language Quarterly,* IX (1948), 298-302.

Nurmi, M. K., "Blake's Revisions of 'The Tyger,'" *PMLA,* LXXI (September 1956), 669-85.

Partridge, E., "Inter-relationships in Blake's Songs," *Modern Language Notes,* XXXVIII (April 1923), 220-23.

Plowman, Max, *An Introduction to the Study of Blake.* New York, 1927.

Pottle, Frederick A., "Blake's 'The Tyger,' 17-18," *Explicator,* VIII (1950), item 39.

Watson-Williams, H., "Blackened Wall: Notes on Blake's 'London' and Eliot's 'The Waste Land,'" *English,* X (Summer 1955), 181-84.

Wicksteed, Joseph Hartley, *Blake's Innocence and Experience.* London, 1928.

Wormhoudt, Arthur, "Introduction to *Songs of Innocence*," *Explicator*, VIII (1950), item 55.

Henry James

Bewley, Marius, "Maisie, Miles and Flora, the Jamesian Innocents," *Scrutiny*, XVII (Autumn 1950), 255-63.

Bowden, Edwin T., *The Themes of Henry James: A System of Observation Through the Visual Arts.* New Haven, Conn., 1956.

Buitenhuis, P., "From Daisy Miller to Julia Bride: A Whole Passage of Intellectual History," *American Quarterly*, XI (Summer 1959), 136-46.

Coffin, Tristram P., "Daisy Miller: Western Hero," *Western Folklore*, XVII (October 1958), 273-75.

Dunbar, Viola R., "Note on the Genesis of *Daisy Miller*," *Philological Quarterly*, XXVII (April 1948), 184-86.

———, "Addenda to 'Biographical and Critical Studies of Henry James, 1941-1948,'" *American Literature*, XXII (March 1950), 56-61.

———, "Revision of *Daisy Miller*," *Modern Language Notes*, LXV (May 1950), 311-17.

Edel, Leon, *Henry James; The Untried Years, 1843-1870.* Philadelphia, Pa., 1953.

———, and Dan H. Laurence, *A Bibliography of Henry James.* London, 1961.

Gargano, J. W., "*Daisy Miller*: An Abortive Quest of Innocence," *South Atlantic Quarterly*, LIX (Winter 1960), 114-20.

Geist, Stanley, "Portraits From a Family Album: Daisy Miller," *Hudson Review*, V, No. 2 (Summer 1952), 203-6.

Hamilton, Eunice C., "Biographical and Critical Studies of Henry James, 1941-1948," *American Literature*, XX (January 1949), 424-35.

Howells, William Dean, "Mr. James's Masterpiece," *Harper's Bazaar*, XXXVI (January 1902), 9-14.

Hoxie, E. F., "Mrs. Grundy Adopts Daisy Miller," *New England Quarterly*, XIX (December 1946), 474-84.

James, Henry, *The Art of the Novel: Critical Prefaces by Henry James*, ed. R. P. Blackmur. New York, 1934.

Kar, Annette, "Archetypes of American Innocence: Lydia Blood and Daisy Miller," *American Quarterly*, V (Spring 1953), 31-38.

Kelley, Cornelia P., *The Early Development of Henry James.* Urbana, Ill., 1930.

McElderry, B. R., Jr., "The 'Shy, Incongruous Charm' of 'Daisy Miller,'" *Nineteenth-Century Fiction*, X (September 1955), 162-65.

Snow, Lotus, "The Pattern of Innocence through Experience in the Characters of Henry James," *University of Toronto Quarterly,* XXII (April 1953), 230-36.

Stafford, William T., ed., *James's "Daisy Miller": The Story, The Play, The Critics.* New York, 1963.

Stone, E., "Further Notes on *Daisy Miller* and Cherbuliez," *Philological Quarterly,* XXIX (April 1950), 213-16.

Volpe, Edmond L., "The Childhood of James's American Innocents," *Modern Language Notes,* LXXI (May 1956), 345-47.

Ward, Joseph A., *The Imagination of Disaster; Evil in the Fiction of Henry James.* Lincoln, Nebr., 1961.

Wegelin, Christof, *The Image of Europe in Henry James.* Dallas, Tex., 1958.

Wright, Walter F., *The Madness of Art.* Lincoln, Nebr., 1962.

Herman Melville

Anderson, Charles R., "The Genesis of *Billy Budd,*" *American Literature,* XII (November 1940), 328-46.

Berthoff, Warner, *The Example of Melville.* Princeton, N.J., 1962.

Braswell, William, "Melville's *Billy Budd* as 'An Inside Narrative,'" *American Literature,* XXIX (May 1957), 133-46.

Chase, Richard, "Dissent on *Billy Budd,*" *Partisan Review,* XV (November 1948), 1212-18.

Fogle, Richard Harter, "*Billy Budd*—Acceptance of Irony?" *Tulane Studies in English,* VIII (1958), 107-13.

———, "*Billy Budd:* The Order of the Fall," *Nineteenth-Century Fiction,* XV (December 1960), 189-205.

Freimarck, Vincent, "Mainmast as Crucifix in *Billy Budd,*" *Modern Language Notes,* LXXII (November 1957), 496-97.

Glick, Wendell, "Expediency and Absolute Morality in *Billy Budd,*" *PMLA,* LXVIII (March 1953), 103-10.

Hayford, Harrison, ed., *The Somers Mutiny Affair.* Englewood Cliffs, N.J., 1959.

———, and Merton M. Sealts, Jr., *Billy Budd, Sailor* (*An Inside Narrative*). Chicago, 1962.

Hillway, Tyrus, *Herman Melville.* New York, 1963.

Howard, Leon, *Herman Melville, A Biography.* Berkeley, Cal., 1951.

Miller, James E., Jr., "*Billy Budd:* The Catastrophe of Innocence," *Modern Language Notes,* LXXIII (March 1958), 168-76.

Noone, John B., Jr., "*Billy Budd:* Two Concepts of Nature," *American Literature,* XXIX (November 1957), 249-62.

Sale, Arthur, "Captain Vere's Reasons," *Cambridge Journal,* V (October 1951), 3-18.

Schiffman, Joseph, "Melville's Final Stage, Irony: A Re-examination of *Billy Budd* Criticism," *American Literature,* XXII (May 1950), 128-36.

Sedgwick, William E., *Herman Melville: the Tragedy of Mind.* Cambridge, Mass., 1945.

Stafford, William T., ed., *Melville's "Billy Budd" and the Critics.* San Francisco, Cal., 1961.

Stern, Milton R., *The Fine Hammered Steel of Herman Melville.* Urbana, Ill., 1957.

Thompson, Lawrence, *Melville's Quarrel with God.* Princeton, N.J., 1952.

Tindall, William York, "The Ceremony of Innocence," *Great Moral Dilemmas in Literature,* ed. Robert M. McIver, pp. 73-81. New York, 1956.

Watson, E. L. Grant, "Melville's Testament of Acceptance," *New England Quarterly,* VI (June 1933), 319-27.

Weir, Charles, Jr., "Malice Reconciled: A Note on Herman Melville's *Billy Budd,*" *University of Toronto Quarterly,* XIII (April 1944), 276-85.

West, Ray B., "The Unity of *Billy Budd,*" *Hudson Review,* V (Spring 1952), 120-28.

Withim, Phil, "*Billy Budd:* Testament of Resistance," *Modern Language Quarterly,* XX (June 1959), 115-27.